PAKIST
– A DREAM
GONE SOUR

PAKISTAN
– A DREAM
GONE SOUR

ROEDAD KHAN

Karachi
Oxford University Press
Oxford   New York   Delhi
1998

Oxford University Press, Walton Street, Oxford OX2 6DP

Oxford New York
Athens Auckland Bangkok Bombay
Calcutta Cape Town Dar es Salaam Delhi
Florence Hong Kong Istanbul Karachi
Kuala Lumpur Madras Madrid Melbourne
Mexico City Nairobi Paris Singapore
Taipei Tokyo Toronto
and associated companies in
Berlin Ibadan

Oxford is a trade mark of Oxford University Press

ISBN 0 19 577980 0

First published by Oxford University Press, 1997
This Edition in Paperback, 1998

Printed in Pakistan at
Mas Printer, Karachi.
Published by
Ameena Saiyid, Oxford University Press
5-Bangalore Town, Sharae Faisal
P.O. Box 13033, Karachi-75350, Pakistan.

For my parents

Contents

Illustrations

Abbreviations

ADB	Asian Development Bank
CGS	Chief of General Staff
CMLA	Chief Martial Law Administrator
COAS	Chief of Army Staff
DGISI	Director General Inter Services Intelligence
DIB	Director Intelligence Bureau
DIG	Deputy Inspector General
ECC	Economic Committee of the Cabinet
FDR	Franklin Delano Roosevelt
FIA	Federal Investigation Agency
ICS	India Civil Service
IST	Indian Standard Time
KANUPP	Karachi Nuclear Power Plant
KESC	Karachi Electric Supply Company
MNA	Member National Assembly
MRD	Movement for the Restoration of Democracy
NAP	National Awami Party
NDFC	National Development Finance Corporation
PIA	Pakistan International Airlines
PICIC	Pakistan Industrial and Commercial Investment Corporation
PINSTECH	Pakistan Institute for Science and Technology
PML (N)	Pakistan Muslim League (Nawaz Sharif Group)
PPP	Pakistan People's Party
PSO (P)	Principal Staff Officer (Public)
PST	Pakistan Standard Time
PTV	Pakistan Television
Sub Judge	Subordinate Judge

Glossary

Achkan	Long coat
Amir	Head of Islamic government
Amirul-Momineen	Head of the Muslim community
Awam	Masses
Bandats	Small dams
Chaddar	Shroud, head covering
Chaks	Villages
Fez	Turkish cap
Gajar ka halwa	A sweetmeat made with carrots
Gulab jaman	A sweetmeat
Imam	One who leads prayers
Janaza	Funeral
Jhuggis	Shanty dwellings
Kamaras	Co-operative arrangements for small village irrigation works
Langar ki dal	Lentils cooked for troops
Majlis-i-Shura	Consultative Assembly
Malik	Headman
Maulvi	Religious learned man
Mishti	A Bengali sweetmeat
Mujahideen	Freedom fighters
Mujra	Dancing
Mullas	Priests
Munshi	Clerk
Naib Tehsildar	Assistant revenue officer
Namazis	Those who pray
Nizam-i-Mustafa	The Prophet's system of government
Paisa	A coin: one hundred paisas make one rupee.
Purdah	Veil
Shamiana	Tent
Shikar	Hunt
Sunnah	Practices of the Prophet (PBUH)
Tehsil	Lowest administrative unit
Wadera	Big landlord

Acknowledgements

No one made a greater contribution to the preparation of this book than my old friends, Jamsheed K. A. Marker and I. A. Imtiazi, who edited the entire manuscript, made innumerable helpful comments, and gave me generously of their time.

This book would not have been possible without the encouragement, help and support of my family, especially my son Riaz Khan, who placed the secretarial facilities of his office at my disposal and was the first to urge me to write this book.

My son Javed Khan read the first draft of the manuscript in Singapore and made useful comments and suggestions.

I benefited greatly from the intimate knowledge and experience of the East Asian tigers of my son Mumtaz Khan and from his valuable suggestions on the Pakistan economy.

My daughter Farida edited the entire manuscript and straightened out many a turgid sentence structure.

Above all, I wish to thank the Presidents I served for giving me the opportunity to participate in and observe the dramatic events described in this book.

Among the books which I have found most useful and on which I have drawn for this work are *Friends not Masters* by Mohammad Ayub Khan; *Ayub Khan: Pakistan's First Military Ruler* by Altaf Gauhar; *Pakistan Chronicle* by Sir Morris James; *Zia's Pakistan* by

Craig Baxter; *Judging* the State by Paula Newberg; *Out of Afghanistan* by Diego Cordovez, and Selig Harrison; *Working with Zia* by General K. M. Arif; *Memoirs of Lt. General Gul Hassan Khan; Nixon* by Stephen E. Ambrose; *Supreme Court Reborn* by William E. Leuchtenburg; *Introduction to the Study of the Law of the Constitution* by A. V. Dicey; and *Character Above All* edited by Robert A. Wilson.

My editor at Oxford University Press, Sabiah Askari, provided sound advice and guidance on the entire manuscript, making essential editorial transformations, reorganizations, and critiques. I owe her an enormous debt of gratitude.

I am indebted to all these people and to many more. The shortcomings of the book are my own.

I want to express my thanks to my long-time secretary, Manzoor Ahmad, who typed the manuscript from my nearly illegible handwriting. My special thanks to Syed Humayun Ahmed Rizvi, who acted as computer and word-processing specialist for the project.

Islamabad   Roedad Khan
May 1997

Preface

The day we see the truth and cease to speak is the day we begin to die.
Martin Luther King

I am not a writer by profession, inclination, or training. Writing a book is a novel experience for me, at once exciting and frightening. I decided to embark on this venture in the evening of my life because for some time I have felt an inner compulsion to present reality as I have experienced it, to re-create some of its scenes and its echoes.

This book is a collection of personal reminiscences and observations based on nearly forty years in the service of Pakistan. I was lucky enough to have witnessed from a ringside seat some of the momentous events in the chequered history of our country and to have participated in some of them. This is not, nor does it attempt to be, a history of Pakistan. Fate placed me at an unusual vantage point at the side of our leaders as they made decisions of incalculable consequences. I have sought to avoid relying on hindsight or passing *ex post facto* judgements on individuals. My appraisal of the men who led Pakistan during this period should not be considered conclusive: it merely represents the opinion of one who had the privilege of working closely with them.

It is in the main the story of six Presidents who guided the destiny of our people from 1958 onwards. I served under five of them, and knew all the six in varying measure: Ghulam Ishaq Khan best, followed, in that order, by Bhutto, Zia, Yahya, Ayub, and Leghari. Leghari I never served under, but circumstances brought us together in 1993 and I got to know him very well. They all displayed vast differences in personality, character, and style. Each one of them, in his own way, has, directly or indirectly, contributed to our generation's anguish and sense of betrayal, to our loss of confidence in our rulers, in our country, in our future, in ourselves, and to the souring of the dream of Pakistan. What is their legacy and how will history judge them?

'History', according to Churchill, 'judges a man, not by his victories or defeats but by their results'. Alexander was driven out of India; Genghis Khan was undone by his sons; Napoleon lost everything, including France. The greater the fall, the greater was a man's height.

'History with its flickering lamp stumbles along the trail of the past, trying to reconstruct its scenes, its echoes, and kindle with faint gleams the passion of former days.' So said Winston Churchill, in his eulogy for Neville Chamberlain in the House of Commons on 12 November 1940. 'What is the worth of all this? The only guide to a man is his conscience. The only shield to his memory is the rectitude and sincerity of his actions. It is very imprudent to walk through life without this shield, because we are so often mocked by the failure of our hopes and the upsetting of our calculations, but with this shield, however the fates may play, we march always in the rank of honour.'

I have tried to throw light on some of the obscure areas of the political history of our country, in the hope that readers will be enabled to see the reality of the Pakistan situation more clearly. The basic questions are: How did the Pakistan dream turn sour? Why this present imbroglio? Where did we go wrong? What has the role of our national institutions been and what is their contribution to the present unpleasant situation? Is it our destiny to be ruled by practitioners of the art of larceny, loot, and plunder? Is there any hope? How can the nation lift itself out of this political morass? How can we raise ourselves from the slough of despondency? Is it too late? Is the nation already passing through its terminal stage? Does a State that has been shamelessly plundered by a succession of rulers have any legitimate claim on the loyalty of its citizenry? Can the nation be reborn, redeemed, and resurrected? These are some of the questions this book seeks to answer. The issues raised will, I hope, be examined dispassionately and with objectivity and frankness. In writing this book I have no desire or intention to defend my own record, or vindicate my position, or to denigrate or create hatred or disaffection against any institution or individual, or to offend the law.

Ruin comes when the trader, whose heart is lifted up by wealth, becomes ruler or when the general uses his army to establish a military dictatorship. The producer is at his best in the economic field, the warrior is at his best in battle; they are both at their worst in public office; and in their crude hands politics submerges statesmanship. For statesmanship is a science and an art; one must have lived for it and been long prepared . . . whereas in simpler matters like shoe-making we think only a specially-trained person will serve our purpose, in politics we presume that everyone who knows how to get votes knows how to administer a city or a state. When we are ill we call for a trained physician, whose degree is a guarantee of specific preparation and technical competence . . . we do not ask for the handsomest physician, or the most eloquent one; well then, when the whole state is ill should we not look for the service and guidance of the wisest and the best?

Plato
428/427-348/347BC

Pity the Nation that is full of beliefs and empty of religion;
Pity the Nation that acclaims the bully as hero,
And that deems the glittering conqueror beautiful;
Pity the Nation that raises not its voice,
Save when it walks in a funeral,
And will rebel not save when its neck is laid
Between the sword and the block;
Pity the Nation whose sages are dumb with years,
And whose strong men are yet in the cradle;
Pity the Nation divided into fragments,
Each fragment deeming itself a Nation.

Khalil Gibran
1853-1931

Prologue

I was born in September 1923 into a Pakhtun family in district Mardan, in the North-West Frontier Province in the village of Hoti on the banks of the Kalpani. The Kalpani rises in Baizai or Lundkhawar 'and flowing southwards joins the Kabul between Nowshera and the village of Pir Sabak. The drainage of Hashtnagar and Yusufzai is ultimately all collected into the Kalpani and by this one channel makes its way into the Kabul.'[1] As a child, the Kalpani, was the centre of my universe. I could never resist its call and remember lying on my back on its sandy beach after hours of swimming, fishing, romping, and playing. It was on the sands of Kalpani that I played marbles in my boyhood.

The Pakhtuns are composed of a number of tribes, each of which is split up into a number of lesser tribes. Each tribe consists of a number of families who confederate under the elders of the senior family. The larger divisions of the tribe bear the adjunct *zai* after the proper name of each such as Yusufzai to which I belong. The lesser divisions are termed *Khels* as for example Babu Khel, the clan of Babu to which I belong. Each *Khel* has its own *Malik*. My grandfather Karim Dad Khan was a Malik. Our village Hoti is divided into *kandis*. Our kandi is Kandi Allah Dad Khel, with its own mosque (*jamaat*) and *hujra* or guest house.

My father Rahim Dad Khan was one of five children, two boys and three girls. My grandfather, Karim Dad Khan, as the village *Malik*, was authorized to collect land revenue from the landowners and to deposit it in the treasury. In return, he got a certain percentage by way of commission. I remember clearly the safe in our house where he kept all this money before transferring it to the treasury. As a child, I thought he was the richest man on earth. Occasionally, on his way to the treasury, he would walk past our primary school accompanied by his *munshi* and would fling a paisa in my direction. I naturally looked forward to such visits. The experience was exhilarating and is etched in my memory.

My father was the first member of our family to be sent to an English-medium school. He joined Islamia Collegiate School, Peshawar, but discontinued his studies in 1923 when he joined government service as a *Naib Tehsildar* (Assistant Revenue Officer) in the NWFP. The appointment was made, presumably, in recognition of my grandfather's services to the British Raj and their appreciation of the contribution he was making in his own humble way to the stability of the Raj. Be that as it may, it was a big event in the area and enhanced the prestige and status of the family. This was also a turning-point in the fortunes of the family and determined the course of events in my life in the years to come.

My father was stern and did not believe in sparing the rod when disciplining his children. He could be exceedingly stubborn, in the best sense of the term — a trait that may have been passed down from father to son. He had a commanding personality and inspired both awe and respect. He was a born fighter and had strong likes and dislikes. He was, as Voltaire said, 'As hard on himself as on others'.

My parents did not openly exhibit their love for me: I was not really a part of their lives, not in the earlier part of my life, at least. In those days, one was not a party to whatever conversation there was when at home. One could listen in silence but one was not expected to speak.

My father was transferred and we left Hoti and accompanied him wherever he was posted.

My most lasting memory of Charsadda is of the civil disobedience movement in 1930. In my mind's eye, I still see the Red Shirts picketing the courts near our house, and the British cavalry charging to disperse the crowds. By the latter half of April 1930, the whole of India was engaged in an epic struggle, following Gandhi's historic Dandi March against the salt laws. The NWFP was in the thick of it. The agitation in the Frontier started on 19 April 1930 from Abdul Ghaffar Khan's house in Utmanzai, Charsadda tehsil, with processions and meetings held all over the province. Abdul Ghaffar Khan was arrested before he could reach Peshawar and was brought to Charsadda jail. I saw thousands of people gathered around the prison, shouting anti-British slogans and demanding Abdul Ghaffar Khan's release. Meanwhile, a bloody drama was being enacted in Peshawar, eighteen miles from Charsadda. On 23 April, Captain Rickett, commanding the Royal Garhwal Rifles, received orders from his superiors to open fire on an unarmed peaceful crowd which had collected in the Qissa Khwani Bazar in Peshawar. Captain Rickett shouted at the top of his voice: 'Garhwalis, three round fire'[2]. Havaldar Chandra Singh, who stood on the left of Captain Rickett, thunderously countermanded it. 'Garhwalis, cease fire'.[3] The heroic hill men from Garhwal responded by putting down the rifles they had held up so long. Captain Rickett hysterically demanded an explanation from Chandra Singh; whereupon Chandra Singh coolly replied that the people were unarmed, and they could not fire upon unarmed men. Meanwhile, the British soldiers posted beside the Garhwalis had started firing, resulting in 200 to 250 dead. The Garhwali soldiers were tried and sentenced to various terms of imprisonment. All this is embedded in my memory and has left an indelible mark on my psyche.

Between 1930 and 1938, we lived in Parachinar, Mansehra, and Kohat and I was exposed to a variety of experiences not shared by my contemporaries in Mardan.

I was sent to Islamia High School, Kohat, but did not like the atmosphere; at my request, I was transferred to Bharatri High School in the same city. I have fond memories of this Hindu school and the devotion and dedication of its teachers.

I joined Islamia College, Peshawar, in 1938 as a first year student. Not many people in Pakistan know how Islamia College was established. The moving spirit behind its establishment was the Chief Commissioner, Sir George Roos-Keppel; he was ably supported by Sahibzada Abdul Qayyum. In a letter to the Viceroy, Roos-Keppel pointed out that the college would keep the Frontier Muslims away from other educational institutions in India, and particularly from Aligarh, which was then regarded as a hotbed of

Muslim political agitation. In another letter to the Viceroy, Roos-Keppel wrote that, 'Fathers of sons are realizing the necessity for education; but family affection is so strong among Pathans that few will send their sons to Aligarh, while they will not send them to Mission Schools, as they, without making them Christians, manufacture agnostics.'

The College was established in the teeth of opposition from the aristocratic circles in the Frontier. Roos-Keppel reported in 1912 that 'among the small educated class of Mohammadans, there is a selfish minority who resist the raising of the proletariat, and urge that the spread of education will endanger the ancient fabric of society by filling the brains of the children of agriculturists with ambitious ideas above their station, and thus unfitting them for the work of hewers of wood and drawers of water for the rich.'

On 5 April 1913, when the opening ceremony of Islamia College Peshawar, was performed, one greybeard rose to give 'an excited extempore harangue in Pushto' the burden of which was 'that this was the first occasion when the Mohammadans of the Frontier had given of their abundance for anything except women and boys.'[4]

I was still at Islamia College Peshawar when the Second World War broke out. I followed the course of the war, glued to the radio set in the common room of our hostel. Whether they were fascists or not, my sympathies in the early days of the war were clearly with the Germans, not because I had any love for Germany but only the desire to see our masters humbled. Nevertheless, I remember joining the protest strike and demonstration against the termination of the services of Mr Holdsworth, the Principal of our College, by the Management Committee.

I saw Lahore for the first time in 1939 when I participated in the Young Speakers' debate at Government College, Lahore. We won the trophy. It was an exhilarating experience. I was overawed by the splendour and sophistication of Lahore.

In 1940, I returned to Lahore to join the Forman Christian College. I thoroughly enjoyed its liberal, tolerant, and progressive environment, which has left a deep imprint on my life. I developed great respect for the American teachers who were running this institution.

At F. C. College, I made friends with B. Sawhney, a Hindu; Bobby Farooqui, son of a Muslim father and a Hindu mother; R.L. Suri, who later became an ace pilot in the Indian Air Force;

and, last but not least, Jamsheed K. A. Marker, who recently retired after a distinguished career in our diplomatic service. I learnt a lot from all of them, but my association with Jamsheed Marker in particular has had a great influence on my life. It was Jamsheed who introduced me to western classical music and I recollect warm, summer evenings spent listening to Beethoven's 'Moonlight Sonata' on the roof of our Garden Town residence. I was fortunate in being exposed to such a talented group of students, belonging to different walks of life, and with a variety of backgrounds, all different from mine. We all lived in a rented house, paying Rs 40 per month, in Garden Town not far from the new F.C. College site on Ferozepur Road. We had a Hindu cook, Mehr Chand.

It was in Lahore that I was first exposed to Marxism and to a small group of students (both boys and girls) who talked about Marxist philosophy, of which I knew nothing. I was overawed by the depth of their knowledge: in political discussions with them, I found myself handicapped by my ignorance. I decided to remedy this. I had little time and no patience to study the works of Marx and Engels. I was, however, stimulated by the Communist Manifesto. I found myself strongly drawn to the idea of a classless society, where life was shared and communal. I subscribed to Marx's basic dictum: 'From each according to his ability, to each according to his needs'. Dialectical materialism seemed to offer both a searchlight illuminating the dark night of class oppression and a tool that could be used to end that oppression. Marxism's call to revolutionary action was music to my ears. What inspired me most and fired my imagination was not the Freedom Movement led by the Indian National Congress, nor the demand for a separate homeland made by the Muslim League, but the October Revolution, aptly described as an unprecedented attempt in Trotsky's words, to 'overthrow the world'. That meant a complete redesign of state, society, economy, and culture all over the world for the purpose of creating a new human being.

Jamsheed and I were watching a matinee show at the Plaza Cinema on 22 June 1941 when, during the interval, we learnt that Hitler had invaded the Soviet Union. We got together and staged Bernard Shaw's Geneva at the Plaza Cinema, Lahore, to raise funds for the Soviet Union. All of us, boys and girls, friends of the Soviet Union, used to meet regularly in a small flat in the Commercial Building facing India Coffee House. Visiting India Coffee House was a stimulating experience in more ways than one. There we met the cream of Lahore society: intellectuals; student leaders like Ramesh Chander and Mazhar Ali Khan; future politicians and revolutionaries like M. N. Roy; and engaged in long discussions over endless cups of coffee. As Orson Welles said, 'A Vienna cafe is the only place in the world where you can sit unmolested for eight hours or longer, drink but a single cup of coffee and still be treated as a king'. India Coffee House was that kind of place. Coffee at the India Coffee House was in the words of Charles de Talleyrand, 'hot as hell, black as the devil, pure as an angel, and sweet as love'. The coffee-house spirit the world over is best summed up by the comment attributed to Austria-Hungary's Foreign Minister, Count Czernin, who, when informed by an aide that Revolution had indeed broken out in Russia said, 'Oh, come, come, good man, who would want to make a revolution there? Perhaps that Herr Trotsky who plays chess at the Cafe Central? Don't make me laugh.'

It was in Lahore that Jamsheed and I were challaned by an Anglo-Indian sergeant for traffic violation. The charge against Jamsheed was of cycling in Lawrence Gardens without a cushion on the carrier and I was charged with allowing myself to be carried on the cycle without a cushion. We were both terrified. When we appeared before the Anglo-Indian magistrate, he took no notice of us. After sometime, his Reader told us that we could go home and that the magistrate had let us off with a warning. We could not believe that we had been let off so easily and suspected foul play. We left only when the magistrate, realizing our reluctance to leave the court-room, told us personally that we could go. For the first time, I had come face to face with the majesty of the law.

I was elected Secretary of the Speakers' Union of F. C. College while Miss V. Z. Singh of 39 Temple Road, the craze of Lahore in those days and much sought-after, was the President.

The Pakistan Resolution of 1940 was passed in Lahore while I was at F. C. College Lahore but, as far as I was concerned, it went unnoticed, made no impact, and left me cold.

I visited Kashmir for the first time in 1941 in the company of our American professors, Dr Sheets and Dr Velte, and my friends Jamsheed and Suri and, on my return, I said goodbye to the politically benign campus of Lahore. Under pressure from my father, I reluctantly joined the Muslim University of Aligarh, which had turned by then into an 'arsenal of Muslim India'. An atmosphere of mystic frenzy prevailed there, as students and teachers poured

'Friends of the Soviet Union' stage Bernard Shaw's Geneva in 1941.
The author, as General Franco, is second from the right

eir idealistic zeal into the emotionalism of Pakistan. My fellow students perceived Pakistan as a bright dream, a passionate goal, the vision of paradise on earth. I did not share this fancy. The contrast with F. C. College was marked and quite depressing. I never took a liking to the achkan and fez (known as rumi topi in India and which Ataturk outlawed in 1925 in Turkey), both essential parts of our uniform. I concentrated on my studies, attending M. A. History classes in the morning and Law classes in the evening. In between, my friend Enver Adil used to carry me on his bicycle to Cafe de Jamil for tea and gajar ka halwa. I saw the Taj Mahal for the first time when I visited Agra as Enver's guest.

One fateful day, while still at Aligarh, I received a letter from my father informing me that I was engaged to be married. My protest that I was not yet ready was summarily overruled. The wedding was to coincide with my final exams, but was postponed to a later date in order to enable me to take my exam. I was now a married man, but without a job and with all the problems of the world to face.

Fortunately, the Government of NWFP advertised the post of a lecturer in History in Government Intermediate College, Abbottabad. I promptly applied, was interviewed by a Selection Committee comprising provincial ministers, and was selected on a pay scale of Rs 120-4-160, subject to a fifteen per cent cut as 'defence contribution', which was my share to the downfall of Hitler.

In July 1944, I reported for duty at the College, which was housed in a rented building on Mansehra Road. Teaching History to young students was an exhilarating experience. I think I enjoyed it partly because I was scared of entering the real world, and life on the campus shielded me from the turbulence raging outside. It was wartime and everything — sugar, kerosene oil, and cloth — was rationed.

One day, a Colonel Ayub Khan, came to our college in the evening, riding a motorcycle, and asked if he could leave his motorcycle in our garage. We had no objection, as the garage was empty and we had no use for it. This was my first meeting with the future President of Pakistan.

In 1946, in response to an advertisement in the Khyber Mail, I applied for appointment to the Provincial Judicial Service, but my application for taking the competitive examination for appointment as a Sub Judge was not entertained by the Public Service Commission on the ground that I was below the minimum age of twenty-three years for appointment in the Judicial Service. The Judicial Commissioner Peshawar, on his own initiative, referred the case back to the Public Service Commission for reconsideration, as in his view, the lower age limit referred to the date of appointment, and not the date of examination. Fortunately, the Public Service Commission relented, reversed its earlier decision, and allowed me to take the examination, which I topped, but, being still a 'minor', was sent for settlement and judicial training.

I was posted to Swabi as a Sub Judge in 1946 on attaining the age of twenty-three. I relieved a Hindu Sub Judge, who left behind three hundred pending cases of pre-emption, redemption of mortgage, restitution of conjugal rights, and declaratory suits. I had a Law degree, but no practical experience of applying law to actual cases. My first day in Court was a daunting experience which I could not have survived without the help of my Reader. I was a nervous wreck when the Court rose for the day.

I kept myself aloof from the Executive and most social functions in Swabi, in accordance with the best traditions of the independent judiciary to which I now belonged.

I was appointed as Presiding Officer at a polling station set up in Swabi for the 6 July 1947 Referendum. The result was a foregone conclusion. The atmosphere of pro-Pakistan frenzy, which I had earlier experienced in Aligarh, now prevailed all over the Frontier.

In September 1948, I decided to sit for the Pakistan Administrative Service Competitive Examination and visited Peshawar to collect some books. I stayed with Ghulam Ishaq Khan, another future President of Pakistan. On the morning of 11 September, we both heard the sad news of the death of Mr Jinnah. I returned to Swabi via Mardan, where I marched through the Mardan Bazar in a pro-Pakistan procession, headed by the Deputy Commissioner, Mardan.

In January 1949, I took the Pakistan Administrative Service written examination in Central Model School, Lahore. After qualifying in the written examination, I went to Karachi for the viva voce examination in July 1949.

Whilst serving as Sub Judge in Charsadda, I received my letter of appointment to the Pakistan Administrative Service. What a thrilling experience! The prospect of stepping into the shoes of the men who had ruled India, was, to say the least, quite exciting.

Of the PAS Academy, where we all reported for training, all that I remember are uninspiring lectures on civil and criminal law, economics, and Islamiat. I did, however, manage to learn to ride sufficiently well to clear the riding test; and I also made many friends. Friendships struck up at the Academy have survived subsequent ups and downs in our careers.

On completion of training at the Academy, in August 1950, I flew to Dhaka via Delhi and Calcutta, accompanied by my friend and colleague Aftab, for training in East Pakistan. In Delhi, I stayed with Professor Abdul Majid Khan, my former teacher at F. C. College, who was now a Member of the Indian Parliament. However, my father's friend Mr Puri, a Prosecuting Inspector in Kohat before Partition, insisted that I move to his house. His wife, who observed purdah, discarded it in honour of my visit and personally cooked a delicious meal for me. I was touched.

A day later, in pouring rain, our Dakota flew into lush green Dhaka. The greenery took my breath away. After nine months in East Pakistan, we left for Australia for overseas training in May 1951. For some reason, although least qualified, I was singled out and elected as member of the Sports and Entertainment Committee on board S. S. Strathnaver. I did whatever I could and thoroughly enjoyed the honour bestowed on me. At sea, the real world fades away and friendships among the passengers flourish.

On my return from Australia in September 1951, I was allocated to serve in the NWFP. I called on the Chief Minister, Khan Abdul Qayyum Khan, a dynamic personality, an able administrator, and a great believer in development — but a ruthless enemy and intolerant of opposition. The sight of senior bureaucrats rigging the election and vying with each other to please the Khan disgusted me. Alas, this was the beginning of the involvement of civil servants in politics in support of incumbent governments.

In August 1952, in the footsteps of Iskander Mirza, I was posted as Assistant Commissioner, Tank. Iskander Mirza was one of the first Indians to pass through Sandhurst and into the Political Service. 'Iskander', as every one called him, enjoyed getting the better of others by cunning strategies. It was Iskander who arranged that the participants in a procession which he thought might cause trouble should be entertained to tea. So tea was served, quite early in the course of its route, by a party of sympathizers, who had, as it happened, included in the strongly sugared tea one of the most powerful of vegetable laxatives. The procession dispersed before reaching its objective.

In May 1953, I found myself back in Peshawar as Registrar Co-operatives and was soon busy organizing sugarcane co-operative societies at village level for the supply of sugarcane to mills on an equitable basis: a very interesting experiment which, unfortunately, was scrapped with the creation of One Unit.

The reaction to the dissolution of the provinces in West Pakistan in October 1955 and imposition of One Unit was very adverse in the NWFP, which had been formed as a separate province in 1901. The move embittered relations with the majority province of Punjab and was looked upon as a political one, and as a conspiracy directed against East Pakistan. On One Unit, my Administrative Secretary and future President, Ghulam Ishaq Khan, and I had identical views. It did not make us very popular with Qurban Ali Khan, the Governor of the NWFP, or with One Unit authorities in Lahore.

In 1956, when I was Political Agent Zhob, Ayub Khan, the then Commander-in-Chief, came for shikar and stayed at the castle, my official residence, as my guest for four days. The drill was to leave early morning and return in the evening. Later, the two of us would sit in front of a roaring log fire, and join the rest for dinner after some time. Ayub's entourage consisted of Generals Burki, Hameed, Yahya, and others. Except Burki, who stayed at the castle, all the others stayed in the Zhob Militia Mess. Mirza was also to come, but had to cancel his visit because of a back problem.

I took no part in the shoot, but before leaving for Rawalpindi, Ayub, who had been watching me all along, remarked upon this and gave me six birds from his bag.

On arrival in Fort Sandeman, I had been told that the guest room in the castle was haunted by the spirit of one of my English predecessors who had been shot dead in his office by his orderly. I mentioned this casually to Ayub before he retired for the night. He laughed and thought I was pulling his leg. Fortunately, it did not disturb his sleep. Or so he told me next morning.

Ayub showed a lot of interest in the civil service and asked many searching questions. Two years later, he was the President and Chief Martial Law Administrator.

In early 1957, I was transferred to Dera Ismail Khan. On my way back home on joining leave, I was shocked when, on arrival in Bannu, my younger brother Yunus told me that our father had been shot. A neighbour, who was a distant relative and a schizo-phrenic, shot my father when he tried to stop him from beating his wife, who was crying for help. His condition, I was told, was precarious. He was already dead when we arrived in Mardan late in the night. My father's passing away changed my whole life in a way that I did not suspect at that time. I had always defined myself through my father, and now I experienced great grief. Suddenly, I felt very lonely and insecure. My father had been a pillar of strength: with him there, I could face the world; now I was alone.

The mourning over, I left for Dera Ismail Khan. Soon, I found myself engrossed in irrigation projects. The winter months were spent on horseback, inspecting *kamaras, bandats* (minor irrigation works), etc., on which the prosperity of the people of the district depended.

October 1958 Martial Law

On 8 October 1958, I heard over the radio that martial law had been imposed and civilian governments with all their parapher-nalia — elected legislatures, etc. — had been dismissed. Ayub Khan was the Chief Martial Law Administrator. I was shocked. It gave the lie to all that I had been taught and all that I had learnt at F. C. College Lahore and at Aligarh. 'There can be no martial law in peace time', so we were taught. I was thoroughly confused: the country was not at war and there was no civil commotion in the country preventing the Judges from going to Court — an essen-tial condition for the imposition of martial law in peace time ac-cording to Dicey.

A telephone call from the local colonel asking me to report to Brigade Headquarters, along with my Superintendent of Police, brought me down to earth. He rattled off a string of directives for compliance within twenty-four hours: all unlicenced arms to be surrendered; all hoarded stocks of wheat to be unearthed; and all prices, including the price of gold, to be controlled. I did my best. I got back to my office late in the evening. All attempts on the part of my Commissioner to get in touch with me had failed. He thought I had been detained by the Assistant Martial Law Administrator, who was now my boss. It took me some time to make the necessary adjustments and to reconcile myself to the new order. In the end, the instinct of self-preservation prevails. The country hailed the new dawn, the deliverers.

Zulfikar Ali Bhutto, the Foreign Minister, greets Egyptian President Gamal Abdul Nasser on his state visit to Pakistan, President Ayub Khan is on the left

One of the priorities of martial law was the 'grow more food' campaign. In pursuance of this, we brought thousands of acres of land under tubewell irrigation in Dera Ismail Khan. Lieutenant General Azam, the new Minister for Food and Agriculture, heard about this and came to see things for himself. Accompanied by the GOC, Major General Fazal Muqeem, Azam went from tubewell to tubewell, saw sparkling water gushing out, and bulldozers removing bushes and levelling the ground. He was thrilled. I remember his words: 'People in Rawalpindi sitting on their haunches must come here and see what is being done on the ground.'

I was posted to Peshawar as Deputy Commissioner in 1959, a prize post in those days. While at Peshawar, I met Gamal Abdul Nasser on his state visit to Pakistan. He has aptly been described as the last great pharaoh of Egypt, successor to Ramses II. He was one of the revolutionaries thrown up after the Second World War whose personalities and ideas had an influence far beyond the confines of the countries in which they assumed power. He was cold and autocratic, a man possessed.

I was in Peshawar when I first met Zulfikar Ali Bhutto, future President and Prime Minister of Pakistan. He was a Minister in the Ayub Cabinet and was on a visit to Peshawar as chief guest at a function at the Rural Academy. I could see that Bhutto was visibly bored. The organizers wanted him to stay on for dinner. Bhutto wanted to get away but did not know how to handle the situation. I rescued him and together we went to the Peshawar Club where we spent a very pleasant evening. I took an immediate liking to Bhutto. He was young, witty, full of life, well-read, and well-dressed, more at home in the company of young civil servants than his Cabinet colleagues.

His next visit to Peshawar was as Acting Foreign Minister. On arrival, he told me that he would like to visit Bada Ber, the American base close to Peshawar, and before leaving for Warsak made it clear that he would like to see everything. I got in touch with the Base Commander who said the Minister would be welcome to visit the cafeteria where he would be entertained and served coffee and sandwiches. He turned down the Minister's request to see sensitive areas of the base but promised, in deference to my wishes, to refer the matter to Washington. Half an hour later, he got back to me and asked me to inform the Minister that, except the cafeteria, no other part of the base could be shown to him. I conveyed this to Mr Bhutto. He was visibly upset and asked me if the Americans knew that he was the Acting Foreign Minister. I said they did. He kept quiet and the matter ended there.

I was still in Peshawar when the U2 incident took place which provoked Khruschev into the dramatic gesture of drawing on the map a red ring around Peshawar. The spy plane, as we learnt later, had taken off from Bada Ber.

In 1960, I left for Hyderabad to take up my new job as Project Director, Ghulam Muhammad Barrage. It was easily one of the most exciting and challenging jobs I ever held. Imagine 2.5 million acres of virgin land, commanded by the G. M. Barrage, placed at my disposal for allocation, development, and colonization. On my first visit to the area, I saw miles and miles of barren, uninhabited land, stretching all the way from Hyderabad down to the sea on both sides of the Indus. Within three years, it was humming with activity. Bulldozers could be seen making roads, earthen tanks being filled with sweet water for the incoming colonists. Peasants from all over the country, including 350 families from East Pakistan, converged on the G. M. Barrage and settled down in their respective chaks. Hospitals, dispensaries, schools, post and telegraph offices were springing up all over the barrage area. Before I left in August 1963, one could see miles and miles of rice and sugarcane crops and flourishing villages, one of them graciously named by the President after me. Before I left the Barrage area, Ayub Khan told the Nawab of Kalabagh, the Governor of West Pakistan, in my presence that he was going to confer a civil award on me and that the case need not be initiated by the provincial government. Ayub made a note of it in a small notebook which he always carried. A few months later, I received my first civil award.

Both Ayub and Kalabagh used to visit G. M. Barrage every alternate month and it was my privilege to show them around. We would spend the whole day driving throughout the length and breadth of the Barrage area, with a break for lunch in the middle of nowhere. I was never to see anything like this again in my career. Never again did I see a President or a Governor taking such genuine interest in a major development project in the country. Never again was I to see another Head of State or another Chief Executive of a province inspiring and motivating field officers by their personal example and by their mere presence among them. We all worked like men possessed, driven by an irresistible force day after day, week after week, month after month, year after year. How was 2.5 million acres of land brought under cultivation in such a short period of time? The answer is surprisingly simple. The magic formula was maximum decentralization, total empowerment of the Project Director and his staff, and total trust and confidence in the local officers. As Project Director, I was the Board of Revenue, Chief Engineer B&R, Chief Engineer Irrigation, Director of Agriculture, Registrar Co-operatives, Conservator of Forests, and Head of every other conceivable department. Believe it or not, I was authorized the grant of five hundred acres of land to one individual, without reference to Lahore or Rawalpindi, and with no questions asked, subject only to one condition: that the allottee must have the will and the means to bring the land under cultivation in the shortest possible time. I was to be judged by performance and performance alone. When I revisited the area in 1983 in the company of the Commissioner Hyderabad, the place had changed beyond all recognition.

Soon after my arrival in Hyderabad, I met Mr Bhutto for the third time, at a lunch given in his honour by the Commissioner, Hyderabad, Mr Niaz Ahmad. He introduced me to Manna, his sister, and her husband Mr Nasimul Islam. Realizing how lonely I was, Bhutto invited me to Bhit Shah for the evening and arranged to have me picked up from my rest-house. From Bhit Shah, we drove together to another village. On arrival there, I was introduced to our host who was none other than Jam Sadiq Ali, the future Chief Minister and strongman of Sindh. The whole place was illuminated. Under a huge *shamiana*, *mujra* (dancing) was in progress and alcohol was being imbibed freely. I got a taste of Sindhi hospitality far superior to anything I had seen anywhere else.

In Hyderabad, I got to know Mr Bhutto's younger sister, Manna, who, in my opinion, was easily the best of all the Bhuttos. She was a very private and reserved person. She had very few friends and even they could not claim to know her well because she revealed so little of herself. She passionately loved her brother whom she closely resembled and was clearly the closest to him. At an hour's notice, Zulfi, as she called him, would ask her to arrange lunch or dinner for twenty friends. Baked beans, his favourite dish, had to be there. Bhutto too loved her. In spite of everything, she never stopped loving him. He was the centre of her existence. Unfortunately, with his rise to power and with a multiplicity of other influences operating on him, the meetings between the brother and sister became more and more infrequent.

I saw a lot of Zulfikar Ali Bhutto in Hyderabad and I grew very fond of him. He could be very charming and it was a pleasure talking to him. He was a great mimic. Both Imtiazi, the District Magistrate, Hyderabad, and I were invited to be his guests in Larkana but we could not make it. We never got another invitation.

I said goodbye to Hyderabad in August 1963 and left by train for Karachi to take up my new appointment as Divisional Commissioner. My friend Jamsheed was busy in Keamari but his gracious wife and my dear friend Diana was there at the Cantonment Railway Station to welcome me. It was quite a change from the G.M. Barrage. Next to 109 Clifton, where Nasim and Manna lived, there was a vast expanse of sand dunes. Northwest of Karachi, all the way from Hawkes Bay to Cape Mons and beyond, there were craggy shelves, caves, and inlets. Jamsheed's hut at Hawkes Bay, although somewhat neglected, was a big attraction, a haven of refuge, and we made full use of it. Karachi in those days was a self-contained peaceful place, a microcosm of Pakistan, home to people from all over Pakistan — Bengalis from East Pakistan, Punjabi businessmen, Memons, Bohras, Parsees, Pathan labourers from the NWFP and Balochistan, well-to-do Sindhis, and millions of Urdu-speaking Mohajirs.

Karachi, a sprawling city of over two million at that time, had a different set of awesome and daunting problems, stemming from the existence of unauthorized *jhuggis*, lack of sanitation, lack of drinking water, absence of municipal facilities and planned development, student discontent and demonstrations. I had two-first class officers, Masood Nabi Nur, Director General, Karachi Development Authority, and Ziauddin, Chairman, Karachi Municipal Corporation. We rolled up our sleeves, visited every part of the city, all its slums, all the *jhuggis*, met the *jhuggi* dwellers, identified their problems, and if, nothing else, at least provided drinking water, electricity, and schools in most of the deprived areas. It was a Himalayan task but we made an honest effort to tackle the most pressing problems, and I think achieved limited success within the short time availabe.

Soon, politics took over. Development took a back seat and the entire city administration was geared up to face the presidential election, the historic contest between Ayub Khan and Miss Fatima Jinnah in January 1965.

The situation generally remained peaceful throughout the run-up to the election. The election itself passed off peacefully. Miss Jinnah brought some minor complaints to my notice over the telephone. These were promptly inquired into and redressed to her satisfaction. To the best of my knowledge, there was no serious complaint of abuse of power by officials or of their involvement in the election for or against either of the two contestants, and certainly no rigging. In Karachi, Miss Jinnah secured more votes than her rival. Ayub also lost in Dhaka. Karachi and Dhaka were the only two 'diseased' cities, as Ayub called them. I heaved a sigh of relief that no untoward incident had taken place. But I was in for a rude shock.

The morning after the election, I was sitting out on the lawn when, at about 10.30 a.m., the telephone rang and somebody — not an official — informed me that a victory truck procession led by Captain (retd.) Gohar Ayub, the President's son, had run into trouble with the residents of the area through which the procession was passing and that there had been some stone-throwing. I had no knowledge of this procession. I tried to contact the District Magistrate and the Police Chief. Both were unavailable, so I contacted Police control who confirmed the incidents and told me that the police were escorting the procession. Police control kept me informed of the progress of the procession. Very soon, reports of more serious incidents started pouring in. By about midday, I finally succeeded in establishing contact with the DIG at his residence. He told me later that he was very tired and had, before going to bed, unplugged the telephone in his bedroom, giving strict instructions that he was not to be disturbed. Together, we toured the area. By this time, armed clashes had taken place between the processionists and the residents of the area, resulting in heavy loss of life and property. Several houses and shops were reduced to ashes. The army had to be called in to restore law and order. The District Magistrate told me that he had authorized the procession and the route it had to follow, but some unauthorized deviation had taken place. The record maintained at the Police control room seemed to confirm this. The inquiry ordered by the government made no headway and was subsequently dropped. Mr Ghulam Nabi Memon, Law Minister, Government of West Pakistan, came down to Karachi to assess the situation. In his railway saloon, he met the DIG Police, the District Magistrate Karachi, and myself. Mr Abdul Qadir Sheikh, a future judge of the Supreme Court of Pakistan, then Assistant Advocate General was also present. One of the sinister suggestions made was that the record kept by Police control should be suitably altered and, if necessary, destroyed altogether. For this, my concurrence was necessary. I refused point-blank and told Ghulam Nabi Memon and others present that this could only be done over my dead body. The matter ended there. The inquiry was dropped, ostensibly due to non-cooperation from the opposition. Soon thereafter, I got my marching orders to Quetta as Commissioner. I have no hesitation in saying that, regardless of who was at fault, as the head of the administration, I had failed to protect the lives and property of the people of Karachi. This was certainly not my finest hour and it has haunted me ever since.

Barring this one incident, Karachi remained generally peaceful. Certainly no part of Karachi, developed or otherwise, inhabited by Mohajirs, Bengalis, Punjabis, Sindhis, or Balochis, was out of bounds for the administration. Wherever we went, people welcomed us. Our relationship was quite friendly and not adversarial. Every now and then, students affiliated with different political parties would come out on the streets, pelt stones, and then disappear in the alleys and lanes. Confrontation was there, but the game was always played according to well-established civilized rules on both sides. On one occasion, a warrant of arrest was issued against Mairaj Muhammad Khan, a student leader and future Adviser to the Prime Minister. He went underground, was not traceable, and could not be apprehended by the Karachi Police. But the Press had no difficulty in contacting him. His press interviews with his photograph were carried daily on the front pages of morning newspapers. When I brought this to the notice of Asif Majid (DIG Police), he was most embarrassed, asked for forty-eight hours to arrest Mairaj, failing which he threatened to resign. Mairaj was still at large, long after the expiry of the deadline. When we met several days later, out of politeness, I did not raise the issue as we had more pressing problems to attend to.

One day I got a telephone call from Major General Rafi, Military Secretary to the President, saying that Ashraf Khan, Begum Ayub's nephew, had applied for a plot of land in Karachi. He said that the file was pending in my office and he recommended its favourable consideration. A week later, Mr N. A. Faruqui, Principal Secretary to the President, made a similar request on the telephone. I sent for the file but did nothing. A week later, Ayub

Khan came to attend a naval function at which I was also present. We were having tea under the shamiana when Ayub Khan beckoned me to join him in a corner of the shamiana. When I went over, he raised the same matter with me. Meanwhile, I had done my homework and knew the facts of the case. I told Ayub Khan that the plot in question had been earmarked by Mr Suhrawardy as Prime Minister for a national theatre and that I could not reverse the Prime Minister's orders. Moreover, it was a gold mine and its allotment to Ashraf Khan would attract the attention of the entire country and bring him a bad name. Ayub Khan did not pursue the matter and I never heard from him or his staff again. What is more important, Ayub Khan never held it against me.

I saw a lot of Zulfikar Ali Bhutto in Karachi and enjoyed his hospitality at his home, 70 Clifton. I remember the dinner he gave for Mr Subandrio, Foreign Minister of Indonesia. Guests were entertained to Sindhi music, while Chham Chham, a pretty young girl from Lahore, danced. In my mind's eye, I still see Mr Bhutto pressing one hundred rupee notes against his guests' cheeks as was customary, till Chham Chham coquettishly snatched them away. Nobody, not even Aziz Ahmad, the austere Foreign Secretary, was spared.

One day, I received the Shah of Iran at Karachi Airport. I found myself facing a shy young man, almost taciturn, in a smart uniform. There was nothing very regal about him at that time. He had to break journey at Karachi for refuelling before flying off to Rawalpindi. We had a cup of tea together. He showed considerable interest in the Midway House, the hotel near the airport, and its touristic potential. I thought he was too young, too schoolboyish, too immature, too inexperienced, to rule over the destiny of the millions of people in Iran. I could not help comparing him to Ayub, who was then at the peak of his power. Ayub towered above him both physically and otherwise. The Shah, it was evident, was on a mission to Rawalpindi to be educated in the art of state-craft, to seek guidance from Ayub, and hear his words of wisdom.

Little did I know that, a few years later, in 1971, this shy young man would stand before the empty but impressive tomb of Cyrus the Great and address it grandiloquently in his flat, featureless voice:

'To you Cyrus, Great King, King of Kings, from myself, Shahinshah of Iran, and from the people, hail!

The author greets Prime Minister Zhou Enlai at Karachi airport in 1964

'We are here at the moment when Iran renews its pledge to History to bear witness to the immense gratitude of an entire people to you, immortal hero of History, founder of the world's oldest empire, great liberator of all time, worthy son of mankind.

'Cyrus, we stand before your eternal dwelling-place to speak these solemn words: sleep on in peace forever, for we are awake and we remain to watch over your glorious heritage.'[5]

And little did he know that eight years later he himself, in Kissinger's words, would be like a flying Dutchman looking for a port of call and final resting place.

I had the good fortune of meeting Prime Minister Zhou Enlai in Karachi in 1964. He landed in Karachi smiling, wearing a light-weight summer tunic. I was the senior-most civil servant in Karachi to receive him. Agha Shahi, then an Additional Secretary, was also there. I sat next to Zhou on a sofa in the VIP lounge at the airport and took full advantage of his brief stay in Karachi. In the words of Edgar Snow, 'Zhou was that rarest of all creatures, a pure intellectual in whom action was perfectly coordinated with knowledge and conviction.' He struck me as a very handsome man with sparkling eyes, a little effeminate, highly cultured, and very easy to talk to. He talked about liberation struggles all over the world. He told me that the Algerians had beaten the Chinese record in their struggle against the French but the Vietnamese had beaten both the Chinese and the Algerians. 'The Americans cannot,' he said, 'win this war. The logistics are against them; the people are against them.' Meeting Zhou was like meeting History.

In Karachi, I also met Foreign Minister Chen Yi, that burly, dashing student from Sichuan. There I was sitting next to the man who, in his student days, had been washing dishes in restaurants and loading barges along the Seine quay. He had a feisty sense of humour. In this, he met his match in Zulfikar Ali Bhutto. I distinctly remember the two of them engaged in a battle of wits and humour at a dinner at the Chinese Embassy. Every now and then Zulfikar Ali Bhutto would raise his glass and exclaim 'Chen Yi: Mao Tai'.

I heard the tragic news of the assassination of President John F. Kennedy while I was having dinner at the American ambassador's residence. We were all stunned.

My posting in Karachi ended shortly thereafter, and I was transferred to Quetta as Commissioner. From there, I reverted to the central government in the Ministries of Science and Technology, and States and Frontier Regions, working directly under Ayub Khan.

I first visited Tehran in 1966 to attend a meeting of the RCD* on the development of the atomic energy programme. I was staying at the Hilton. Zulfikar Ali Bhutto was also there. I went to see him early in the morning before going to the RCD meeting. Over a cup of tea, we discussed the domestic political situation threadbare. Before I left, he asked me to keep my evening free. He took me to the house of the Iranian Foreign Minister for an exclusive dinner party. A pretty young Iranian girl was singing in different languages. I was sitting next to an Iranian lady. Bhutto came up to me and whispered in my ear: 'Be careful. She is the wife of the Savak chief.'

After the fall of Ayub Khan, I was appointed Managing Director, Pakistan Television Corporation. On 14 March 1971, I was in Karachi attending a meeting of the General Managers of Television Corporation when the telephone rang and Vaqar Ahmad, the Establishment Secretary, informed me that President Yahya had appointed me as Information Secretary and that I should report to the President who was in Karachi. I suddenly realized that fate was drawing me into the eye of the storm that was fast building up. Vaqar gave me a telephone number at the Presidency to contact. I wrote the number on a piece of paper, put it in my pocket, and left my office for a lunch engagement with my friends Mahmoud Haroon and Altaf Gauhar. I told them what had hit me. They both sympathized with me and wished me luck.

After lunch, I rushed to the Presidency, only to be told by the Chief of Staff, General Peerzada, that the President had left and that he had selected me for this very sensitive appointment in spite of my friendship with Altaf Gauhar, and that the file on the subject was lying on the President's table. I left for Rawalpindi in the evening. Next morning, I took over charge and met all my colleagues in the Ministry of Information. Two days later, before I could familiarize myself with my new responsibilities, I was summoned to Dhaka. I knew that the moment of truth had come. Accompanied by Jalal, an officer of the ministry, I landed in Dhaka. An army officer received us and took us in his jeep to the army

* Regional Co-operation for Development, an organization comprising Pakistan, Iran, and Turkey.

rest-house in the cantonment. I did not meet Yahya before 23 March, when I was asked to meet him at the official residence of General Tikka Khan. When I got there, a number of other senior army officers were also present. Yahya was wearing a bush-shirt and white trousers. I did not know that 23 March would virtually mark the end of united Pakistan. Yahya did not tell me that negotiations with the Awami League had failed and that resort to force was the only option. He talked in generalities and asked me to prepare for all eventualities. Yahya said to me: 'Two old women thoroughly demoralized a first-class army'.

Tikka had arranged lunch for the President and his party. Yahya asked Tikka to arrange *langar ki dal* (lentils cooked for the troops). The resourceful Tikka produced *langar ki dal* from somewhere. After lunch, Yahya left and we all dispersed. I headed for the army rest-house, not knowing what had been planned and what was in store for us, and in particular, for the innocent people of East Pakistan.

On 23 March, I telephoned my Bengali friend and colleague, Sanaul Haq. We agreed to meet at the Intercontinental Hotel. From the Intercontinental, he took me home in his own car. There was absolutely no feeling of hostility on either side, although we knew that Pakistan as we knew it was on its deathbed. 23 March is a national day in Pakistan. In Dhaka, however, it was observed as Resistance Day. Nobody was allowed to fly the Pakistan flag.

Meanwhile on 19 March, I had been asked by General Peerzada to telephone Bhutto in Karachi and ask him to come to Dhaka. At first, Bhutto was somewhat reluctant to do so as he thought it would serve no purpose. But then, wiser counsels prevailed and he arrived with all his principal party leaders.

As we felt somewhat isolated in the army rest-house, we booked a room at the Intercon Hotel, where we could better watch the fast unfolding tragic drama. On the evening of 25 March, Qaiser Rashid, a foreign service officer and a friend of Zulfikar Ali Bhutto, came to my room at the Intercon. Later, as there was nothing much to do, he took me to Akhtar Ispahani's house for dinner. A number of foreign journalists were also there. While dinner was still in progress, Arnold Zeitlin of the Associated Press was called to the telephone. When he came back, he told us that the Army operation had been launched. I hurried back to the rest-house, driving past several barbed wire barriers, and established contact

radio station remained operational and that the morning
programme was broadcast on schedule. All the Bengali staff had
vanished. With great difficulty, we were able to round up a few
key persons — mostly West Pakistanis and Biharis — and take
them to the radio station under army escort. I distinctly remember driving in an army jeep on a deserted road. All I saw was one
or two stray dogs barking as we drove past. Mercifully, I saw no
action and I saw no dead bodies. A trembling maulana recited the
Holy Quran, with an army captain standing behind him.

At daybreak, I left for General Tikka's Headquarters. On the
tarmac at Dhaka Airport, I met Brigadier Jehanzeb who told me
that Yahya had left for Karachi on the night of 25 March and
Bhutto and his party were in the VIP lounge, waiting to take off
for Karachi. Bhutto was sitting on a sofa, accompanied by Mubashir
Hasan, J. A. Rahim, and others. The first question he asked was
how many had been shot dead. I could not tell him anything because I did not know anything myself nor was I particularly keen
to know the exact figure. He then told me that the army action
would have to be followed up with political initiatives, and that
army action alone would not solve the crisis. Having said this, he
got up, boarded the aircraft, and took off for Karachi where he
made the public announcement, 'Thank God, Pakistan is saved'.

My instructions were to stay back for a few days and assist Tikka.
Suddenly, in my own country, I felt lonely, isolated, threatened,
and very insecure. How was all this to be explained to our own
people and to the world at large? Our task was not made any easier
when, without consulting me, all foreign correspondents were
forced to leave East Pakistan, taken by the army to the airport,
thoroughly searched, and then put on a plane leaving the country.

On 30 March I left Dhaka and flew to Karachi and on to
Rawalpindi.

On arrival, I headed for home. Ghulam Ishaq Khan, the future
President, was sitting on the lawn of my official residence in Civil
Lines, waiting for me. He was then Cabinet Secretary and recipi-
ent of cypher messages from our ambassadors all over the world.
They all wanted to know what had happened; what our side of the
story was and how it was to be explained. All that we had was
Yahya's broadcast in which he said, 'The Proclamation that Mujib
proposed was nothing but a trap . . . The man [Mujib] and his
party are enemies of Pakistan and they want East Pakistan to break

away completely from the country. He has attacked the solidarity and integrity of the country. This crime will not go unpunished'.

With material mainly supplied by the Inter Services Public Relations, we prepared a White Paper, which gave details of the armed rebellion as we called it. By then, a lot of damage had been done. Our White Paper lacked credibility and the world at large was mostly left unconvinced.

On arrival in Rawalpindi, I was told that I had to attend an early morning meeting in the GHQ which the President would chair. Lieutenant General Gul Hassan and Major General Akbar, DG ISI represented the Army. The Foreign Secretary, Sultan Khan, and myself were the only two civilians. The impression conveyed to us was that the army had the situation in East Pakistan well under control; that the rebellion was a conspiracy between Mujib and the Indians; and that the people of East Pakistan were with us. There was an element of truth in all this, but in the military operation, many innocent persons — men, women, and children — lost their lives; excesses and atrocities were committed by the army and, as a result, we lost the people of East Pakistan. Almost till the end, whatever may have been Mujib's own designs, the people of East Pakistan did not want to break up the country and it was only a vocal minority which was in favour of total secession.

We were told in the GHQ meetings that Tikka's aim was to seal the border — as Tikka described it — in order to seal off the routes from India and hold important towns. General Gul Hassan talked about the reinforcements required by Tikka and how these were being dispatched by PIA which did a wonderful job. He was not satisfied with the GHQ meetings, to which relevant Secretaries were now being invited. He complained that in the absence of the Principal Staff Officer to the President, there was no machinery for implementation of decisions taken at the GHQ meetings and that there was no co-ordination with the CMLA Headquarters.

All Bengali secretaries to the government were now suspect and, on their arrival at the GHQ meetings, all discussion would suddenly become constrained, less open and frank. They were in a most unenviable position and I felt sorry for them, the unfortunate country, and everybody else, including ourselves.

By August, we were told in the GHQ that Tikka had almost restored the authority of the central government; that the rebels were fleeing to India; and that troops were moving towards the border.

I soon realized that the GHQ meetings were unproductive. No serious discussion really took place in these meetings. I never left these meetings feeling either more enlightened or better informed. Major issues confronting the country were never raised or addressed. We started losing touch with reality. East Pakistan was too far away; in West Pakistan it was business as usual. I liked to believe that there was no cause for concern as the army-wallahs knew what was to be done and the country was in safe hands. But the feeling of unease, that something was wrong, a sense of foreboding, gripped me and I decided to get out and see things for myself in East Pakistan. I felt suffocated in West Pakistan and somehow felt drawn towards East Pakistan. I therefore made it a point to visit East Pakistan once a month if possible and I did not confine my visits to Dhaka alone. After a day or two in Dhaka and after meeting my civilian colleagues, I used to go to the interior, visit the troops in their forward positions, and also meet my Bengali civilian colleagues. At Khulna, I was delighted to meet Colonel Shams, a fellow Pakhtun.

I always came back from these tours feeling terribly depressed and unhappy at the turn of events and not knowing how it was all going to end. On the one hand, I never felt so close to the troops and so proud of the soldiers in their forward positions facing the Indians and defending the territorial integrity of the country against heavy odds. On the other hand, they were pitted against their own people in a civil war in which innocent men, women, and children were being killed and atrocities were being perpetrated on them. How the hell had we landed ourselves in this mess? On one occasion, on a troop train taking ammunition to Jessore, I saw a solitary, old, bearded Bengali facing the Kaaba, saying his evening prayers. I said to myself, 'How can he be my enemy? He is a better Mussalman than I am. How can he be unpatriotic? How can he join hands with the Indians against his own country, his own people?' I could never find answers to these questions which were constantly agitating my mind.

On my return from these trips, I used to brief the President at the GHQ meetings. I noticed that the meetings were becoming less and less frequent, and the President's interest was flagging. I did not know that all was not well in the inner army circle surrounding the President. There was no love lost between the COS General Hamid and the PSO (P) General Peerzada, between the COS and the CGS General Gul Hassan, between the CGS Gul

Hassan and the PSO (P). It was a house divided. Even Gul Hassan did not know about the army action on the night between 25 and 26 March until Yahya told him on his arrival in Karachi. When Yahya spoke to him, Gul Hassan thought he was speaking from Dhaka. Gul Hassan did not know how East Pakistan, if attacked by India, was going to be defended, and how the political crisis was going to be solved. So I was in good company. In fact, I knew even less.

The Indians attacked several places on the border in East Pakistan on 2 November. On 22 November, I was invited to attend a meeting with the President at his residence. After some discussion, it was decided to send a message to our permanent representative at the UN to the effect that India had committed aggression against our territory. We were all along led to believe that, in its own national interest, China would never allow the Indians to attack and overrun East Pakistan. In order to boost the morale of the people, we fed them this line of thinking. We did not know and we were never told that the Chinese had made no such commitment. In fact, it later transpired, the Chinese had told our delegation led by Bhutto that we should settle the crisis politically. (In the 1965 war, the Indians had spared East Pakistan which, if attacked we were told, would be looked after by China. This led East Pakistan to believe that if China was going to defend them against India, they should not bear the burden of maintaining and financing the Pakistan Army.)

On 3 December, I was asked to meet Gul Hassan in his office in the GHQ at about 3 p. m. When I got there, he was not in his office. In a little while, he came in and sat next to me. He was in a very agitated mood. He told me that we had no choice but to attack from the West; that time was against us; that people were getting restive and wondering why we were not attacking the Indians in the West; and that he could no longer appear in public in his uniform anywhere in the West. I totally agreed with Gul Hassan and told him that our feedback in the Ministry of Information was the same and that people were wondering why we did not regard an attack on East Pakistan as an attack on Pakistan.

After this depressing talk, we went to the OPS room in the GHQ. The President was already there. Air Marshal Rahim was also there. Our attack aircraft had already taken off and the movement of aircraft was being shown on the board. A suitable news item about the Indian attack was broadcast over the radio, minutes before the

Indian version. Whatever the outcome of the war, Radio Pakistan had scored its first point. The President had a transistor radio with him and was monitoring both Pakistani and Indian radio broadcasts and was visibly relieved that we had beaten the Indians to it.

Later in the evening, we reassembled at the President's House. Air Marshal Rahim and General Hameed were there; I was the only civilian present. Rahim told us that all our planes had returned safely. The President inquired about the damage inflicted on the enemy. Rahim told him that it had all been photographed and the result would be available next morning. Hameed told the President that all our formations had attained most of their objectives.

By 13 December, the Indians were on the threshold of Dhaka which was poorly defended. Dhaka fell on 16 December 1971. On the basis of information supplied by the ISPR, we broadcast the news that, as a result of a local arrangement between the two commanders, Indian and Pakistani, a cease-fire had been arranged.

When I met Yahya next day, I was in tears. What we did not know was that Yahya had told Niazi to remain in touch with Governor Malik, to whom the President had delegated authority to take any action he deemed fit to bring a halt to hostilities. Terrible confusion followed because Dhaka asked the UN for a cease-fire but this was contradicted by Rawalpindi. President Yahya went on the air and assured the people that we had only lost a battle and that the war in the West would go on. He was given a draft based on Churchill's heroic words (We will fight on the beaches etc.) after the retreat from Dunkirk, but we found next morning that these words had been deleted. We were not British and Yahya was no Churchill. When I raised the matter with Yahya and told him that nations do not fight wars by halves, he told me that he was not going to endanger West Pakistan 'for the sake of Bengalis'.

To share my sorrow, I called on the Vice-President, Mr Nurul Amin, who was staying in East Pakistan House. Mr Mahmud Ali, his friend and constant companion was also there. I had never seen Mr Nurul Amin, a true Pakistani and a great patriot, in such an angry mood. He said he had been trying in vain to meet the President for two days. I immediately contacted Yahya on the green line and arranged a meeting that very evening. Yahya asked me to accompany Mr Nurul Amin to the President's House. When we got there, General Hameed was already there and they were all having drinks. Nurul Amin burst out and told the President, 'So

Dhaka has fallen and East Pakistan is gone, and you are enjoying whisky'. For a moment, there was a hush. When Yahya recovered, he tried to explain all that he had done, the various steps he had taken to avert the catastrophe, and put the entire blame on Mujib. It was one of the most painful meetings I have ever attended.

On 19 December, two army officers in uniform, one of them a brigadier, came to my office in Chaklala. I was in a meeting with senior officers of the Ministry and the heads of radio and television. Coffee was ordered. After the usual pleasantries, the Brigadier asked me if some kind of a Constitution was going to be broadcast in the evening. I confirmed it. He then expressed the opinion that, in the background of the tragedy being enacted, it was hardly the time for such broadcasts. I let it pass and tried to change the subject. But he brought up the subject again and suggested cancellation of the broadcast. At that point, I realized that it was not an academic discussion and that the two army officers were deadly serious and were on a dangerous mission. I told them that the broadcast had the approval of the President and could not be cancelled without his explicit orders. It made little impact and he advised me to take the bit in my teeth and go ahead with the cancellation of the broadcast. They left when they realized that I was in no mood to oblige. We were stunned: what they wanted was that I should defy the President's orders. For a moment, I thought a coup had already taken place and Yahya had been toppled. The realization suddenly dawned on me that the situation was fraught with all kinds of dangerous possibilities.

Later in the evening, the Emergency Committee, of which I was a member and which acted as Yahya's Cabinet or Council of Advisers, met in the Ministry of Defence. Other members present were Ghulam Ishaq Khan, Cabinet Secretary; Qamrul Islam, Secretary, Petroleum and Natural Resources; and Mumtaz Alvi, Additional Foreign Secretary. The green telephone in the Defence Secretary's office rang. He picked up the receiver and told me that the call was for me. The CGS Gul Hassan was on the line. Speaking in Pushto, since both of us are Pakhtuns, he asked me to cancel the evening broadcast. This is how Gul describes the conversation in his *Memoirs*, 'I picked up the phone next to the President, contacted the Secretary [meaning me] and passed on the message. On hearing it, he asked me where I was speaking from. In order to set his mind at rest, I requested the President to speak to him. General Yahya Khan took the phone and told the Secretary, "I have told Gul what is to be announced immediately and he will convey it to you". This I did. The announcement came within minutes while we were still with the President.' [6]

This is basically correct but Gul Hassan seems to have mixed up a few things. After he had spoken to me and told me where he was speaking from, I called the President. The ADC on duty answered the call. I asked him to put me on to the President, which he did. When the President came on the line, I conveyed to him what Gul had earlier told me. He confirmed it and asked me to go ahead with the cancellation of the broadcast. This was done within minutes and we succeeded in stopping the broadcast.

After the fall of Dhaka, the President called a meeting to review the situation. Those present included Ghulam Ishaq Khan, Cabinet Secretary; Sultan Khan, Foreign Secretary; Qamrul Islam, Secretary Petroleum; and S. Ghiasuddin Ahmad, Secretary General Defence. After some discussion, it was decided that I should explain the circumstances leading to the fall of Dhaka to the editors of newspapers in Lahore and Karachi. I suggested that, since military matters were involved, a senior army officer should accompany me to explain the debacle in East Pakistan. On hearing this, Yahya flared up, ticked me off, and told me that I had used a wrong word to describe the situation. I was stunned. How else could it be described? He still lived in a world of make-believe and thought it was a problem of semantics. Nobody present said a word.

After Mrs Gandhi's unilateral offer of a cease-fire, the Emergency Committee met as usual in the Ministry of Defence, to formulate our response to the offer. A draft was approved and one of us picked up the phone and arranged a meeting with the President. When we got there, the President was sitting in the verandah of the President's House. Among those present were Sultan Khan, Foreign Secretary; General Hameed, COS; Air Marshal Rahim Khan; Lieutenant General Peerzada, the PSO (P); and some others.

Before any one of us could say a word, the President recapitulated the events leading to the catastrophe. I do not think he used that word, but that is what it was. When he had finished, he asked Sultan Khan, the Foreign Secretary, to read the draft prepared by him in response to Mrs Gandhi's unilateral offer of a cease-fire. Sultan Khan took a piece of paper out of his pocket and started reading. It conveyed our unconditional acceptance of the offer. Nobody raised any objection to the substance of the draft but a heated and animated discussion followed on how the timing of the cease-fire was to be described, in terms of IST, GMT, or PST; and, if PST, in terms of West Pakistan Standard Time or East Pakistan Standard Time. The implications in each case were discussed threadbare. This went on for sometime. Yahya Khan got bored and in utter exasperation observed that if only we had adopted the proposal on the subject of a standard time contained in the summary which had come up before the Cabinet a month earlier, we would not have had this problem!

Before discussion on our response to the Indian cease-fire offer, the President asked the Foreign Secretary to read President Nixon's letter addressed to him (the President). In it, Nixon, describing himself as a friend of Pakistan, had advised the President to accept the offer and undertaken to make up our losses in military hardware. This clinched the matter and our acceptance of the cease-fire offer was conveyed to New Delhi on 17 December.

It was the most painful moment of my life when on 16 December we watched with anguish the humiliating spectacle of the surrender in Dhaka, officially described as a 'cease-fire agreement between local commanders'. There have been many surrenders in history, and I recalled the German surrender to the allies at the end of the Second World War: '. . . at 2.35 Strong escorted Jodl (General) and two aides through the entrance and down the corridor into the blinding klieg lights. Jodl bowed stiffly before taking his seat . . . . After signing the surrender documents, Jodl stood and attempted to lend dignity to the German position with a brief statement, "With this signature", he said, "the German people and German armed forces are for better or worse delivered into the victor's hands. In this war which has lasted more than five years, they achieved and suffered much more than any other people in the world. In this hour, I can only express the hope that the victors will treat them with generosity."' [7]

Jodl was tried at Nuremberg and hanged. This was indeed a surrender but it was exercised with dignity. On an earlier occasion, Matthias Erzberger, the Chief German Delegate, after signing the surrender document at ten past five in the morning of 11 November 1918 at Compiegne, declared: 'A nation of seventy million suffers but does not die.' [8]

By contrast, our surrender in Dhaka was a travesty, a clownish exercise in self-humiliation. Never in my life had my spirits been so low. The generals responsible for this humiliation reminded me of Wellington's famous observation on the eve of the battle of Waterloo. He said 'Really, when I reflect upon the character and attainment of some of the General Officers of this Army, and consider that these are the persons on whom I am to rely to lead columns against the French Generals, and who are to carry out my instructions into execution, I tremble'; and as Lord Chesterfield said of the Generals of his day 'I only hope that when the enemy reads the list of their names, he trembles as I do.' To rub salt in the wound, the surrender film was shown on Pakistan Television on the orders of Zulfikar Ali Bhutto, who assumed power on 20 December 1971 as President and Chief Martial Law Administrator, but was quickly withdrawn under public and army pressure.

I hit it off very well with Hafeez Pirzada, my new Minister, but Bhutto had decided to have a more committed man as his Information Secretary. I left for Sindh, home province of Mr Bhutto, to take up my new appointment as Chief Secretary. When I mentioned this development to Mr Bhutto's sister in Karachi, she was not very enthusiastic, in fact a little apprehensive, and advised me to try and get a low-profile job in the Centre. She knew her brother and her talented cousin, Mumtaz Bhutto, the new Martial Law Administrator and Chief Minister of Sindh, much better than I did. Trouble was not far.

Karachi was soon plunged into a wave of serious ethnic trouble, when the government in its wisdom decided to make Sindhi the official language of the province, in the teeth of opposition from non-Sindhis. The reaction of the Urdu-speaking people was sharp. There were violent clashes with the law enforcement agencies, resulting in many deaths.

At the very outset it became clear that the new PPP rulers had scant regard for the rule of law. Any civil servant who quoted the book to them aroused their anger and suspicion. I knew my days in Sindh were numbered. Meanwhile, my brother Khaliq Khan had joined a small group of rebel PPP MNAs who defied Mr Bhutto who was becoming more and more authoritarian, intolerant of criticism, and despotic. Khaliq Khan frontally attacked Bhutto on the floor of the House in his Budget speech. Bhutto was furious. I was made to suffer mainly for the sins of my brother and soon found myself back in the Centre as Secretary Labour.

One morning in 1974, I lost my job as Secretary Labour and found myself in the wilderness for the first time in my career. A week or two before this happened, I had made a presentation before the Cabinet on labour laws. At the end of the presentation, the Cabinet Secretary walked up to me, shook my hand, and congratulated me on my excellent performance. I was very pleased with my performance and with myself. Just when I felt most secure, the blow fell when I least expected it. I knew the reason. My brother was being troublesome and not falling in line. This was Bhutto's way of conveying the message. Five months later, when I was getting ready for premature retirement, I was recalled from the wilderness and appointed Secretary, Ministry of Tourism, a job I thoroughly enjoyed. I felt like a convict who had just come out of jail after serving his full sentence and felt very safe and secure.

I was soon made to realize how wrong I was. Mr Bhutto had just finished addressing the Secretaries to the Government and I was seated in the front row. As he was leaving the dais, he stopped, looked at me and said, within the hearing of my colleagues, 'I have given you a second chance, but you still keep bad company. You meet Altaf Gauhar and visit Peshawar' (implying that I intrigue with his political opponents). Altaf Gauhar was an old friend and Peshawar the capital of my home province. I was stunned. The tragedy of Bhutto was that he could at times be very petty and vindictive. In fairness to him, I must add that three times, according to the Establishment Secretary, Bhutto ordered my premature retirement from service but on each occasion, perhaps for old times' sake, he relented and reversed his order.

My stint as Secretary Tourism was the happiest of my entire career. Mr Bhutto enabled me to see the world, including many exotic places. One day, I found myself in outer Mongolia, the fabled land of Genghis Khan, sitting at the hearth of a Mongolian yurt and sipping fermented mare's milk, talking to my nomad hosts. A pretty young Mongolian girl was playing a two-stringed horse fiddle. Early every morning, I would leave the yurt and go for long walks in the Gobi desert. Mongolia is a nation of two million people, whose President once said that his favourite pastime was sleeping. When I visited Mongolia, it was under communist control and wherever one went, one saw huge portraits of the Great Leader.

Thanks to Mr Bhutto, I spent a pleasant fortnight in Spain on the Costa del Sol at Torremelinos, attending a WTO Conference, mixing a lot of pleasure with a moderate amount of work. On the summary seeking approval for my visit, Mr Bhutto wrote: 'Approved. Have fun'. (Sd.) Zulfikar Ali Bhutto.

One day, Mr Bhutto sent for me and said: 'One of the ambitions of my life is to have a Geneva-type fountain installed in the Kinjhar lake in Sindh. Go to Geneva; meet the consultants and see that work on the fountain is started without delay. Funds will be no problem.' I went to Geneva twice and had detailed discussions with the consultant. He advised against the implementation of the project on the ground that conditions at Kinjhar Lake were different from Lake Geneva. He added that Pakistan was a poor country and could ill afford such a luxury. In the summary submitted to the Prime Minister, armed with the consultant's report, I opposed the proposal. Very reluctantly, Mr Bhutto wrote on the margin 'Approved. Drop it'.

One day, Mr Bhutto sent for me and at great length narrated all my acts of omission and commission which had soured our relations and then said: 'Now you know why I have sent you to an unimportant Ministry like Tourism. But that is all in the past. I am thinking of giving you an important assignment.' I thanked him profusely and immediately sought an appointment with Begum Bhutto. I told her that the Prime Minister was threatening to give me an important assignment and requested her to intercede on my behalf and tell the Prime Minister that I was quite happy where I was. Her intervention produced the desired result. Before I took leave of her, she told me that, in spite of everything, Mr Bhutto must have a lot of regard for me, otherwise, if he could sack Qamrul Islam, an old friend, what prevented him from throwing me out of service?

Field Marshal Muhammad Ayub Khan

Chapter 1

Ayub

> No Constitution can be absolutely safe from Revolution or
> from a *coup d'état*.
> **Dicey**

On 4 October 1958, Ayub recalls in *Friends Not Masters*, the hour
had struck. The moment so long delayed had finally arrived. The
responsibility could no longer be put off. And yet, in the same
breath, he asked Iskander Mirza in Karachi on 5 October: 'Have
you made up your mind, Sir?' 'Yes', he replied. 'Do you think it is
absolutely necessary?' 'It is absolutely necessary,' Mirza said firmly.
Ayub never told Mirza that he disagreed with him and that he
would not be a party to such a drastic action. In order not to take
responsibility for what was about to be done with his full connivance, support, and collusion, he told Mirza, 'I want two things
from you in writing: one, that I will administer Martial Law; and
the other, a letter to the Prime Minister that *you* have abrogated
the Constitution and declared Martial Law and that *you* have
appointed me to administer the Martial Law. I wanted him to write
the letter to the Prime Minister so that he should assume full
responsibility for his decision. He, as the constitutional head of
government had come to the conclusion that the country could
not be run any more on a constitutional basis. At least you have
done something and I believe you have done the right thing. But

I feel that I must have it from you in writing. He hummed and hawed but finally agreed to give me the letter after two or three days.'[1]

Ayub knew fully well that the Constitution contained no provision for its own abrogation; that it contained no provision for declaration of martial law and appointment of a Chief Martial Law Administrator; that it constituted treason in the eyes of the law; and that the piece of paper he was demanding from the President would not absolve him of the enormity of the crime he was about to commit. Instead of taking his share of responsibility for the assault on the Constitution and the civilian set-up, he desperately tried to distance himself from the operation and throw the entire responsibility on the shoulders of Mirza, knowing fully well that it was jointly conceived, planned, and executed.

Now that the decision to murder democracy had been taken, everything had to be done in strict conformity with propriety. 'From that time onwards, emotion had no place in the proceedings. Now that this job had to be done, it must be done properly. A simple plan was formulated and put into operation. I advised Mirza, "you had better inform your Prime Minister about the situation". He thought it was unnecessary as he had no doubt about the legality of his action.'[2] He conveniently omits to mention whether he himself had any doubts about the legality of his action. Ayub was aware of what he was going to do. 'Another worry I had was, how if the Army once got drawn into political life — and this seemed inevitable — it could withdraw itself from the situation. The outside world was going to interpret the action of the Army in terms of the *coup d'état* which frequently occurred in certain other countries. This would have had a damaging effect on the image and reputation of Pakistan. A well-organized, trained and disciplined army would find it distasteful to be turned into an instrument for securing political power. But as conditions were, the army alone could act as a coercive force and restore normalcy.'

Aware of adverse foreign reaction, Ayub describes what they did on 7 October not as a *coup d'état* but as a revolution, to which he devotes a whole chapter in *Friends Not Masters*. 'Revolutions take long and painstaking preparations, detailed planning, clandestine meetings and countrywide movement of troops. In our case, there was very little preparation. It was handled as a military operation. What happened was that a brigade was moved, actually two brigades.'[3] Such detailed military preparations, Ayub knew,

President Iskander Mirza

were not really necessary because it was not an insurrection on the part of the civilians against the security apparatus of the state. It was not a revolution but a *coup d'état* by the armed forces, a seizure from within, and a politically neutral operation. Experience shows that the army chief does not have to move even one brigade to capture power and topple a corrupt, unpopular civilian government. A jeep-load of soldiers led by a major armed with the authority of the Chief will suffice. Resistance to usurpers is not part of our culture nor in accordance with the best traditions of our society.

'Ayub introduced a range of reforms in the hope that the benefits flowing from these reforms would reach the people and they would come to recognize the merits of his system of government. Some of the reforms never got off the ground; others like the land reforms, lost their purpose in the course of implementation. Still, the introduction of the reforms created an atmosphere of rethinking which constituted a challenge to vested interests. The *ulema* were particularly alarmed when family laws came into operation. These laws gave married women certain rights which acted as a restraint on male freedom to divorce at will or acquire more than one wife. While women welcomed these laws, the conservative classes considered them an assault on the Islamic structure of society. When Ayub's reforms came to be questioned he began to wonder whether he had not pushed the people too hard into the modern age.'[4]

Ayub will be remembered for the development of the atomic energy programme in Pakistan which received a shot in the arm when he converted the Pakistan Atomic Energy Commission from a semi-government body into a statutory body in 1965. It then attained a great measure of autonomy to fulfil its statutory obligation in respect of internal administration as well as international co-operation.

To support the nuclear power programme, a big national centre for advanced studies and research, PINSTECH, was established at Nilore near Islamabad, with a 5 MW swimming-pool research reactor, a sub-critical assembly, and other tools like the neutron generator and a cobalt source. It went critical in December 1965. PINSTECH is equipped to take care of the problems in nuclear technology that the Commission has in hand. PINSTECH is building around the reactor and other tools, large laboratories in the field of electronics, nuclear materials, radioisotope production and application, nuclear physics, and radiation chemistry.

Another important development during this period was the construction of KANUPP, eighteen miles west of Karachi, the country's first atomic station with a generating capacity of 137,000 KW gross. The plant is now operating on full power. KANUPP marks the beginning of the gradual induction of nuclear energy in Pakistan to fill the gap between the growing power demand and its limited available supply.

These two, KANUPP and PINSTECH, are the focal points of Pakistan's peaceful nuclear energy effort. The engineering research laboratory, ERL, later renamed Dr A. Q. Khan Research Laboratories, was established much later in July 1976, long after Ayub had left the stage, but at the policy level, Ayub's contribution to Pakistan's nuclear programme cannot be ignored. For me, personally, it was a very exciting experience to be associated with this programme in my capacity as Ayub's Science Secretary.

Ten years later, as he crumbled toward collapse, he told his former Ministers, 'I am sorry we have come to this pass. We are a very difficult country structurally. Perhaps I pushed it too hard into the modern age. We were not ready for reforms. Quite frankly, I have failed. I must admit that clearly. Our laws were for a sophisticated society.'[5]

In the letter addressed to Yahya, on 25 March 1969, Ayub did not say he was resigning. He chose his words very cleverly. All he said was that he was stepping aside and, without abrogating the Constitution or declaring martial law, called upon Yahya to save the country from internal disorder and chaos as it was his legal and constitutional responsibility. He conveniently forgot that under his own Constitution which he did not abrogate, the Speaker of the National Assembly alone could fill the vacuum left behind by him. The Speaker was not called upon to play any role. Ayub shirked responsibility for abrogating the Constitution and declaring martial law. He left this dirty job to be done by Yahya and Yahya did not ask Ayub to abrogate the Constitution or to sack the Assemblies and the central and provincial governments as Ayub had asked Mirza ten years earlier. Why did he not resign? Why did he leave everything so vague? Did he hope that after the restoration of law and order he would be called back to rule the country?

Before leaving, Ayub saw his entire constitutional edifice crumbling before his eyes and all his reforms denounced. In an effort to appease the opposition, he even agreed to demolish the Basic Democracies system, and revert to adult franchise. Too late: nothing worked. His departure from the President's House reminds one of the Shah's departure from Tehran into exile, both looking very lonely and abandoned by everybody, not knowing what had hit them.

'Miss Jinnah had lost the Presidential Election but during the campaign, she had mercilessly portrayed Ayub as an interloper and a dictator. She attacked him and his family for corruption, particularly Gohar Ayub, a retired captain from the army who had acquired an assembly plant from General Motors to which he gave the name Gandhara Motors through the influence of his father'.[6] Throughout the campaign Gandhara was used as the ultimate symbol of corruption in Ayub's government and in his family. 'Nothing destroyed Ayub's prestige and credibility more than "Gandhara". . . His land reforms were seen as an elaborate design to consolidate the power of landlords and bureaucrats and his Islamic reforms, especially the family laws were criticised as deviation from the Sunnah.'[7]

Ayub's reputation and authority received a severe blow as a result of the 1965 war with India. The Tashkent Declaration was ill received in West Pakistan. Pakistanis were disillusioned, lied to, and cheated. They held Ayub responsible for leading them into a war with India and then losing it. It was clear that Ayub could not survive Tashkent. It was only a question of time. Bhutto exploited it fully and gave him the *coup de grâce*.

In the end, like the Shah, all the steps Ayub was willing to take politically were always too little and too late. By that time, the Revolution — the real Revolution because it involved the masses — had gathered such momentum that nothing Ayub did could have averted it.

Like the Shah, as he went on making concessions, he only whetted the appetite of the people for further concessions. He was on the run. But unlike the Shah, Ayub's impending fate caused very little concern in the US State Department. No emissaries were sent to stiffen Ayub's resolve and no assurances of American support were conveyed to Ayub. Like the Shah, Ayub's face toward the end had become ashen, his former physical vigour had clearly gone.

President Ayub Khan signs the Tashkent Declaration on 10 January 1966. Foreign Minister Zulfikar Ali Bhutto is on his right

Ayub, according to Altaf Gauhar, 'had one advantage over most other military rulers. His accession to power was generally and quite genuinely acknowledged as the only way out of the mess which the politicians had created during the first eleven years of Pakistan's existence.'[8] Ayub failed not because his military rule was a complete negation of democratic principles and fundamental human rights. He failed because he could not demonstrate to the people that the assault on democracy and the abrogation of the Constitution was justified by his subsequent performance; that he was qualitatively superior to the deposed politicians, and that military rule was an improvement on civilian rule. He failed because his performance fell far short of the promises he had made to the people and the expectations he had aroused. Unlike his democratic predecessors, he commanded absolute power and had no excuses. Why then did he fail to bring about an egalitarian social and economic order? Why did his long rule make no dent in the system he had inherited? Why did he not identity himself with the poor people of Pakistan who listened to him and believed in him? What prevented him from confronting their main anxieties? Why did he promise them a new heaven and a new earth? Is it surprising that, when he was on the ropes, nobody stood by him? Like the Shah's white revolution, Ayub's revolution, if it can be called a revolution at all, collapsed like a house of cards. Unlike the Shah, Ayub rests in peace in his ancestral village Rehana, which he loved.

Towards the end, Ayub symbolized a hated regime. He was the first to stab Pakistan's democracy in the back. It was Ayub who committed the original sin. It was Ayub who inducted the army into the politics of Pakistan. It was he who set a bad precedent. Others merely followed his example. In the process, he did incalculable harm to the country and to the army. He knew that if the army once got drawn into political life — and this he knew was inevitable — it could not withdraw itself from the situation. What a mess he left behind.

Chapter 2

Bhutto outcast

In March 1966, Ayub removed Bhutto, as Secretary General of the Muslim League and in June from the Cabinet, saying that Bhutto was going abroad for medical treatment. I was attending a dinner party at the house of Altaf Gauhar, the Information Secretary, when he told me that Bhutto had received marching orders from Ayub earlier in the day. After dinner, I told Ghulam Ishaq Khan who was also there that we had to go and see Bhutto. He agreed but suggested that we visit him next day. I told him that would be too late. So we left Altaf Gauhar's house together and went straight to Bhutto's official residence in Civil Lines, Rawalpindi. The atmosphere prevailing there was one of gloom and depression. Bhutto was sitting all alone on the lawn with a glass of whisky in his hands. Ghulam Ishaq Khan extended his hand. Bhutto, instead, threw his arms around Ghulam Ishaq Khan and broke down. He then embraced me and told us in an animated voice, 'The way Ayub treated me today you would not treat your orderly.' Ghulam Ishaq Khan consoled him and said, almost prophetically, 'You are still very young. Your future is ahead of you.' We both felt very depressed and left Bhutto still holding the glass of whisky in his hand. A few days later, when I met him again, he had recovered and was sitting on the verandah, busy sorting out his papers. Benazir, then a very young girl, asked him in Urdu, 'Papa, have we become *awam* now?'

President Zulfikar Ali Bhutto

A few days later, he left Rawalpindi by train from the cantonment railway station. I went to see him off. One or two persons
from the Foreign Office were there in their official capacity. Altaf
Gauhar, Secretary Information and Broadcasting, was also there.
The railway platform was enveloped in darkness. I was there in
my personal capacity. I had grown very fond of Bhutto since my
first meeting with him in Peshawar six years ago and I would not
have forgiven myself if I had not seen him off. I distinctly remember him standing at the door of the railway saloon in shalwar
kameez, waving to the small bunch of sleepy civil servants who had
come to see him off. I do not think anybody realized what a tumul-
tuous reception was awaiting him at the Lahore railway station.

I next met Bhutto when he came to Rawalpindi on his way
back from Europe via Peshawar. I came to know about his visit
from Begum Bhutto. Bhutto was staying at Flashman's Hotel. I
spent the whole evening with him and he asked me to stay for
dinner. After dinner he asked me if I could drive him to the airport to catch his flight for Karachi. Driving is not my strong point
but I managed somehow. On the way to the airport, we found the
railway crossing closed. Bhutto was getting late for his flight so I
got out and used all my powers of persuasion. The gate was opened
and we drove on to the airport. On arrival, we were told that the
flight was delayed. We went back to Flashman's. Just before dawn,
he left for Karachi and I drove back home. It had been a pleasant
evening, and the obtrusive shadow of the intelligence agencies
which were now keeping track of Bhutto did not deter my enjoyment of his company.

Every time I went to Karachi, I made it a point to meet Bhutto,
sometimes at 70 Clifton, but mostly at 109 Clifton, the residence of
his younger sister, Manna, who was an excellent hostess and knew
what her brother liked most. Bhutto wanted to know what was
happening in Islamabad. I was not an insider and knew nothing.
The discussions were therefore mostly academic. Very soon, the
frequency of my visits, the carefree manner in which I used to
meet him, aroused his suspicions. I got the shock of my life when
Manna told me that he could not understand how a civil servant
could meet him so freely and so fearlessly and that I must therefore be one of Ayub's agents, deputed to spy on him. Bhutto was a
highly suspicious person and could never understand that I could
have other motives, and that I was risking my job, only because I

felt drawn towards him and because I admired him and regarded
him as a friend. This soured our relations and the meetings
became less and less frequent.

Ayub knew all along that I was meeting Bhutto quite frequently.
The Intelligence agencies kept him fully informed. He was not
only the President: he was also my Minister in charge of States
and Frontier Regions and Science and Technology Divisions. In
that capacity, I used to meet him two or three times a month; but
he never brought up the question of my meetings with Bhutto
and never suspected my basic loyalty to him, and he never held it
against me. This shows the greatness of the man.

I was pleasantly surprised one day when the Establishment
Secretary, the late Agha Abdul Hamid sent for me and told me
that in spite of my frequent meetings with Zulfikar Ali Bhutto, the
President had decided to appoint me as Head of the Intelligence
Bureau, a post generally held by senior police officers. This
confirmed Bhutto's suspicions and he thought it was all directed
against him. Fortunately, senior police officers represented against
my appointment and Ayub changed his mind. If it had gone
through, if nothing else, I would have gone straight to jail, as the
new DIB did, after Ayub's fall.

Soon after elections in December 1970, Bhutto came to our
house in Mardan. There was a heated argument between Bhutto
and my brother over party matters. My brother Khaliq Khan took
the PPP manifesto too seriously. He thought under the manifesto
there was no place for landlords and *waderas*, etc. in the PPP. He
got a shock when told that other extraneous factors had to be taken
into consideration. Bhutto left our house in a huff, without eating
dinner. At a public meeting next day, Mr Bhutto tried to belittle
the significance of my brother's electoral success and also said some
uncharitable things about me. After the public meeting, my brother
raised this matter with Mr Bhutto at the Mardan Circuit house.
This again led to a heated argument and they nearly came to blows.
This was the beginning of our troubles with Bhutto. Khaliq Khan
was kept out of all committees constituted by Bhutto in preparation for taking over the administration of the country. When I
raised this matter with him in Dhaka at the residence of the
Iranian Consul General, he asked me if I knew how Awami League
MNAs treated their leader Sheikh Mujibur Rehman. Before I could
say anything, he said, 'they take off their shoes before entering his

room; bend down, touch his feet and don't sit on the chair unless permitted to do so by the leader.' I knew bad days were ahead for both of us.

Yahya announced on 13 February 1971, that the National Assembly would meet in Dhaka on 3 March 1971. Bhutto reacted sharply and made it clear that, unless there was prior understanding between him and Mujib on the fundamentals of the Constitution, he would not allow the National Assembly to meet. When I met him at the Intercontinental Hotel, Rawalpindi, he was very critical of Yahya whom he accused of betraying national interests and being soft on Mujib. He said, 'Here I am defending the vital interests and honour of West Pakistan, and Yahya is creating difficulties by calling the session of the National Assembly without prior understanding between me and Mujib.' I asked how, after solemnly agreeing to hold the session on 3 March, Yahya could wriggle out of this commitment. I distinctly remember Bhutto's reply: 'A law and order situation could be easily created in Dhaka resulting in tear-gassing and firing, etc., a few dead bodies and that would more than justify postponement of the National Assembly session.' I was stunned. How Machiavellian! I had never thought of it.

On 1 March 1971, under pressure from Bhutto, Yahya announced postponement of the Assembly, without fixing a new date. The reaction in Dhaka was violent. Between 3 March and 23 March, the central government writ did not run in East Pakistan. With that fateful announcement, both Yahya and Bhutto set in motion the tragic course of events which inevitably led to civil war and the breakup of Pakistan.

President Agha Muhammad Yahya Khan

Chapter 3

Yahya

I first met Yahya in 1956 when he came to Fort Sandeman as a member of Ayub's entourage, a few months after I had been posted there as Political Agent. Unlike Ayub, Yahya was an extrovert, full of life, and a bon vivant. He was from my province of NWFP, but spoke Persian, and, like Ayub, no Pushto. I did not see much of him then because he was not staying at the castle, my official residence, but in the Zhob Militia Mess, along with General Hameed and others.

I met him again at Fort Sandeman when we flew together from Rawalpindi by helicopter to attend the Frontier Corps Reunion. As the evening wore on, he drank champagne from a huge silver cup. After dinner, there was typical Pakhtun dancing in which we all participated. Yahya was undoubtedly immensely popular with the young officers at that time.

I distinctly remember one of the young officers telling him that army requirements were not being met for want of foreign exchange. He looked at the young officers surrounding him and said, 'You are my foreign exchange.' Next morning, we flew back to Rawalpindi. Yahya was sober and remained quiet throughout.

Soon after Yahya took over, I was appointed Managing Director, Pakistan Television, a job for which I was least qualified. My sole qualification, if it can be called a qualification at all, was that I owned a television set. My mother was most upset. I met her soon after taking over charge of my new job. In the absence of my relatives and in an embarrassed tone, she cursed the powers that be and said, 'Is this musician's job the only job they could offer my son?' She could not believe her ears when much later I told her that I was thoroughly enjoying the job. I was introduced to the world of producers, musicians, eminent dancers, and artistes from both wings of the country, people who had dedicated their lives to their profession. I did whatever I could to raise the level of the programmes, plays, etc.

Yahya used to come to the Chaklala television station for the recording of his addresses to the nation. He always had problems with the make-up men. Every now and then, he would yell at them if they touched some part of his face which he did not want to be touched. He was very particular about his eyebrows and God help the man who tried to touch them. He told me that he derived all his strength from his brows; while the make-up man was busy, he looked at me and said, 'You have one thing in common with me. You too have thick bushy eyebrows. Don't let anybody touch them.'

When Ayub wrote to Yahya that he was stepping aside and expressed his belief that he (Yahya) had the capacity, patriotism, dedication, and imagination to deal with the formidable problems facing the country and called upon him to discharge his legal and constitutional responsibility to defend the country, not only against external aggression but also to save it from internal disorder and chaos, I am inclined to believe he meant what he said. Ayub was aware of Yahya's weaknesses and knew he was an extrovert and a bon vivant appreciative of the good things of life. What Ayub failed to realize was that he was giving Yahya an impossible task for which he was ill-suited both by experience and temperament. Ayub was leaving behind a mess of his own creation. How could Yahya succeed where Ayub had failed? Yahya's only advantage over Ayub was that his hands were clean and his record untainted. Ayub knew that Yahya would be pitted against two most unscrupulous politicians and that he was no match for them. After eleven years of absolute rule, he was leaving behind a country on the verge of total collapse, and deserted his post saying, 'I could not sign away the future of the country.'[1] He conveniently left that to Yahya, knowing that the task was beyond him.

Yahya started very well. The disturbances in the country came to an abrupt end; law and order was restored without any difficulty; the country rallied round him and gave him full support.

His initial moves were very popular. He dissolved One Unit, which had been imposed on the people of West Pakistan, and earned the gratitude of at least the three minority provinces. He sacked most corrupt officers. He held the first free, fair, and impartial election Pakistan ever had. He allowed the government-controlled media, both radio and television, to cover the election without any interference from the government.

Within twenty-four hours of his accession to power on 25 March 1969, Yahya pledged to transfer power to the elected representatives of the people, elected on the basis of direct adult franchise, and announced that it would be for the representatives of the people to give the country a workable Constitution. This was, in a sense, a revolutionary development in the politics of Pakistan.

Yahya did not ban political parties when he imposed martial law on 25 March 1969. In one of his speeches in 1970, he said, 'This caused both surprise and relief. The first action of any martial law regime is to ban political parties, for the existence of martial law regime side by side with political parties is a most unusual phenomenon'. There were guidelines for political activity contained in MLR 60, but these were honoured more in the breach than in the observance.

'The Government decided to give facilities to the leaders of various parties to project their political manifestoes and policies through radio and television. This was the first time that politicians were freely and impartially given the chance to use the Government-controlled radio and television for their political activities.'[2]

Political broadcasts began on 28 October and continued until 19 November 1970. The series began with Mujib, who was given the chance to speak first, and ended with the leader of the Sindh United Front, G. M. Syed. Bhashani alone spoke in the two national languages, in Bengali from Dhaka, and in Urdu from West Pakistan. His speech was a masterpiece and it met with a very good reception in both Wings, especially West Pakistan. Bhashani spoke not as an East Pakistani or a West Pakistani, but as a true Pakistani. Mujib emphasised regionalism. Bhutto's main emphasis was on Islamic socialism, confrontation with India, etc.

I met all the political leaders and discussed their scripts with them. I met Mujib at his residence in Dhan Mandi in Dhaka. This was my very first meeting with him. He gave me the impression of being an angry young man in a hurry. His script contained references to Bangladesh. I suggested their deletion, because it clashed with the guidelines and the Legal Framework Order. He did not agree. I suggested its substitution by East Bengal. This too was unacceptable to him. In the end, he was allowed by Rawalpindi to have his own way. He threatened not to say anything on radio and television if the government insisted on the deletion of the word Bangladesh. He was otherwise very courteous and very hospitable. He entertained me to tea and *mishti*. When the tension eased, I suggested that, being a national leader, he should come to West Pakistan, tour the four provinces and meet the people who, I was sure, would welcome him. His reply stunned me. He said, 'West Pakistan is too far away and it costs a lot of money to go there.' Mujib seemed uninterested in visiting West Pakistan. Whatever the reasons, Mujib had lost faith in a united Pakistan.

Next on my list was the 'Red Maulana'. I met Bhashani in his village. When I got there, he was lying on a cot. He sat up, shook hands, and began the conversation in a very weak, inaudible voice. I thought he was seriously ill and did not expect the conversation to last too long. Very soon, he warmed up and gave me a brilliant exposé of the political situation in chaste Urdu, punctuated with verses from Iqbal and the Quran, for one whole hour. I was most impressed. He told me that in the course of his electioneering campaign, he had met Mujib somewhere on the roadside and a brief conversation followed in which he warned Mujib that, although he was drawing big crowds, because he was spreading venom against West Pakistan, these very people would one day hang him and drag his dead body in the streets of Dhaka. Prophetic words, although the end did not come exactly the way Maulana had predicted. In the midst of this exposition, he asked one of the hangers-on to catch some fish in the local pond near his cot. I thoroughly enjoyed the lunch and then took leave of him.

Nothing gave me greater pleasure than to see our leaders appear one by one on national television and explain their manifestos and programmes unedited and uncensored in a martial law regime. I had sold this idea to the martial law government and I am glad they accepted it. I regard this as one of my proud achievements. I succeeded in obtaining Yahya's approval for unrestricted, uncensored, and completely objective coverage of the election results without any interference from the government.

Our commitment to covering the election results from Chittagong to Karachi and Peshawar on television and bringing them to the viewers as they became available without any break-down or interruption was viewed with scepticism. In an atmosphere full of tension and political activity, the television broadcasts provided the people with a good picture of the intensi-fying election campaign. The BBC sent a team of observers to watch our performance. The result was beyond our expectations and theirs. People remained glued to their television sets for more than twenty-four hours. Nobody slept. There were no breakdowns. Our engineers kept the equipment going. 'PTV had come of age', *The London Times* reported. It was undoubtedly PTV's finest hour.

Television had done a wonderful job but for days we did not hear one word of appreciation from the martial law authorities. I have no doubt that they were taken by surprise and it took them some time to recover from the shock.

My Minister, Major General (retd.) Sher Ali, was a great cham-pion of the Islam *Pasand* (Islam-loving) parties (as they were then known). He was most upset at the turn of events when I met him in his office. He told me, almost prophetically, that the election results would lead to the breakup of the country and must there-fore be scrapped. His prophecy unfortunately turned out to be correct, but how could the result of an election universally recog-nized as free, fair, and impartial be scrapped with a stroke of pen?

I watched the election results on television in our studio in Chaklala. Early in the morning I left to see what was happening in Karachi. There I got the good news that my brother, Abdul Khaliq Khan, had won his National Assembly seat as a PPP candidate against two stalwarts, Colonel Amir Khan, the Nawab of Hoti, and Mehr Dil Khan, the veteran Red Shirt leader. Like most Pakis-tanis, I had not had a wink of sleep for twenty-four hours. It was good to be alive. That is how I felt on that day and on that day I was proud of being a Pakistani.

When my brother won his National Assembly seat on a PPP ticket — the only PPP candidate to win a seat in the Frontier prov-ince — I thought Bhutto would be very happy that at least one seat had been won in the NWFP. I got a shock when I sat next to him on board a PIA flight to Karachi and he made no reference to my brother's victory. Just before landing at Karachi, I brought up the matter myself. He responded by saying that Khaliq had se-cured an easy victory as both the rival candidates were lame ducks. I realized that Bhutto was basically a small man, not prepared to give credit to his own party man, even where credit was due.

Yahya had redeemed his pledge to hold free and fair elections on the basis of direct adult franchise. The Awami League led by Sheikh Mujib obtained 160 out of the 162 seats allotted to East Pakistan. In West Pakistan, it could not secure a single seat. The Pakistan People's Party headed by Mr Bhutto won 82 out of 138 seats for West Pakistan. It had not nominated a single candidate in East Pakistan. Yahya did not have the political vision or capacity to handle the complex situation arising out of the election results and the emergence of two unscrupulous politicians, who had neither political honesty nor any broad vision and statesmanship. The result was the total collapse of his plan to transfer power to the elected representatives of the people, eventually culminating in a bloody civil war and the secession of East Pakistan. I never had any doubt that Yahya genuinely wanted to transfer power to the elected representatives of the people within the framework of a single, undivided Pakistan. In fairness to Yahya, it must be said that he had inherited from Ayub a discontented, disillusioned, and highly agitated Bengali population, and an explosive political situation, not of his making.

Neither Ayub nor Yahya had the statesmanship or political skill required to resolve the East Pakistan crisis in accordance with the aspirations of the people of East Pakistan. Commenting on President Ayub, a 'Muslim de Gaulle', *The Economist* wrote that the President wanted essentially what his brother soldier sought for France. But faced with a similar situation in Algeria, de Gaulle 'realizing that whatever aspiration of grandeur he might hold for France, it would come to nothing as long as the nation remained mired and locked in the draining and divisive Algerian crisis', in a moment of inspiration, took off for Algeria to 'grasp the Algerian nettle'[3] and to speak to the people himself. 'By the end of the afternoon a crowd of 20,000, almost entirely European, had massed in the open square, the Forum in front of the Government General Building to greet General de Gaulle with a mighty roar when at last he stepped out on a balcony, arms outstretched and fist clenched in the defiant gesture of exhortation that was his permanent hallmark. But he responded to the cheers with one of the most famous and most elusive utterances of his life. "Je vous ai compris"'[4] — I have understood you. On his return to Paris, de Gaulle held a referendum on the future of Algeria in the teeth of opposition from hawkish generals, the so called ultras. In June 1962, 99.7 per cent of Algerians voted for independence and

Algeria emerged as an independent state on 3 July 1962. Without settling the Algerian crisis, all else for de Gaulle would have been failure. 'Of all the services de Gaulle rendered to France, extraction from Algeria was the most difficult and decisive. It was his masterpiece in the skilled exercise of political power, and if he had failed, history would have been far different and his stature diminished.'[5]

Both Ayub, the 'Muslim de Gaulle', and Yahya, his fun-loving successor who used to describe himself as a part-time President, failed to comprehend the rising tide of Bengali nationalism and failed to meet its challenge in a realistic and flexible manner, with disastrous consequences for Jinnah's Pakistan. This was their greatest failure, and this, in my view, was also their greatest disservice to Pakistan.

Yahya was a true hedonist and believed that the art of life was to crowd in as much enjoyment as possible into each moment. His detractors and enemies charged that he was drunk day and night and that, in his scheme of things, all good things had reference to the belly. This is an unfair assessment of the man. There are innumerable instances of Yahya's unsurpassable kindness. He was devoted to his family, generous and gentle to his servants, loyal to his friends, and he lived without pretence. Yahya derived a lot of happiness from friendship and human relationships. His creed was a likeably honest creed. His friendships were proverbial for their permanence.

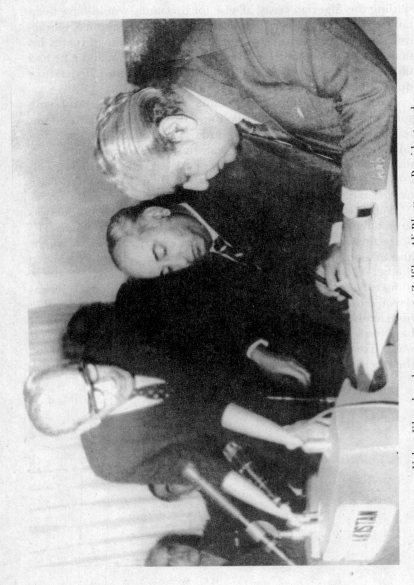

Yahya Khan hands over power to Zulfikar Ali Bhutto as President and Chief Martial Law Administrator at the Presidency, Rawalpindi, on 20 December 1971

Chapter 4

Bhutto — triumph and tragedy

After the surrender in Dhaka in December 1971, and our uncon-ditional acceptance of the cease-fire, the junta initiated action for the future governance of the half of Pakistan which now remained with us. Bhutto, now Deputy Prime Minister and Foreign Minis-ter, had gone to New York as leader of Pakistan's delegation to the UN and had made his dramatic, tearful intervention before the Security Council. He had then stopped in Rome, awaiting a signal from Ghulam Mustafa Khar, and not without trepidation, the course of developments at home. The ruling junta decided to hand over power to Bhutto and, on 20 December 1971, sent a PIA plane to fetch him from Rome. I witnessed the transfer of power from a deflated, humiliated Yahya to Bhutto, the man of the hour who possessed all the qualities of leadership — courage, drive, energy, eloquence, and a sense of history. His hour had struck. The man of destiny had at last arrived. As President and Chief Martial Law Administrator, he was about to exercise absolute power which no military dictator or civilian President had ever possessed in Pakistan. At last, Bhutto had the authority to enforce his will upon the people of Pakistan. At that hour, people forgot his con-troversial past, his contribution to the loss of East Pakistan; and nobody reproached him. Like Churchill on the eve of acquiring power in the state, Bhutto felt as if he too was walking with destiny and, like

Churchill, he felt as if all his life had been but a preparation for this hour and for the task that lay ahead.

I was asked to arrange radio and television coverage of the swearing-in ceremony of Bhutto as President and Chief Martial Law Administrator in place of Yahya. When I arrived at the President's House, Ghulam Ishaq Khan, the Cabinet Secretary, was already there. He had made all the formal transitional arrangements for transfer of power from Yahya to Bhutto. We both walked up and down on the lawn, waiting to be called in. When the call came, we went in and there on the verandah we saw Yahya Khan, Zulfikar Ali Bhutto, Air Marshal Rahim Khan, General Hameed (the COS), General Peerzada (the PSO[P]), J. A. Rahim, and Mumtaz Bhutto. It was a tense moment. We had just lost half of our country and had left behind over 90,000 prisoners in Indian captivity. My personal relations with Bhutto were strained and we were hardly on speaking terms. When the ceremony was over, I bade Yahya farewell and took my leave of him. As I was leaving, Bhutto told me that I would be hearing from him. I was terribly depressed and thoroughly demoralized. We had lost the war and half the country. The President, the man we had served and worked for, was in disgrace, about to be thrown into the dustbin of history. The future looked uncertain and full of foreboding. How could I work under Bhutto?

With all these thoughts assailing my mind, I left for my office, waiting for the new President's call. About 3 p.m., the green telephone rang. The caller said 'Roedad, this is Zulfikar Ali Bhutto. I want you to make arrangements for my address to the nation in the evening. I want you to meet me in the Punjab House at 5 p.m. and I want to address senior Secretaries in the evening.' After making all the necessary arrangements, I left for the Punjab House. There were many people outside the compound wall. I was ushered in. The first person I met was Ghulam Mustafa Jatoi. I was led upstairs, where Bhutto was sitting alone. We shook hands and then he introduced me to Hafeez Pirzada, the new Information Minister. Bhutto was very civil and there was no rancour in his conversation. He told me he had nothing against me but that some changes had to be made and that I would be shifted to another ministry.

Bhutto started very well. His informal talk with the Secretaries in the Punjab House on that cold wintry evening created a very good impression and we all thanked God that a man of Mr Bhutto's

President Zulfikar Ali Bhutto with some Cabinet Ministers in the early hours of 24 December 1971

calibre was now at the helm of affairs in Pakistan's darkest hour. The same evening, he addressed foreign correspondents. He spoke with apparent conviction. My spirits rose and I felt proud of him. I thought of Arnold Toynbee's description of the phenomenon of withdrawal and return of historical figures in his *Study of History* and Ghulam Ishaq Khan's prophetic observation when we had met Bhutto after he was given his marching orders by Ayub. After five years of wandering, Bhutto was back in the saddle, called back from Rome by the army to pick up the pieces and lead Pakistan at a critical time. He told the Secretaries that he was going to seek the help and co-operation of every political leader. Ghulam Ishaq Khan asked him to establish contact with Wali Khan. Bhutto replied that he was going to invite Wali Khan and enlist his support in the reconstruction of the country. Not a bad beginning. We dispersed, feeling a little more hopeful about the future of what Bhutto called the new Pakistan.

The 1973 Constitution, which had the approval and support of all the political parties in the country, was undoubtedly one of Bhutto's greatest achievements. It is unfortunate that Bhutto violated its sanctity by a series of unilateral amendments in the teeth of opposition from his political opponents.

The credit for putting Pakistan on the nuclear road also goes to Bhutto. In 1974, soon after India had conducted its first underground test, Bhutto declared that impoverished Pakistan would 'go for nuclear status even if we have to eat grass'. Again, it was Bhutto who, in 1976, laid the foundation of what is today known as the Khan Research Laboratories at Kahuta, an institution which has enabled Pakistan to join the select nuclear club.

In the December 1970 elections to the National Assembly, the PPP had won 62 seats out of 82 in the Punjab and 18 out of 23 in Sindh. But it won no seat in Balochistan and only one in the NWFP, i.e., the seat won by my brother Khaliq Khan. Thus, in the two provinces of NWFP and Balochistan, PPP had hardly any representation. This caused considerable trouble to Bhutto throughout his tenure. In February 1973, Bhutto dismissed the NAP government in Balochistan, sacked governor Bizenjo, and imposed President's rule. The NAP government in the NWFP resigned in protest. Bhutto was now on the warpath. Armed confrontation between the army and Baloch and Marri tribesmen followed in the wake of the dismissal of the NAP government. Bhutto was intolerant of opposition and did not believe in sharing power, a trait inherited by his daughter Benazir. Till the end, he was not able to find a solution to the Balochistan crisis. In a bid to crush the NAP, he banned the Party, arrested all its top leaders, and put them on trial for conspiracy and high treason before a special court in Hyderabad. This was the biggest political blunder he committed and one which he was soon to regret.

The other disastrous move made by Bhutto was his undue interference in the Civil Service of Pakistan. Bhutto abolished service guarantees, and compulsorily retired as many as 1400 civil servants without any inquiry or reason. In 1973, he created the Federal Security Force, a fascist praetorian guard, designed to victimize his political opponents, and to crush civil commotion and labour discontent without having to rely on the assistance of the army.

By 1977, he felt strong enough to seek a fresh mandate and announced that fresh elections to the National Assembly and the Provincial Assemblies would be held at the beginning of March. The PPP secured a sweeping victory. The combined opposition, however, cried foul, claimed that the elections had been rigged, and demanded fresh elections. They started a country-wide agitation, resulting in prolonged rioting in Lahore and other cities. In order to stem the tide of popular discontent and to appease the religious elements who had joined hands with the politicians, Bhutto announced that drinking of alcohol, gambling, etc. would be banned. He also took the extraordinary measure of declaring the Ahmedis non-Muslims. But nothing he did seemed to satisfy the people. He went on making concession after concession but nothing worked.

On 4 July 1977, I saw Bhutto at the American Ambassador's reception. He was smoking a cigar and was huddled up with the Afghan Ambassador. I was standing next to the Chief of Army Staff, General Ziaul Haq; Ghulam Ishaq Khan, Secretary General Defence (both future Presidents); and Hafeez Pirzada, who held the portfolio of Finance. Hafeez asked his Finance Secretary and my friend Aftab Ahmad Khan to draw up a ten-day tour programme for him in the Middle East. The same day, the Chinese Ambassador had invited me, all my family members, and my friends, Mr and Mrs V. A. Jafarey to dinner at his residence. It was a very relaxed evening and we all enjoyed ourselves, totally oblivious of the political storm about to burst.

On 5 July, General Ziaul Haq, the COAS promoted by Bhutto in 1976 over the heads of several more senior officers, struck; he staged a military take-over, arrested Bhutto and other members of his government, sacked the federal and provincial governments, dissolved the Assemblies, and imposed martial law.

Bhutto had been in the wilderness before, but had staged a comeback. This time, the stakes were high. He had overplayed his hand and the army had moved against him. There seemed no chance that he might return to power.

Bhutto's trial

> Woe to the Revolution which has not enough courage to behead the symbol of the ancient regime.
>
> **Marat**

Mr Bhutto was arrested on 3 September 1977 on the charge of the murder of Nawab Muhammad Ahmed Khan, father of Mr Ahmed Raza Kasuri, MNA. The arrest was made on the basis of the confessional statement of Masud Mahmud, Director General, Federal Security Force. On 10 October 1977, in a radio and television address to the nation, General Zia said, 'After much deliberation I have come to the conclusion that to hold the election on 18 October in the present circumstances would be inviting a crisis.' On 13 September, Mr Justice Samdani of the Lahore High Court granted bail to Mr Bhutto. I was in a meeting with Zia at GHQ when the news was conveyed to us. Three days later, Mr Bhutto was detained under a Martial Law Order.

The decision to arrest Mr Bhutto was not taken in consultation with the Ministry of Interior, of which I was now the Administrative Secretary. The most likely forum where the decision of such immense importance and fraught with all kinds of possibilities and implications might have been taken would have been the Martial Law Administrators' Conference which, in the words of General K. M. Arif, 'was a perennial policy-making organ which took major policy decisions on all matters of substance. These meetings were normally held one day before the Cabinet meetings at an interval of four to six weeks, except when some urgent business demanded an early session. Towards the middle of 1984, and more significantly after the referendum of December that year, the frequency of holding the MLA's Conference decreased appreciably.

The President increasingly preferred to discuss important issues with the Governors concerned individually rather than dealing with them in the open full house'[1].

According to Arif, 'Mr Ghulam Ishaq Khan, Secretary General-in-Chief, invariably attended meetings of the Military Council'[2] but not the Martial Law Administrators' Conference. It is doubtful if the decision to arrest Mr Bhutto was taken by the Military Council which gradually became a dormant body and died a natural death. The FIA initiated fresh investigations into the murder case and, in the words of General Arif, unearthed sufficient incriminating evidence against three officers of the FSF and Mr Bhutto; but we, in the Interior Ministry, were not privy either to the decision or to subsequent developments, even though the FIA was administratively under the control of the Ministry of Interior. The FIA was, throughout, in direct contact with the martial law authorities. The Interior Minister was not a part of the kitchen Cabinet and I do not know if he was ever co-opted to participate in the Council discussions relating to the arrest and subsequent trial of Mr Bhutto. Who should be co-opted and who not to participate in Council discussions was decided on a need-to-know basis. As Secretary Interior, I attended all Cabinet meetings, but not the Military Council meetings.

I headed a Joint Security Committee comprising all Home Secretaries, Heads of Provincial Special Branches, the DG ISI, and the DIB. The Committee was given the responsibility of assessing and reviewing the law and order situation and forecasting future developments in the event of the Supreme Court convicting or acquitting Mr Bhutto.

A full bench of the Lahore High Court headed by the Chief Justice, Mr Justice Mushtaq Hussain, in a unanimous judgment convicted Mr Bhutto and sentenced him to death. The appeal against the High Court judgment was heard in the Supreme Court by the full court of nine Judges headed by Mr Justice Anwarul Haq. The Supreme Court dismissed Mr Bhutto's appeal by a majority decision of four to three. On 30 June 1978, Mr Justice Qaiser Khan retired from the Court on attaining the age of superannuation. Justice Qaiser Khan, an old friend and colleague and a relative of mine, was reluctant to be associated with the hearing of the appeal because he knew the case could not be decided before his superannuation but was prevailed upon to join the Bench on the clear understanding that his retirement would take effect after the disposal of the appeal. Qaiser Khan retired during the pendency of the appeal and one can only speculate on whether he would have held Mr Bhutto guilty of murder and awarded him the death penalty on the uncorroborated testimony of Masud Mahmud who had turned approver and who was generally regarded as an unreliable witness. Knowing him as I do, I have my doubts, but this is an academic exercise. With Qaiser Khan gone, Mr Bhutto's fate was sealed. With due respect to the late Chief Justice Anwarul Haq, not many people agree with his observation: 'I am left with no doubt that the prosecution has fully succeeded in establishing the case. There is absolutely no support for the contention that the present case was politically motivated.'

The Ministry of Interior came into the picture when we received a number of mercy petitions on behalf of Mr Bhutto. We received the record of the case from Lahore at about 11 a.m. one day. The drafting of the summary began almost immediately. In the summary, we referred to the observation of the Supreme Court on the review petition: 'Although we have not found it possible in law to review the sentence of death on the grounds urged by Mr Yahya Bakhtiar, yet these are relevant for consideration by the executive authorities in the exercise of the prerogative of Mercy', and pointed out that the recommendation of the Supreme Court, although not binding and not to be honoured in every case, had to be taken into consideration. While analysing the political implications, the summary read: 'This is an unprecedented case which has caused deep concern at home and has generated a lot of interest abroad. The general reaction, particularly in the USA and Western Europe, to the execution of the sentence would be strong and adverse and would cause aversion, and do immense damage to the image of Pakistan.'

'According to the guiding principles, cases in which there are special or political considerations, are to be dealt with on the merits of each case. It may sometimes be necessary to take account of public opinion and to commute the sentence in deference to a widely spread or strong local expression of public opinion lest the execution should arouse sympathy for the murderer than otherwise.' We made it quite clear in the summary that the judgment of the Supreme Court or the High Court and their finding of guilt did not stand in the President's way and his power to remit or commute the sentence was absolutely unfettered.

While we were busy giving final touches to the summary, the CMLA's Secretariat was getting impatient and we were getting repeated telephone calls to hurry up and dispatch the summary by the fastest means possible. This was done late in the evening on 1 April 1979. My Joint Secretary Law, Mr Irshad Khan took the summary (Appendix 1) first to the residence of the COS, General Arif, and then the two of them headed for the Army House, the official residence of the President, for the fateful decision. Irshad told me later that when the driver of his car accidentally took a wrong turn, General Arif pounced upon him and the mistake was immediately corrected. I cannot vouch for the veracity of this story as I have not had the opportunity to check it with General Arif but, since the entire country was on the verge of a nervous breakdown, I am inclined to believe it.

Irshad told me that the President rejected the mercy petition without reading it. General Arif, on the other hand, says in his book *Working with Zia* that the President read it carefully. Whatever the truth, the file came back to me with the fateful words: 'Petition is rejected'.

In my considered opinion, Bhutto was a doomed man once it became clear that he continued to remain popular with the masses even after loss of office and that nothing could stop him from staging a comeback in the free, fair, and impartial election which Zia had promised to the people of Pakistan. Bhutto was now like a wounded animal and his political opponents were mortally afraid of him. They dreaded the prospect of his return to power and were demanding his death in the name of justice.

When we referred the summary on Bhutto's mercy petition to the Law Division for their comments, it came back with their views in red ink, endorsed by the Law Minister Mr A. K. Brohi: 'legally it is humane to kill the killer, more so when he is found so by the superior-most court. In fact, the authority that allows merciful commutation etc. of a sentence is merciless to the deceased, his heirs, and his relatives. Mercy, remission or commutation is negation of justice and justice is not only to be done to the killer who is surviving because of legal formalities but is also to be done to the deceased who cannot be heard but whose soul looks for justice the revenge, death for death and that in fact is the humanitarian consideration.'

The fatal mistake made by the PPP leadership was to fight the battle for saving Bhutto's neck in the court-room only. They fondly hoped that, like any other murder case, it would be decided purely on merit. They forgot that Bhutto's fate was going to be decided not in the court-room but in the streets, throughout the length and breadth of Pakistan. After all, the Agartala Conspiracy Case was withdrawn not because the prosecution case against Mujib was weak, but because over a million people were out on the streets of Dhaka, several government offices and the houses of ministers — including Khawaja Shahabuddin's house — were burnt. The situation in Dhaka was completely out of control. Curfew was being openly violated. Confronted with this situation, Ayub had no choice but to withdraw the case. Again, after the army action in Dhaka on 25 March 1971, Mujib was arrested and, militarily, the situation in East Pakistan was brought under control; but the matter did not end there. The Bengalis kept up the struggle, organized the Mukti Bahini, internationalized the struggle, converted it into a liberation movement, invited foreign help, and declared themselves independent. Of course, the two situations were not identical. Mujib, in 1971, was in a much stronger position than Bhutto was in 1977. In 1971, Mujib's hands were clean and his record was untainted. Bhutto, on the other hand, had discredited himself in the eyes of the people during his five years in office and had been corrupted by power. Instead of mobilizing street power, the PPP concentrated on collecting appeals for mercy from foreign heads of government, appeals which were not going to influence Zia at all.

The rejection of the mercy petition did not come as a surprise to me. On one occasion, Zia had told me, 'Roedad Sahib, it is his neck or mine.' 'Woe to the revolution which has not enough courage to behead the symbol of the ancient regime.' So said Marat. Zia knew this and was not going to take any chances. He and he alone had the courage to take Bhutto to the gallows. Ceasar had his Brutus; Charles I, his Cromwell; Zulfikar Ali Bhutto had his Zia.

It is said that in sending Bhutto to the gallows Zia was guided by justice, which outweighed all other considerations, and that, as a matter of principle, Zia never commuted death sentences awarded by superior courts and was not prepared to make an exception in the case of Bhutto. This is factually incorrect. In a number of murder cases, both before and after Bhutto's execution, Zia disagreed with Interior and, in disregard of the judgments of the Supreme Court, commuted death sentences.

On 2 April 1979, I went to Rawalpindi Club in my official car to meet Mr Bhutto's only surviving sister, Manna, and her husband, Mr Nasimul Islam. As good friends, they had stood by me through thick and thin and I knew that in doing so, they had incurred the displeasure of Mr Bhutto, and their relations with him had become somewhat strained. Rawalpindi Club was ringed by intelligence agencies representing the IB, the ISI, Military Intelligence, and the Special Branch. I took Manna and her husband home for dinner, aware that we were tailed by a convoy of intelligence vehicles. On that day, I knew when Mr Bhutto was to be executed. The least I could do was to tell Manna when the tragedy was going to be enacted, but I did not know how to utter the dreaded words. I was still debating this with myself when she realized that something was wrong. She broke down and began to cry. She wanted to leave for Karachi to be in Larkana as soon as possible to receive the dead body. She asked me if before leaving she could meet her brother one last time. I knew it was too late but there was no harm in trying. Dinner was left uneaten and we drove straight to the PIA booking office in Rawalpindi. I got them priority seats for Karachi and Larkana and dropped them at the Rawalpindi Club. Next day, i.e., 3 April, I met them again. Predictably, Manna's application for permission to meet Mr Bhutto had been turned down. There was nothing more to be done by them in Rawalpindi. I drove them to the airport in time for the evening flight to Karachi, saw them off, and drove back home with a very heavy heart.

Meanwhile, the final touches were being given to the arrangements for Mr Bhutto's execution by the jail staff under the supervision of the martial law authorities. Mercifully, I was kept out of all this and not involved in the final act of this tragic drama. I was, however, kept informed as the countdown began. In my mind's eye, the whole night long, I pictured Mr Bhutto spending his last few hours before being taken to the gallows. The pressure inside me was building up and I could not take it any more. I took two tablets of Valium to soothe my nerves, but to no avail. All night, I was pacing up and down in my bedroom. Just before Mr Bhutto was taken to the gallows, I remembered the last words of Socrates as recorded by Plato in The Apology: 'The hour of departure has arrived, and we go our way. I to die, and you to live — which is better, God only knows.'

Just before daybreak, as I was getting ready to go to the CMLA Secretariat to review the situation arising out of Mr Bhutto's execution, I was told that Mumtaz Bhutto, Zulfikar Ali Bhutto's cousin and a former Chief Minister of Sindh, was waiting downstairs in the drawing-room. The first question he asked me was if Mr Bhutto was dead or alive. I told him that he had been hanged at four minutes past 2 a.m. Having said that, I broke down and wept. Mumtaz placed his hand on my knee. His nerves were much stronger than mine. He was calm and in control of his emotions.

When I went to the CMLA Secretariat, almost all the army officers had reddened eyes. After a brief discussion, a press note was drafted and issued. The press note read: 'Mr Zulfikar Ali Bhutto was hanged to death at 2 a.m. this morning in Rawalpindi Jail. The dead body was flown on 4 April in a special aircraft from Rawalpindi and handed over to the elders of the family who buried him after Namaz-i-Janaza-[funeral prayers] in the ancestral graveyard at Garhi Khuda Bakhsh near Naudero, Larkana at 10.30 a.m. in accordance with the wishes of the family. The funeral was attended by relatives, including his two uncles, Nawab Nabi Bakhsh Bhutto, Sardar Pir Bakhsh Bhutto, his first wife Shirin Amir Begum, friends, and residents of the area.'

The coup against Bhutto and the imposition of martial law were not justified in the circumstances prevailing just before the promulgation of martial law. The resurrection of the murder case against Bhutto, his arrest and subsequent trial were politically motivated. Bhutto did not get a fair trial. He was a doomed man once the army decided to topple him.

Zia made a serious attempt to ban the People's Party. A senior army officer was detailed and sent to the Ministry of Interior to collect relevant material in support of the decision to ban the party In the face of opposition from the Ministry of Interior and the Law Division, the plan was abandoned. In spite of his best efforts, Zia failed to destroy the Party which survived him and bounced back to power.

The French political philosopher, Le Comte Alexis de Tocqueville (1805-1859) made an observation in his treatise, *The Ancient Regime and the French Revolution*, which is appropriate to other governments past, present, and future, in particular to the fall of both Ayub and Bhutto. He said, 'Experience teaches us that, generally speaking, the most serious moment for a bad government is when it seeks to mend its ways. Only consummate statecraft can enable a king to save his throne when after a long spell of oppressive rule, he sets to improve the lot of his subjects; patiently endured so long as it seemed beyond redress, a grievance comes to appear intolerable once the possibility of removing it crosses one's mind.' Events have proved that both Ayub and Bhutto, despite all their other qualities, lacked the vital requirement of 'consummate statecraft' of which de Tocqueville spoke, and therefore could not save their thrones.

In a bid to wheel and deal his way out of the crisis, Bhutto tried to pacify the *mullahs* and announced his decision to introduce complete prohibition, to ban all gambling, night-clubs, bars, movie houses, and other 'unIslamic' activities, and to bring all laws into complete conformity with the Quran and *sunnah* within six months. 'He understood by now', writes Wolpert, 'that the most powerful, implacable opposition confronting him was the *mullah*-led force of tens of millions of devout Pakistanis, both inside the army and ones who believed that the laws of Islam were higher and far mightier than the laws of any land. And if it was necessary for him to stop drinking within Pakistan and remain in power, he was even ready to try that just as he had abandoned construction of a huge gambling casino on Karachi's seashore — where its concrete whale-like skeleton remains a forlorn symbol of Zulfi's unrealized dream. He would give up all the wine and the waltzing for power was far sweeter and more important. He thought that a ban on alcohol would convince the *mullahs* who hated him that he should stay on the throne, even as he believed that by donating a solid gold door for the shrine of Lal Shahbaz in Sehwan, all his sins would be forgiven.'[3]

Under pressure from orthodox Muslims, Bhutto went to the extent of referring the religious status of Qadianis to the National Assembly and got them declared a non-Muslim minority. Even this could not save him from the gallows.

Ayub had met the same fate. Instead of defending his reforms and the institutional structure he had raised with such care, he demolished brick by brick the elaborate facade of indirect election with his own hands in order to pacify the people and save his throne. Nothing worked.

Bhutto was Winston Churchill's puzzle inside a riddle wrapped in an enigma. He was a human dynamo, a whirlwind, a magnificent, inspiring leader one minute and a mean and petty person the next. Like Lyndon Johnson as described by Robert Dallek, Bhutto 'too was driven, tyrannical, crude, insensitive, possessed by demons, petty. And like LBJ, Bhutto was empathetic, sophisticated, and could be uproariously funny.'[4]

Writing about LBJ, *New York Times* columnist, Russell Baker, concluded: 'Johnson was a character out of a Russian novel, one of those human complications that filled the imagination of Dostoyevsky, a storm of warring human instincts: sinner and saint, buffoon and statesman, cynic and sentimentalist, a man torn between hungers for immortality and self-destruction.'[5] It is amazing how much Bhutto resembled LBJ. 'Johnson', in the words of Robert Dallek, 'was much loved and greatly hated, not just liked and unliked but adored by some and despised by others. Some people remember him as kind, generous, compassionate, considerate, decent and devoted to advancing the well-being of the least advantaged among us. Others describe him as cruel, dictatorial, grandiose and even vicious.'[6]

Bryce Harlow, a House and Senate staffer and later White House Counsel under Eisenhower, remembers LBJ in these words. 'He could not stand not being the cynosure of all eyes. He had to be at the head of the table. And people had to do what he thought they should do. And ordinarily he made them do it. How many people do you know like that? None. You never know anybody like that, because they don't make them. But, yes, they do, once in a millennium. That is Lyndon.'[7]

I knew at least one person like that: Bhutto.

Bhutto like Johnson suffered, in the words of Robert Dallek, 'from a sense of emptiness; he could not stand to be alone; he needed constant companionship, attention, affection and approval. He had insatiable appetites; for work, women, drink, conversation and material possessions.'[8]

Like John F. Kennedy, Bhutto, more than any other President of Pakistan — in the beginning at least and especially during the years spent in the wilderness — embodied the nation's romantic dream of itself.

While opinions about Bhutto's role and place in Pakistan history differ violently, there can be no two opinions that he continues to be incomparably the most dominant figure on the Pakistan scene. He occupied centre-stage even when out of power. In a manner of speaking, Bhutto continues to influence the course of events from the grave. He is the principal point of reference for most Pakistanis, including his bitterest critics and political opponents. He could be capricious and imperious; he was indifferent to the means adopted in pursuit of his ends. Yet, his empathy with the people of Pakistan, especially the poor, the deprived, and the downtrodden had to be seen to be believed. His radical rhetoric was phony, his populist promises utterly unmatched by performance but, right until the end, the poor never lost faith in him. Bhutto did what no other political leader of Pakistan, with the exception of Mr Jinnah has done: he mobilized the people. His political career from 1966 to 1970 was a grand love affair with the people of Pakistan. For a short period of four years it appeared as if Zulfikar Ali Bhutto and the people of Pakistan were made for each other.

Bhutto suffered from a common failing: his ego blinded him. He became dangerously certain and ludicrously vain, like Robespierre. 'That man', said Mirabeau about Robespierre, 'will go far; he believes all that he says'. He went to the guillotine. Whether Bhutto believed all that he said or not, he too went too far, too soon, and met the same fate, although for different reasons. He went to the gallows.

Bhutto was too immersed in politics to have time for friends. Friendship implies a near equality of give and take. Bhutto found it hard to concede equality in any form. Like Napoleon whom he admired, Bhutto thought friendship was but a name and, like Napoleon, he loved nobody. Bhutto was like a man possessed. Like Napoleon, there was a fire within him that was fast consuming him He was full of energy, drive, unbridled ambition; he was unprincipled, thoroughly unscrupulous, reckless, arrogant, suspicious — basically a lonely man, desperately wanting to be loved, but on his own terms, intolerant of opposition. There was an inner compulsion to alienate old friends, to humiliate them for no rhyme or reason. At times, he could be very petty and highly vindictive. He could not live with a whisper of opposition, either within his party or outside it. Criticism invited brutal reprisal from him.

By destroying the constituency that made him, Bhutto hastened his own demise and, in the process, maimed the left. It has still not recovered.

To the objection that the activity of such individuals who consider themselves chosen flies in the face of morality, Hegel replied, 'World history occupies higher ground than that on which morality has properly its position, which is personal character and the conscience of individuals . . . Moral claims which are irrelevant must not be brought into collision with world-historical deeds and their accomplishment. The litany of private virtues, modesty, humility, philanthropy, and forbearance, must not be raised against them. So mighty a form must trample down many an innocent flower, crush to pieces many an object in its path'. This describes very well the belief Bhutto held that he was chosen to play such a role and therefore exempt from the ordinary canons of human conduct.

It was a part of his character to lose his temper and turn angrily on anyone who crossed or even irritated him. An abrupt withdrawal of confidence was all too often followed by arrest and incarceration. Bhutto harboured a strange resentment against anyone who appeared to have better education, better upbringing, greater sophistication, or even better dress. He could not rid himself of an inferiority complex that threatened the image he had formed of himself. A master of dissimulation, he was a model of Machiavellian politics in which every device and ruse recommended by the Florentine master found a place. There is no doubt that he had great abilities as a leader, flawed by faults of character and temper. He was cast in the mould of heroic leadership. Referring to such leaders, Nietzsche says, 'Such beings are incalculable, they come like fate without cause or reason inconsiderably and without pretext. Suddenly, they are here like lightning, too terrible, too sudden, too compelling, and too different even to be hated . . . what moves them is the terrible egotism of the artist, who knows himself to be justified for all eternity in his work as the mother is justified in her child'.

After he acquired almost absolute power, Bhutto reacted sharply to anything — criticism, opposition, even unwelcome news — and exhibited symptoms associated with paranoid states: chronic suspicion, self-absorption, jealousy, hypersensitivity, megalomania. He would attribute to others motives and attitudes that he refused to admit to himself. He would betray a friend or an ally and then justify it to himself and others by accusing the victim of the treachery he was himself intending. He had delusions of grandeur, with *l'idée fixe* that he was the victim of persecution and conspiracy. Like Stalin, Bhutto saw enemies everywhere and suspected his closest collaborators.

Stalin's daughter Svetlana writes: 'When the "facts" convinced my father that someone he knew well had turned out "badly" after all, a psychological metamorphosis came over him . . . At this point, and this was where his cruel, implacable nature showed itself, the past ceased to exist for him. Years of friendship and fighting side by side in a common cause might as well never have been. He could wipe it all out at a stroke . . . and X would be doomed. "So you have betrayed me", some inner demon would whisper. "I don't even know you any more"'. Svetlana said this about Stalin but it as aptly describes the character and personality of Bhutto.

Like Nixon, Zulfikar Ali Bhutto was 'devious, manipulative, driven by an unseen and unknowable force, quick as a summer storm to blame, passionate in his hatreds, self-centred, untruthful, untrusting. Nor is it news that this same man could be charming considerate, helpful, or that he was blessed with great talent, a superb intellect, an awesome memory and a remarkable ability to see things whole, especially on a global scale'.[9] If he was a prime minister without principle in domestic politics, he was also a prime minister without peer in foreign affairs. Why these contradictions? He was a very complex man.

To sum up, like Nixon, Bhutto was 'as great as man can be without virtue, without principles and he was as wise as a man can be without modesty, humility, tolerance and respect for others.'[10] Pakistan would not see the likes of Bhutto for many years. It must have been a terrible thing to be Zulfikar Ali Bhutto.

In 1966, when I met him late at night at his Civil Lines residence in the company of Ghulam Ishaq Khan, he had earlier in the day received his marching orders from Ayub. At that time, many people, his friends and foes alike, thought that Zulfikar Ali Bhutto as a political force was spent. Many thought he would turn to drink or any of those other escapisms. Some even wrote his political obituary. Bhutto, however, had no intention of ending up as a drunk or of walking out of history. He was already planning his future. There was nothing miraculous about his resurrection. He used his assets shrewdly and succeeded with his qualities of hard work, courage, risk-taking, and by relentlessly attacking Ayub.

What then went wrong? Did Bhutto have to end like he did? Was there some inevitability about it? Like de Gaulle in France, Bhutto had exercised supreme power over Pakistan but that power was never consolidated politically. At the peak of his power, Bhutto was almost unrecognizable. He was arrogant, not the man I first met in 1959, in Peshawar; he had grown high-handed and intolerant of opposition. If you went to see him, you did not know how much of your self-respect you would be left with when you came away. Power corrupts and absolute power corrupts absolutely. Some it corrupts more absolutely than others. Bhutto had betrayed the common people who regarded him as their champion and who shared his ideals and his dreams. Once they were his power base. With the loss of that base, he was totally isolated and at the mercy of the khaki.

Churchill used his power to the fullest to defeat England's enemies, to lead England to victory. 'Power for the sake of lording it over fellow creatures or adding to personal pomp, according to Churchill, is rightly judged base. But power in a national crisis when a man believes what orders should be given is a blessing'. At the end of five years and three months, Churchill had at least the satisfaction that all England's enemies had surrendered unconditionally. Bhutto, on the other hand, was on the ropes, fighting his political opponents who had succeeded in rallying the people behind them, all his dreams shattered, accused of rigging the election, and clinging to power which was fast slipping out of his hands. In spite of all his undoubted achievements, Churchill was merely dismissed by the British electorate from all further conduct of their affairs. Bhutto, on the other hand, with no such achievements to his credit, was sacked, tried for murder like an ordinary criminal, thrown into a prison cell, and taken to the gallows on a stretcher.

The army did not have to make elaborate arrangements to dislodge him from power. The security apparatus of the modern state, as events in France in 1968 and in Pakistan in 1977 have shown, cannot be defeated by civilian agitation alone, however intense and prolonged. The PNA on its own could not have toppled Bhutto. Towards the end, Bhutto had everything against him: the armed forces, the security agencies, the bureaucracy, the police, and, last but not least, his own party. All the elaborate security arrangements we had made to deal with the post-execution situation were not really needed.

Chapter 5

Ziaul Haq

On the death of Roosevelt, the *New York Times* editorialized: 'Gone is the fresh and spontaneous interest which this man took, as naturally as he breathed air, in the troubles and hardships and the disappointments and hopes of little men and humble people.'[1] Among all our leaders today and of all the six Presidents discussed here, without any doubt Ziaul Haq alone will earn such a tribute.

When, on 17 August 1988, he died in the crash of a C-130 aircraft, there was a spontaneous outpouring of emotion, unequalled in the history of Pakistan since the death of Mr Jinnah. All around Faisal Mosque where he was to be buried, I saw a sea of humanity. Thousands of people had gathered to bid him farewell. They came from the fields, the farms, the twin cities of Islamabad and Rawalpindi. There were Pakhtuns, Uzbeks, Tajiks, *mujahideen* from across the border, people he had helped throw the Russians out of their country. They thronged in their thousands to pay their last respects.

Like Roosevelt, Zia was deeply receptive to the needs of people he met. He made them feel that he was interested in their lives and their families and he encouraged them to talk about themselves and always listened with deep attention. He made them feel that he cared about them, that he understood their concerns, and that he would protect them.

President Muhammad Ziaul Haq

Zia was a good listener. He always made you feel that you had something very important to say. He would then ask you if you could put it down in writing and send him a brief note. People spent weeks writing such notes — which Zia never read. Zia would ask for your opinion and then listen to you and, when you left him, you thought you had been at your best. Zia never resented it if you told him not what he wanted to hear but what he needed to hear.

Zia was not a garrulous person. He was a great believer in bringing people together in marathon sessions in the cabinet room to discuss complex issues. He enjoyed clash of views, conflicting opinions, discordant notes. Everyone was given a chance to speak; everyone was heard. When he got bored or thought he had had enough, he would just doze off in cabinet meetings, without interrupting the discussion.

During cabinet meetings, one of the attendants would regularly come at the appointed time and remind Zia that it was time for midday prayers. He would then walk to the Presidency mosque, accompanied by one or two persons. Meanwhile, all the non-*namazis* would be walking up and down the lawn in full view of Zia. He never asked anybody to join him for prayers and he never held it against you if you did not.

Zia like Stalin and Hitler was a nightbird, and, like Hitler, rarely appeared much before noon. He did not go to bed until the early hours of the morning. He would wake up for the early morning prayers and then go to sleep again. Often, at around midnight when you were fast asleep, the green telephone (hot line) would ring and the operator at the Army House would tell you that the President wanted to speak to you. Zia would come on the line, apologize for disturbing you at that late hour, hope you were not asleep, and then inquire about some minor matter.

In personal matters, Zia was a very helpful and humane person. If you had a human problem and you brought it to his notice, he would, if necessary, break or bend rules in order to help you out. He commanded respect, not awe, and he knew how to win your loyalty. Altaf Gauhar, one of his detractors has a different view of Zia:

'From the ashes rose a great hypocrite, General Ziaul Haq. He promised to hold elections and reneged on that promise. He set out to establish what he called an Islamic system of government and for eleven long years the country remained enmeshed in the bushes of obscurantism and sectarianism. General Zia surpassed all other politicians in corrupting the democratic process. He exploited the politicians, including some leading ulema, with great skill, humility and piety. His grin concealed his arrogance and his cold-blooded nature. He too met a tragic end but by then he had distorted and mangled every institution, the opportunity of guiding the political process along Islamic lines was betrayed.'[2]

It was in 1976 that Bhutto took a fateful decision when he promoted Lieutenant General Muhammad Ziaul Haq over the head of a number of more senior officers and appointed him Chief of Staff of the Pakistan Army. I caught a glimpse of Zia for the first time in that year when we were both attending a reception at the Islamabad Club on the occasion of the wedding of the daughter of Mr Ghulam Ishaq Khan, Secretary General Defence. I was standing next to the late Mr Sarwar Jan Khan, father-in-law of Ghulam Ishaq Khan. Pointing in the direction of Zia, Sarwar Jan Khan told me in a tone of derision: 'There stands our new Commander-in-Chief'. He looked very unimpressive — physically at least — and we could not help commenting on the sharp contrast with his two predecessors, Ayub and Yahya.

I was a daily visitor to Ghulam Ishaq Khan's house near Masjid Road in Islamabad. He had no other friends and he did not encourage unwanted visitors. The fast deteriorating political situation used to dominate our discussions. On 28 April 1977, we had a very animated discussion. A day earlier, a joint statement had been issued by the Chairman of the Joint Chiefs of Staff Committee and the three Service Chiefs including, Ziaul Haq. It read:

> While the military code prohibits the soldiers, sailors, and airmen to have anything to do with politics, the armed forces who belong to the nation have to remain on call to safeguard the country's integrity when threatened on account of external aggression or internal subversion. We wish to make it absolutely clear that the Pakistan Army, Navy and Air Force are totally united to discharge their constitutional obligation to support the present legally constituted government.

The message was loud and clear. The armed forces had clearly decided to intervene on behalf of Bhutto and bail him out. Eight years earlier, Ayub had asked Yahya to discharge his legal and constitutional responsibilities, not in support of his government, but to defend the country — as he put it. Now the Service Chiefs were coming out openly in support of a beleaguered government whose credentials were being widely challenged. This was an unprecedented move on the part of the armed forces, and I made my views known to Ghulam Ishaq Khan in unambiguous terms. Ghulam Ishaq Khan maintained his silence and, cautious as he always is, made no comments.

I am an early riser. On that fateful day on 5 July 1977 when I switched on the radio to listen to the 6 a.m. news bulletin, I was stunned. 'The Armed Forces of Pakistan', the news bulletin said, 'have taken over the administration of the country this morning. It has been announced by a military spokesman that top political leaders belonging to the PPP, including the former Prime Minister, Mr Zulfikar Ali Bhutto, and PNA leaders have been taken into temporary protective custody'. It did not say who the coup leader was and why this drastic action had to be taken. This was a significant departure from earlier such announcements. If the COAS was the coup leader, why was he not coming out into the open? Was a power struggle going on? Many such questions assailed my mind and I thought of the worst. The position became clear when General Ziaul Haq, the COAS, came on air and addressed the nation. He said 'I want to make it absolutely clear that I neither have any political ambitions nor does the army want to be distracted from its profession of soldiering. I was obliged to step in to fill the vacuum created by the political leaders. I have accepted this challenge as a true soldier of Islam. My sole aim is to organize free and fair elections which would be held in October this year. Soon after the poll, power will be transferred to the elected representatives. I give a solemn assurance that I will not deviate from this schedule'.

On 5 July 1977, General Zia promoted Ghulam Ishaq Khan as Secretary General-in-Chief with the rank of Cabinet Minister and charged him with the responsibility of formulating plans for the manning of the federal and provincial governments.

On 6 July 1977, Zia addressed the Secretaries to the government in the auditorium of the Planning Division in Islamabad. He was accompanied by Ghulam Ishaq Khan. Zia was not the man I had seen earlier at the Islamabad Club. He was now impressively clad in the dashing cavalry uniform; with his jet black hair, eyebrows, and moustache, and his steely eyes, he radiated strength and self-confidence, and appeared to be in total command. His manner was mild. But what impressed me most was his humility.

He expressed his views on the working of the government, its short-comings, etc. Of all the ministries, he singled out the Ministry of Religious Affairs and Haj Arrangements for sharp criticism. This was a clear indicator of his priorities.

The very next day, Ghulam Ishaq Khan asked me to meet him in the Ministry of Defence. The moment I entered his office, Ghulam Ishaq Khan told me, 'The Chief wants you to be his Secretary, Ministry of Interior.' For a brief moment, flashes of all the exotic places, Acapulco, Torremelinos, Costa del Sol, raced through my mind. I loved what I was doing, and I knew that Interior was not a bed of roses, certainly not at the time when an elected government had been sacked, national and provincial Assemblies dissolved, the Prime Minister and all other top political leaders held in what was called protective custody. I had earlier held a high profile job under Yahya and been through the traumatic experience of the tragedy of East Pakistan. I knew from experience the tensions, the demands on time, energy, emotions, etc. that go with such jobs. But civil servants, unlike politicians, have no choice in such matters. I told Ghulam Ishaq Khan, 'I am on board.'

A few days later, I was called to GHQ for a meeting with the COAS and CMLA. My predecessor, M. A. K. Chaudhry, was already there. A tall young man in uniform introduced himself as Arif. The three of us went in. Zia shook hands with us and we all sat down. My predecessor was briefing Zia on action taken on a number of tasks which Zia had assigned to him. I soon realized that it was a serious business meeting and not the customary courtesy call. I quickly took out my notebook and recorded Zia's instructions. I had worked with Ayub and Yahya, but Zia's style and approach were quite different. He knew his priorities. He was down-to-earth and business-like. I came away convinced that this man had an agenda and he knew how to carry it out.

My next meeting with Zia took place in GHQ in the presence of Ghulam Ishaq Khan. The Hyderabad Conspiracy Case came up for discussion. Mr Bhutto had earlier banned the National Awami Party, arrested the top Pathan and Baloch office-bearers of the Party, thrown them into Hyderabad Jail, and put them on trial under the Criminal Law (Amendment) Special Courts Act of 1976. Mr Bhutto's administration was in a state of armed confrontation with the people of Balochistan. Under orders from Bhutto, the army had been deployed to crush what was officially described as

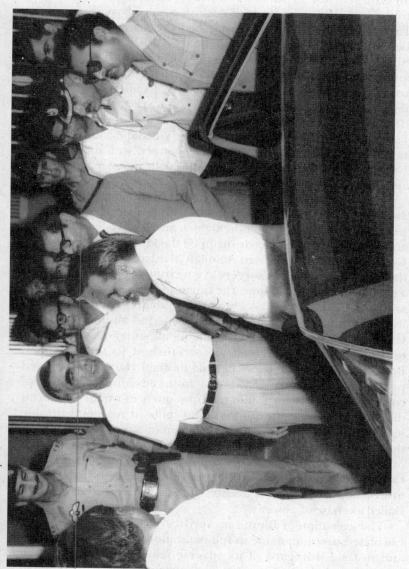

The author with President Ziaul Haq

an insurgency and both sides had suffered serious causalties. We told Zia that the people of Balochistan were basically patriotic Pakistanis; that Bhutto had launched the army operation, not because there was any insurgency, but because he had quite unjustifiably sacked an elected government, just because it was non-PPP and he could not reconcile himself to such a government. He was using the army to punish the people of Balochistan for not electing a PPP government. We advised Zia to reverse this process, drop the Hyderabad Conspiracy Case, release the Baloch and Pathan leaders, and defuse the situation. We told Zia that he would never regret this decision. He said he agreed with us but would have to discuss the matter with his army colleagues. When we met again, he told us that his colleagues did not agree. We pressed him again to ask his colleagues to reconsider the matter dispassionately. When we met again, Zia had secured their agreement. He went to Hyderabad, met all the Baloch and Pathan leaders in jail, and had lunch with them. He dropped the Hyderabad Conspiracy Case and what is more, sent Ataullah Mengal, a heart patient, to the United Kingdom for surgery at government expense. This had a dramatic effect. In no time, the situation returned to normal. All military operations in Balochistan were ended and troops were withdrawn; a general amnesty was granted to all those who had taken up arms against the government; all sentences were remitted; properties confiscated were returned to their owners. Balochistan never gave any trouble to Ziaul Haq and remained peaceful throughout. If Zia had followed Bhutto's policy of confrontation in Balochistan, the consequences would have been disastrous for the country. Like de Gaulle in Algeria, with one masterly stroke, Zia turned confrontation into reconciliation, won the hearts of the people of Balochistan, and foiled the evil designs of the enemies of Pakistan. He never regretted his bold decision. Of all the decisions Ziaul Haq took, extrication from the Balochistan insurgency was the most decisive. It was his masterpiece in the skilled exercise of power.

The execution of Bhutto in April 1979, however, was a cold, calculated decision, made in full realization of all its implications and in total disregard of its adverse reaction abroad and the immense damage it was to cause to the image of Pakistan. At home, the message conveyed to Zia's enemies was loud and clear: anybody who stood in his way would be eliminated. When he entered the cabinet room to preside over the first cabinet meeting after the execution of Bhutto, I remember how he stalked forward, his hair, jet-black, his eyes steely, radiating strength and exuding a self-confidence I had not observed before. Zia was now in total command. On that day, the realization came to all of us that, with no one left to challenge his authority, Zia was going to be around for a long time.

A deliberate policy of hounding and persecuting PPP leaders and workers was conceived and ruthlessly followed with no holds barred. From then onward, a state of undeclared war existed between Zia and the PPP. Under no circumstances was he going to allow the PPP to ever return to power. He was shrewd enough to realize the consequences for him personally, if the PPP ever staged a comeback. He led himself to believe that the PPP was a threat not only to himself but also to Pakistan. He genuinely believed that the PPP and Pakistan could not co-exist and that he had done a great service to Pakistan by sending Bhutto to the gallows. This belief was reinforced by Zulfikar Ali Bhutto's political opponents, so-called democrats, a large number of sycophants and flatterers, who told Zia what he liked to hear: that election was not the answer to the problem of Pakistan; that the Bhuttos were a potential threat to the integrity of the country; that accountability, not of themselves, but of the PPP must precede elections in the country. It is ironic that when the Benazir government was dismissed in November 1996, and the entire country was demanding ruthless accountability of corrupt politicians, the very same people reversed their earlier position and pressed for elections before accountability.

Some wanted Zia to make structural changes in the Constitution along Islamic lines, scrap the Westminster-type of democratic government, declare himself *Amirul Momineen*, and introduce an 'Islamic' system of government. They harped on how he was the best person to rule; that nobody wanted elections; that the demand for election and transfer of power was articulated by a few senior bureaucrats only. All this was music to Zia's ears. In fact, Zia had nothing but contempt for the Constitution and democratic norms.

It is, therefore, not surprising that while addressing a press conference in Tehran, Zia said, 'What is the Constitution? It is a booklet with ten or twelve pages. I can tear them up and say that from tomorrow we shall live under a different system. Is there anybody to stop me? Today the people will follow wherever I lead. All the politicians including the once mighty Mr Bhutto will follow me with their tails wagging'. Almost two hundred years before Zia made these observations, another soldier of fortune, that disturber of the world and devastator of Europe as he was called, was asked by Moreau de Lyonne: 'And of the Constitution?'. 'The Constitution!' replied Bonaparte, indignantly, 'What is it but a heap of ruins? Has it not been successively the sport of every party? The Constitution ! Has not every kind of tyranny been exercised in its name since the day of its establishment? Is not its insufficiency manifested by the numerous crimes which have been committed in its name, even by those who are swearing to it a contemptuous fidelity? All the rights of the people have been indignantly violated. I speak with the frankness of a soldier.'!

After the execution of Bhutto, active politics went into the background. All the principal PPP leaders disappeared from the scene. Some went underground; others decided to come to terms with the new reality. With Bhutto executed and Begum Bhutto and Benazir in jail, no PPP leader worth the name had the will or the courage to mobilize the masses, organize street power, and confront martial law. All the elaborate arrangements that we had made to deal with such a situation were not put to the test. What must have shattered Bhutto and hurt him most was that in his hour of greatest need, his Party had deserted him. For this he himself was mainly to blame. His record during his five years in power had certainly not endeared him to the people of Pakistan. His party was no longer a party of the masses and he was no longer the charismatic leader that he had once been. Some of the people around him were secretly desirous that Bhutto should be eliminated so that they could take his place. When the moment of truth came, everybody except his family members had deserted him. There were no protest demonstrations and no processions anywhere in the country. This came as a big surprise to those of us who were charged with the responsibility of monitoring law and order. If only the PPP knew how apprehensive we were and how we were hoping and praying that there would be no serious resistance and no confrontation between the people and the security forces anywhere in the country, especially the big cities. If such a confrontation had taken place and clashes had occurred, the history of Pakistan might well have been different.

By 1981, the politicians had recovered from the shock. Realization soon dawned on them that Zia had no intention of transferring the substance of power to them. Zia had his own political agenda. In February 1981, twelve opposition parties, from one end of the political spectrum to the other, including the PPP, joined hands and formed a Movement for the Restoration of Democracy. On 14 August 1983, the MRD declared its intention of holding protest rallies against the government.

At my suggestion, the government had set up a Joint Security Committee under my chairmanship to review and monitor the law and order situation, anticipate events, make intelligence forecasts, take preventive action, and keep the President and the Cabinet fully informed. The other members of the Committee were: all Home Secretaries; all Heads of Special Branches; the Director, Intelligence Bureau; and the Director General, Inter Services Intelligence.

The Committee met several times to anticipate law and order problems arising out of the MRD call for agitation. Among the provinces, the provincial government of Sindh was the most optimistic and they assured us that they did not expect any serious trouble. The three other provinces were cautiously optimistic but had prepared themselves for all eventualities. The matter was discussed in a Cabinet meeting a week or so before the MRD D-Day. The views expressed by the provincial representatives and heads of Intelligence agencies were confirmed by the Martial Law Administrators and Governors. Lieutenant General Abbasi, Governor of Sindh, assured the Cabinet that Sindh would remain peaceful. We were in for a rude shock. In Sindh, the agitation started with a bang and was like a volcanic eruption. The urban areas generally remained quiet but the spectacle of peasants marching up and down in the interior of Sindh in protest demonstrations, in violation of prohibitory orders and facing the Frontier Constabulary, the Frontier Corps, and other law enforcement agencies, was unprecedented and hard to believe. Nothing like this had ever happened in the interior of Sindh. An interesting dimension to this rural agitation was that it had the moral, material, and political support of the *waderas*, who had always supported the Establishment and had never participated in agitational politics. We had not realized that all our assumptions, all our intelligence forecasts were out of date; that a fundamental change had taken place; that, as a direct consequence of the execution of Bhutto, Sindh was now highly politicized — the level of political awareness had risen unperceived.

The movement, however, failed to evoke much response in the rest of the country. Ironically, it was the intensity of the agitation in the interior of Sindh which aroused the suspicion of the people in the other three provinces, especially the Punjab. It began to be viewed as a Sindhi movement for the redressal of Sindhi grievances and removal of their sense of deprivation, and therefore lost its national appeal.

Like all military dictators, Zia also had a legitimacy problem. He was conscious of the fact that he derived his power not from the people, but from the barrel of a gun, and was desperately trying to gain public approval for retaining power. With this end in view, he decided to hold a referendum on 19 December 1984. The question put to the voters was: 'Do you endorse the process initiated by the President of Pakistan, General Muhammad Ziaul Haq for bringing the laws of Pakistan in conformity with the injunctions of Islam as laid down in the Holy Quran and Sunnah of the Holy Prophet (Peace Be Upon Him) and for the preservation of the ideology of Pakistan, and are you in favour of the continuation and further consolidation of the process and for the smooth and orderly transfer of power to the elected representatives of the people?' Every voter was required to answer 'Yes' or 'No'. On 1 December 1984, Zia had said, 'If the majority of the electorate responds to the question in "Yes", it will be taken to mean that the people of Pakistan have expressed confidence in the present Government, have endorsed its policies and have elected General Muhammad Ziaul Haq as President for the next five years.'

The turn-out for the Referendum was embarrassingly low. Accompanied by the Director, Intelligence Bureau, I visited a number of polling stations in and around Rawalpindi. They were all deserted. At one polling station for ladies in Lalazar, I complimented the Polling Officer and her staff on the quick and efficient disposal of voters in record time as I saw no voters waiting to cast their ballot papers. On hearing this, they all said with one voice that they had not seen a single voter since early morning and had been sitting idle.

Faced with a similar problem of legitimacy, Ayub too had resorted to a national referendum. The question he had formulated and put to the members of the electoral college on 15 February 1960 was: 'Have you confidence in the President, Field Marshal Muhammad Ayub Khan, Hilal-i-Pakistan, Hilal-i-Jurat?' The fraud practised on the people of Pakistan in both cases fooled nobody and the subterfuge backfired. If Zia thought that the referendum would provide him with a popular mandate for another five years, he was sadly mistaken.

Zia was now coming under increasing pressure from his colleagues, both civil and military, to initiate the political process for the transfer of power to the elected representatives of the people. As early as 1980, some of us had got together, prepared a scheme for the transfer of power to the people, and submitted it to Zia. But, realizing that it would be the beginning of the end, he turned it down. He was aware of the fact that he had to associate the people with the running of the government but he was disinclined to transfer the substance of power to them. Following quickly on the heels of the referendum, Zia announced on 12 January 1985 that partyless elections to the federal and provincial Assemblies would be held on 25 February 1985. The elections were boycotted by the MRD, since Zia had not acceded to their demands for the restoration of the 1973 Constitution. Three days later, elections to the four provincial Assemblies were held. In order to ensure that the President remained powerful after the restoration of an elected government and did not become just a Constitutional figurehead, Ziaul Haq amended the 1973 Constitution by the Constitution (Eighth Amendment) Act 1985, which gave the President the power, in his discretion, to dissolve the National Assembly, dismiss the government, and appoint Service Chiefs. This was a structural change in the Constitution which brought about a major shift in the relative positions of the President and the Prime Minister. When the Amendment came up before the Cabinet, the draft proposed was not circulated; only its contents were read out by the Law Minister Mr Sharifuddin Pirzada, who explained the salient features of the proposed Amendment. In answer to my question as to who would be the Chief Executive under the amended Constitution, Mr Pirzada said that it would be the Prime Minister. I pointed out that, if that was the position, it should be clearly understood that the Secretaries to the government would submit their cases to the Prime Minister and not to the President. The President remarked that the Chief Executive would be the Prime Minister but he would be the Super Chief Executive. I knew this was not going to work, as a working relationship between an indirectly elected powerful President and a directly elected Prime Minister with different political affiliations is not easy to establish, as the French experiment has demonstrated. Ziaul Haq was now determined to curtail the powers of the Parliament and the Prime Minister. He was dead against the parliamentary form of government and expressed his preference quite openly for the election of a powerful *amir*, assisted by consultants nominated by him to help him in the performance of his functions. I was reminded of de Gaulle's speech on 16 June 1946, at the town of Bayeux to mark the second anniversary of the landing in France after D-Day at the place where he first addressed the French on his native soil. Addressing the constitutional problem, he warned that only under a system based on a strong Chief of State could France achieve stability, cope with the problems and dangers it was facing, and avoid the threat of dictatorship. What had been the fate, de Gaulle asked, 'of the First, Second and Third French Republics, of the Weimar Republic, of Italy's democratic experiments and of the Spanish Republic? All had ended in dictatorships because the parliamentary systems on which they were based were too weak to govern. But dictatorship was not the answer.'[3] The system de Gaulle outlined at Bayeux in that speech was almost identical to the one he eventually ensured was written into a Constitution when he returned to power and established the Fifth Republic, as President of the Republic, chosen by a 'Grand Council' of electors, with power to appoint the Prime Minister, preside over the government, dissolve parliament, make treaties, conduct foreign policy, and command the armed forces. Parliament would have a purely legislative role, and the President could take questions of great national importance directly to the voters through referendums. Without similar powers, Zia, an Islamic de Gaulle, had no intention of restoring democracy to Pakistan.

Zia lifted martial law on 1 January 1986 after the newly elected Assembly had agreed to give him those powers which he wanted to retain and had passed an indemnity bill, retrospectively legitimizing all the measures taken by Zia and his regime since 1977. With the lifting of martial law and the return of Benazir from abroad in April 1986, the people became more vocal, the tempo of political activity escalated, and Zia came under heavy fire. When I went to see him in his new office at the Presidency, the place looked deserted. The old hustle and bustle was missing and there were very few people around. Zia was clad in the same cavalry uniform in which I had first seen him eight years ago but he no longer exhibited strength, vitality, and self-confidence. He still possessed all the perquisites and trappings that go with the office of the Head of State but something was missing. There was not a scrap of paper on the table in front of him and he appeared most definitely underemployed.

Apart from a divergence of views on issues of substance, Junejo, the new Prime Minister, irritated the President by insisting on asserting his authority and vetoing the President, even in petty staff matters relating to the Presidency.

On 29 May 1988, Zia dismissed the Junejo government, ostensibly for incompetence and lack of interest in Islamization, but in reality he was disillusioned with the democratic experiment. Things had not gone the way he had planned and the experiment had produced unintended results not to his liking. Zia and Junejo were strange bedfellows. A marriage of convenience had brought them together. But Zia realized that he had chosen the wrong partner. Each had his own political agenda. Junejo refused to play second fiddle. Temperamentally, they were poles apart and incompatible. Zia and Junejo could not co-exist. The time for the parting of ways had come. Zia was not going to be a Hindenburg who called Adolf Hitler to power in 1933. With one stroke of the pen, Zia sacked the Prime Minister, dissolved the national and provincial Assemblies, and dismissed the federal and provincial governments. He formed a caretaker government — but without a prime minister — to run the affairs of the state until the elections.

Junejo did not challenge his dismissal. In fairness to Junejo, nobody in Pakistan challenges a President if he is also the Chief of Army Staff, and no court declares him a usurper: not if he is alive and in uniform, even if he abrogates the Constitution, dissolves the national and provincial Assemblies, and dismisses elected governments.

After Zia's death, the Lahore High Court in its judgment on 17 September 1988 on the dissolution of the Assemblies by Zia, *inter alia*, held that, 'The grounds given for the dissolution of National Assembly and the Provincial Assembly of Punjab are so vague, general or nonexistent that the orders are not sustainable in Law'. The court ruled that while the dissolved Assembly could not be restored, polls should be held in November 1988 as announced by Zia. The Supreme Court of Pakistan upheld the decision of the Lahore High Court. In 1993, on the other hand, the dissolved Assemblies were restored and the dismissed government was reinstated by the Supreme Court. People found it difficult to comprehend such double standards and why a similar course of action had not been followed in both cases.

If I were to name two individuals who kept the Zia administration on an even keel and helped in prolonging his rule, the first name would be that of Ghulam Ishaq Khan, for his sound, although somewhat conservative, economic and financial policies, and his bold and fearless expression of views on vital national issues, not always to the liking of the military. The other was General Khalid Mahmud Arif, who, as Zia's Chief of Staff, acted as a bridge between the military and the civil government. Arif was easily the best of all the Chiefs of Staff that I have worked with.

'Of the three military dictators, Zia was the first to declare that Pakistan could not survive without Islam and that the sole justification, the *raison d'etre* for the establishment of Pakistan was the introduction of the Islamic system.' There had been military coups before, but now, for the first time, a *maulvi*, a deeply religious person, was the head of state, the head of government, and the army chief — a frightening combination — and he seemed determined to recreate the Islamic legal and social order which had originated in tribal Arabia more than a thousand years earlier.

As against this, in 1923 another Muslim, General Mustafa Kemal, became the first Muslim ruler openly to assault and vanquish an orthodox religious institution, and declared as his objective the final separation between the spiritual and the temporal power, the abolition of the Caliphate — the tumour of the Middle Ages as he called it. Kemal disbanded the Ministry of Religious Affairs. All religious schools were transferred to the secular arm, the religious courts of the Shariat which administered the law relating to marriage, divorce, and inheritance were closed, and a civil code based on the Swiss system was planned to replace it.

Kemal Ataturk created a new secular but ideologically 'torn' country out of the ruins of the Ottoman Empire. Whether the Kemalist model is the right one for Turkey or for any other Muslim country remains to be seen. But it cannot be denied that Ataturk transported his country from the Middle Ages to the threshold of the modern era. What did Zia achieve and what is his legacy? His Islamization was a non-starter. He has left behind no durable institution. Nothing that he introduced survives as a living force in the Pakistan of today. If he had had his way, he would have taken Pakistan back to the Middle Ages. He had no idea of law or Constitution or the requirements of a modern government. The changes that he made in the civil and criminal laws in order to bring them in conformity with the principles of Islam have led to judicial chaos, with the result that in most cases people do not know what the law is. The resultant confusion was fully exploited by the police who abused their discretion to register criminal cases under a variety of conflicting laws. Zia's Islamization was limited to symbolic measures of peripheral importance which have had no impact whatsoever on our society. Zia himself soon realized that Islamization was not working and was merely creating more problems. The whole thing simply petered out.

My guess is that if Zia had lived, after sacking Junejo and dissolving the Assemblies, he would have taken serious steps to institute his brand of Islamic state, governed by his own concept of *Nizam-i-Mustafa* and 'led by an *Amir* to be chosen by some form of election from among those who are faithful to Islam and who would be advised by a *Majlis-i-Shura* of faithful persons but would not be bound by its advice.'[4] His experiment with democracy had not produced positive results.

Zia made conscious efforts to further strengthen and develop brotherly relations with all the Muslim states, especially those in the Middle East. His emphasis on Islamization of the orthodox brand endeared him to the conservative Muslim rulers. They felt much more comfortable with Zia than they had with Bhutto, whose radical rhetoric was not to their liking.

Under Zia, Pakistan's relations with India showed distinct improvement. At the drop of a hat, Zia would speak to Indira Gandhi on the hot line and consult her on various issues of common interest to both the countries. Zia thoroughly enjoyed this telephone diplomacy, but Indira, I am told, was not very enthusiastic. Zia went out of his way to cultivate Indian journalists, intellectuals, judges, etc., all of whom enjoyed his hospitality at the Army House and admired his easy-going manner, his friendliness, informality, and modesty. Zia enjoyed meeting Sikh leaders whenever they came to Pakistan on pilgrimage to their holy places. Against the advice of the Interior Division, Zia allowed them to go wherever they wished. On one occasion, in my presence they invited Zia to Amritsar and promised that thousands of *khalsa* would welcome him. Zia thanked them but pointed out some technical difficulties which his guests thought could be easily overcome.

The unfortunate burning of the US Embassy in Islamabad on 21 November 1979, following the desecration of the Holy Kaaba and rumours of US involvement, had soured Pakistan's relations with the US. Bismarck used to say that a statesman's main task was to listen until he heard the rustle of God's robes, then leap up and grasp the hem of the garment. Zia was listening. In December 1979, when the Soviet Union invaded Afghanistan, Zia heard the rustle. He leapt up, grasped the hem of the garment, and, almost overnight, became the darling of the West, especially the United States. The Soviet invasion of Afghanistan in 1979 not only brought about a dramatic transformation in Pakistan's relations with the US, but with skilful manipulation by Zia also transformed him overnight, in Western eyes, from a military dictator and despot to a brave and courageous leader, a valiant fighter, a David pitted against a Goliath, and a champion of the free world.

Zia handled with skill and firmness the situation created for Pakistan by the Soviet intervention in Afghanistan, which had taken him and everybody else completely by surprise. Everyone had proceeded on the assumption that the Soviets would never cross the Oxus and enter Afghanistan. Very courageously, Zia refused to accept the *fait accompli*. He called for immediate withdrawal of all Soviet troops. Pakistan's position was supported by the Organization of Islamic Countries, at a special Conference attended by 36 out of a possible 40 Muslim countries. 'At the UN Pakistan led a large majority of the non-aligned States in condemning the Soviet action.'[5] Pakistan agreed to serve as a conduit for the gradually expanding aid. The price exacted from Washington was a US commitment to provide $ 1.5 billion in military aid for the armed forces. 'Zia had acquired powerful leverage in his dealings with the U.S. by agreeing in 1979 to permit the installation of U.S. electronic monitoring facilities in the northern border areas adjacent to the Soviet Central Asian missile testing and anti-satellite launch sites. One of the most serious problems posed for American intelligence agencies by the fall of the Shah in January 1979 was the loss of critical monitoring facilities in Iran. Neighbouring Pakistan was a natural place to turn to for alternative location.'[6]

For Pakistan, as for Iran, the invasion of Afghanistan resulted in the immediate escalation of the Afghan refugee influx, putting a strain on the social and economic fabric of the two frontline provinces, the NWFP and Balochistan.

An Afghan Cell had been created in the Foreign Office in 1973 but had become dormant. It was revived in 1978. As Secretary Interior, I was a member of the Cell. At the beginning, discussions were quite open and frank. Very soon we realized that the Cell meetings were called to discuss peripheral matters only. More sensitive issues were discussed in restricted meetings. The security implications of the Soviet invasion of Afghanistan for Pakistan were discussed threadbare in the Afghan Cell meetings. What were the Soviet objectives? The majority view was that the ultimate objective was to reach the warm waters of the Arabian Sea and that aggression against Pakistan was inevitable and only a question of time. General Zia's view was that, after crushing Afghan resistance, the Soviets would turn their attention toward Pakistan. It was his assessment that it would take the Soviets about two years to control the situation in Afghanistan, before continuing their march to the Arabian Sea. He told us that the pot must therefore be kept boiling for at least two years so that he could set things in order and prepare himself for the inevitable blow. The Soviet Ambassador, in one of his informal discussions with me, dismissed this theory, saying that the Soviet Union had plenty of warm waters of its own and was not interested in the warm waters of the Arabian Sea.

My first direct exposure to the tragedy of Afghanistan was after the Soviet withdrawal — on 20 January 1988. Abdul Ghaffar Khan, the veteran Red Shirt leader and freedom-fighter had died after a protracted illness. In accordance with his wishes, his body was to be buried in Jalalabad. Along with thousands of his admirers, I joined the cortege at Peshawar. We crossed the Torkham border without any travel documents. But on arrival at Jalalabad, all hell broke loose when a series of bomb explosions occurred all around us in the parking lot near the burial site. I was thrown off my feet and on to the ground but luckily escaped unhurt. When I looked around, I saw dead bodies scattered all over the fields. Scores of injured persons, bleeding profusely, their limbs blown off were crying for help. In a state of shock, I ran across the fields to the burial site and contacted the Afghan authorities. Dr Najibullah, the Afghan President, was delivering his funeral oration. While I was busy arranging medical help for the injured, I suddenly realized that my compatriots had left for Peshawar, leaving me alone with the dead and the injured. I therefore felt very relieved when I met Haji Ghulam Ahmad Bilour and Muhammad Afzal Khan, two high-ranking Awami National Party leaders, near the Jalalabad hospital. We spent the night at a hotel, as guests of the Afghan government. The next morning, we left for Peshawar in a convoy of vehicles, carrying the dead and the injured. As we approached the Pak-Afghan border, nothing gave me greater pleasure than to see the Pakistan flag fluttering in the breeze atop our check-post at Torkham. This was my closest brush with death and also my closest encounter with the traumatic events in Afghanistan.

Little did Zia know that on 13 November 1986, the Soviet leadership had decided, for internal reasons, that the war must be ended within one to two years and the troops brought back home. 'You had better be ready,' Gorbachev told Najibullah, 'in twelve months because we will be going whether you are ready or not.'[7] When the decision became known in the fall of 1987, Zia was caught unprepared, with no contingency plan for the fast-changing situation. Zia and all his advisers proceeded on the assumption that, since the Soviets had not given up territorial acquisition under military challenge since the Second World War, the question of withdrawal of troops from Afghanistan except on terms favourable to the Soviets simply did not arise. 'What the bear has eaten', so says a Chinese saying, 'he never spits out.' All our plans were based on this wrong assumption.

Zia made another wrong assumption while assessing the post-withdrawal situation in Afghanistan. He thought, as did everybody else, that Najib would not survive after the Soviet withdrawal. They all thought he would flee Afghanistan on the first available Soviet helicopter. They were in for a rude shock. Subsequent events showed how we had completely misjudged Najib and overestimated the power of the *mujahideen* (or Muj, as the Americans called them). However, the fatal error Zia and (in fairness to him) all his advisers committed was to view the Afghan conflict not as a nationalistic movement, as it largely appears in hindsight, but as evidence of a major communist drive for access to warm waters and for hegemony in South Asia. We badly misread Soviet objectives. We did not realize that Soviet leadership was sharply divided and that the decision to intervene did not have the support of the entire leadership. What is worse, we branded all the Afghan leaders as Soviet stooges. We saw them first as communist and only second as Afghan nationalists. We did not realize that the Afghans are Afghans first and Afghans last. We misjudged Daoud, Hafeezullah Amin, Taraki, and Dr Najib. We did not know — or did not want to know — that they were desperately struggling to secure their release from the Bear's embrace. We did not know that Daoud had clashed with Brezhnev on 12 April 1977 during his Moscow visit which led to the tragic events which followed. 'Recalling this encounter, Abdul Samad Ghaus, then Deputy Foreign Minister and Daoud's long time confidant, writes that the Soviet leader objected to what he called a "considerable increase" in the number of experts from NATO countries working in Afghanistan. In the past, Brezhnev said, the Afghan government did not allow experts from NATO countries to be stationed in the northern part of the country, but this practice was no longer followed. The Soviet Union took a grim view of these developments and wanted the Afghan government to get rid of these experts who were nothing more than spies.

'A chill fell on the room. Some of the Russians seemed visibly embarrassed. In a cold, unemotional voice Daoud told Brezhnev that what was just said could never be accepted by Afghans who viewed his statement as a flagrant interference in the internal affairs of Afghanistan — Daoud said, and I remembered clearly his words: we will never allow you to dictate to us how to run our country and whom to employ in Afghanistan. How and where we employ the foreign experts will remain the exclusive prerogative of the Afghan state. Afghanistan shall remàin poor, if necessary, but free in its acts and decisions'. After saying this, Ghaus concludes, Daoud and all the other Afghans present abruptly stood up and were starting to walk out when Brezhnev, 'rising from his chair with some difficulty', hurried after him. Reminding Daoud of his request for a private conversation, the Soviet leader offered to meet, 'whenever convenient to you', whereupon Daoud replied, in a clear loud voice for all to hear, 'I wish to inform Your Excellency that there is no longer any need for that meeting.'[8] This episode sealed Daoud's fate, but we did not know it and we did nothing to help him. Hafeezullah Amin met the same fate for standing up to the Soviets but we refused to do business with him.

From the very inception of Pakistan, we played into Indian hands by treating the Afghans as our enemies and their leaders as Indian or Soviet stooges. We failed to analyse our assumptions critically with the result that the foundations of our decision-making were seriously flawed. Is it, therefore, surprising that Afghanistan today is in a mess and Pakistan has no Afghan policy worth the name?

President Ghulam Ishaq Khan

Chapter 6

Ghulam Ishaq Khan

Ghulam Ishaq Khan was born in village Ismail Khel in Bannu District in January 1915. He joined Islamia College, Peshawar in 1930. He left Islamia College after getting a B.Sc. degree and joined the prestigious Provincial Civil Service (Executive Branch) in 1940 as a gazetted officer on the basis of a competitive examination held by the Punjab and NWFP Joint Public Service Commission. For some time, he served as Assistant Commissioner, Nowshera, a prize post under the British Raj. Even as a young provincial civil service officer, Ghulam Ishaq Khan impressed his colonial masters with his hard work, clarity of views, analytical mind, unimpeachable financial and moral integrity, and devotion to duty. He was always a stickler for rules, and honest to a fault.

After independence, Ghulam Ishaq Khan was inducted into the newly created Civil Service of Pakistan cadre, successor to the old Indian Civil Service. He came to the notice of the powers that be at inter-provincial meetings, where he used to outshine senior ICS officers. From then on, his climb to the top was meteoric. His exceptional talent was recognized by successive governments, both civil and military. In his various assignments, as Chairman WAPDA, Finance Secretary, Governor State Bank of Pakistan, Secretary General Defence, Finance Minister, and Chairman Senate, Ghulam Ishaq Khan acquitted himself with great distinction and left the imprint of his personality and his exceptional talent on some of the key institutions of Pakistan. In international conferences, Ghulam Ishaq Khan could hold his own against the best.

I inherited my acquaintance with Ghulam Ishaq Khan from my father. I have known him for more than half a century. I first met him in 1941 in Bannu in the company of my father. He was posted there as a Treasury Officer. Two things about him struck me: he was very handsome and he was immaculately dressed in western clothes.

Three years later, I met him again in Haripur, a sub-division of Hazara District. Ghulam Ishaq Khan was now Extra Assistant Commissioner and I was on my way to Abbottabad to take up my first job as lecturer in history. I spent two delightful days as his guest at his official residence on the main Haripur-Abbottabad Road. I always think of those days every time I drive past that house.

I stayed with Ghulam Ishaq Khan at his official residence in Islamia College whenever I went to Peshawar. He had been specially selected by the Governor Sir George Cunningham and sent as Bursar to straighten out the financial problems of the college. I remember him sitting on a sofa in front of a roaring log fire on a cold wintry morning, busy dictating lengthy reports on the finances of the institution. I did not know the ABC of what he was saying. I was most impressed.

We were both in Srinagar on 14 August 1947, the dawn of independence. The fate of Kashmir was hanging in the balance. While driving through Srinagar, Ghulam Ishaq Khan would, every now and then, ask the driver to slow down. He would then address the nearest Kashmiri and ask him to say 'Pakistan Zindabad', and pay him a rupee. When we returned to Mansehra, there was a message awaiting him. He was directed to take over as Secretary to the Chief Minister of the NWFP, Abdul Qayyum Khan.

On 10 September 1948, I went to Peshawar to collect some books in connection with the Civil Service of Pakistan Examination I was going to take in January 1949. I was staying with Ghulam Ishaq Khan at his official residence on North Circular Road. Early the next morning, we heard the sad news of the passing away of Quaid-i-Azam Mohammed Ali Jinnah. GIK accompanied Qayyum Khan to Karachi to attend the funeral and I, with a heavy heart, left for Mardan on my way back to Swabi where I was posted as a sub judge.

In 1953, I was posted at Peshawar as Registrar Co-operative Societies NWFP. Ghulam Ishaq Khan was my Administrative Secretary. I knew nothing about co-operative societies and co-operative banks, but Ghulam Ishaq Khan was always there to help, guide, and assist. I learnt a lot from him. Together, we organized a network of sugarcane co-operative sale and supply societies throughout Peshawar District. This was a unique experiment in the history of co-operatives in Pakistan. Unfortunately, all these societies were scrapped after both of us left Peshawar at the time of the establishment of One Unit in October 1955. Ghulam Ishaq Khan left for Lahore to take up his new job as Secretary Irrigation and Development in the government of West Pakistan. I was posted to Kohat as Deputy Commissioner, my first district assignment.

From 1966 onwards, when both of us reverted to the federal government, we used to meet two or three times a week, generally at Ghulam Ishaq Khan's residence in Islamabad. I have fond memories of hours of animated discussions over endless cups of tea with Ghulam Ishaq Khan. Together we saw the rise and fall of first Ayub, then Yahya, and subsequently the tragic end of Bhutto. We were not always in agreement in our assessments of the principal characters in the tragic drama which was unfolding itself but our discussions were always totally honest and uninhibited.

Ghulam Ishaq Khan knew that I wanted nothing from him and he did not have to be on guard in my company. I think my old-shoe quality helped him relax. We would spend hours swapping stories, gossiping, reminiscing, talking about anything and everything.

I had witnessed Ghulam Ishaq Khan's meteoric rise to the highest position that a civil servant could aspire to. As Finance Minister, Ghulam Ishaq Khan exercised practically veto power in all matters having financial implications. Zia at times disagreed with Ghulam Ishaq Khan but he rarely overruled his Finance Minister whom he held in high esteem.

'It is amazing how a sudden, unexpected, unforeseen turn in the road can', in the words of Ronald Reagan 'lead you a long way from where you intended to go — and a long way from where you expected to go.'[1] For Ghulam Ishaq Khan, this unexpected turn in the road occurred one day in May 1985, when the green telephone in his office rang in my presence. Ghulam Ishaq Khan picked up the receiver and from the sudden change in his tone and his responses, I realized that the President was on the line and offering him the chairmanship of the Senate, the number two slot in the hierarchy, next only to the President. It was quite obvious from the way Ghulam Ishaq Khan reacted that he was taken by surprise, a little hurt, and not at all impressed by the offer. Neither of us realized then how this unexpected turn in the road would affect his career and the future of the country.

★   ★   ★

In August 1985, I retired from the Civil Service of Pakistan. Like most civil servants, I did not know how to confront not old age but retirement. I always thought — and still do — that age really is a question not of how many years a person has lived but of how much he has lived in those years. I had been involved in national affairs of great importance. I had lived a full and rich life. I had always believed in keeping fit, keeping active, and keeping up with what was going on in the world. I therefore felt very young even when I retired — and still do. I do not know what it is that is still keeping me young but power never kept me young. I was therefore a little surprised to learn that to Churchill's question, 'How do you keep so young?' Tito replied 'I know what it is. It is power. It is power that keeps a man young'. I never missed power after retirement and loss of power never prevented me from keeping young. I never missed the files, the endless meetings, or the Secretariat. I never lost interest in life and all that it has to offer. Oddly enough, I experienced a strange feeling of liberation after retirement. In search of nirvana, my early morning walks in the Margalla Hills which always brought me in close communion with nature and created a feeling of exhilaration, inner peace and tranquillity, now became longer and longer and a lot more enjoyable.

At the crack of dawn, seven days a week, with Wordsworthian enthusiasm when most of Islamabad was fast asleep, I began to wander about the Margalla Hills, enjoying nature's richness and its luxurious fecundity. Fatigue, frustration, and disillusionment would all drop away. In solitude among nature's works and away from the selfishness of man, I began to seek in the Margallas communion with nature and a place to lose myself. The scented and invigorating air and the sight of the distant snows acted like an elixir.

The Margalla Hills, which form the backdrop of Islamabad, comprise largely subtropical, dry, semi-evergreen forest and pine forest. No less than 1,700 species of flowering plants and 53 ferns occur in a diversity of habitats. In spring, the Margallas are carpeted with flowers such as tulips, dandelions, buttercups, poppies, calchicums, mints, and many more annual and perennial plants.

Once within their embrace, the Margalla Hills are designed by nature to dispel from the minds of visitors, all thoughts of business, politics, government, and all memories likely to sadden or oppress. To be in the Margallas is not to be in Islamabad but to be suspended magically beside it, freed from the city's tensions, protected from the bureaucracy. The Margalla Park is where people go to seek asylum from the mandarins.

Unfortunately, although the entire area was declared a national park by the federal government in 1980, it is exposed to activities, undertaken with the full support of government, which are prejudicial to its preservation, are environmentally hazardous, and incompatible with the objectives of a national park. A cement factory was established in 1984 in the green area. Its requirement of raw material — i.e., limestone — is quarried in the national park. Consequently, the park's features, its rock, soil, fauna, flora, are being gradually destroyed; besides, the factory is creating serious pollution.

Hundreds of stone-crushers have been installed in four of the beautiful valleys of the national park and rock-mining allowed. This has totally destroyed the landscape, the natural geological formations, the archaeological features, and native plant communities. An industrial atmosphere has been created in an otherwise pristine environment by the noise of motors and machinery, dynamite-blasting, heavy truck traffic, workers' camps, and polluted streams. Rawal Lake, a part of the national park and the main source of drinking water for Rawalpindi, is threatened by pollution caused by unauthorized human habitations all around the lake.

I believe that there are urgent moral and practical reasons to conserve the Margalla's natural resources, not only for the benefit of the people today, but also to meet the needs and aspirations of our future generations.

The Margalla Hills Society, of which I have been the President since 1989, is campaigning in the teeth of opposition from powerful political elements and vested interests against this deliberate degradation and decimation of the environment. Against heavy odds, we have achieved some limited success but the problem persists. In the process, I have lost some good friends and made many enemies. How can we protect the national park or, for that matter, anything else, when the gamekeeper has become the poacher?

After retirement, I spent a lot of time catching up on my reading and enjoying western classical music. I suddenly realized that all those years when I was in service, I had neglected my family and had become a stranger to my children. When a former Bulgarian communist dictator, Todov Zhirkov, asked Nixon how many grandchildren he had, Nixon replied he had three. Zhirkov said, 'You are a very rich man. Having grandchildren is the greatest wealth a man can have'. I could not agree more. I have thirteen: it is a pleasure watching them grow up.

It was June 1990. I was enjoying my new life and, above all, my newly won freedom. I had just come back from a long and very pleasant morning walk in the Margalla Hills when someone came into my room and told me that the Military Secretary to the President was on the line. I was a little intrigued when told that I had an appointment with the President, Ghulam Ishaq Khan, at 11 a.m. that day. I generally keep away from people in power, especially if they are friends. We had not met for about two years and some tension had developed in our relations since my retirement. The meeting was very emotional. Needless to say, I was very happy to see my friend in his exalted new position, occupying the highest office in the country. Flags and standards of various colours framed the desk on both sides, symbolizing the President's military and civil powers. Ghulam Ishaq Khan embraced me very warmly and we reminisced for a while and then, as the President surveyed the domestic situation, I could see that he was gripped with a sense of urgency and crisis. He wanted me involved right away. I soon realized that the President and the Prime Minister, Benazir Bhutto, were on a collision course. The fateful decision to sack her and dissolve the Assembly had already been taken. I was sorry to hear that things had come to such a pass and that I had been such a poor prophet. My mind flashed back to 1988.

★   ★   ★

At her request, I met Benazir on the eve of the elections in November 1988, at her aunt's house in Karachi. I was staying at the Karachi residence of my friend, Jamsheed Marker. Early one morning, her cousin, Tariq Islam, whom I had met the evening before at his parents' home in Clifton, came to see me and told me that Benazir wanted to meet me and wanted to know if it was okay by me. When I told him that I looked forward to meeting her, he said that he would get back to me and left. A little later, he came back and asked me if I had any objection to meeting her at her residence at 70 Clifton. I had none. He then asked me if I would meet her openly or incognito, as most people preferred. I told him that I had never in my life met anybody incognito and that I would meet her openly and in broad daylight, just as I used to meet Mr Bhutto, even when he was *persona non grata* with Ayub Khan. He came back again and asked me if I had any objection if the meeting took place at 6.30 in the evening at his parents' home at 18-D Clifton, instead of at 70 Clifton. I had none. I got to 18-D Clifton a little before 6.30 p.m. Manna had been duly informed and was busy arranging dinner for seven, including Benazir, her husband Asif, myself, the host and hostess, Tariq, and his wife Yasmeen. I did not know how the meeting would go and awaited Benazir's arrival with some trepidation.

Benazir turned up a little after 6.30 p.m., accompanied by her husband Asif whom I had never met before. She introduced her husband and reminded me that we had last met twelve years earlier. Benazir has an awesome memory.

Benazir had seen her father elevated to the exalted position of President, Chief Martial Law Administrator, and Prime Minister of Pakistan; and then incarcerated as a convict in the condemned person's cell; taken to the gallows; and hanged by Ziaul Haq. During most of this period, I was Secretary Interior, looking after internal security, law and order, etc. Zia had died in the mysterious C-130 crash and Ghulam Ishaq Khan had stepped into his shoes and assumed the office of President. Benazir asked me how I viewed the political situation and made searching inquiries about Ghulam Ishaq Khan. I told her that she would come out on top in the election and that nothing could stop her from coming to power. I could see that, deep down, Benazir viewed Ghulam Ishaq with a considerable measure of wariness. She was obviously aware of Ghulam Ishaq Khan's problems with her late father, his close association with Ziaul Haq and Ayub, and she shared the popular perception that Ghulam Ishaq Khan was involved in all their major policy decisions. Knowing all this, I told her that she was lucky in having an honest man like Ghulam Ishaq Khan at the helm of affairs, a workaholic who was totally committed to Pakistan, and that in him she would find a friend, philosopher, and guide. I remember telling her in so many words that if she just shut her eyes and followed his advice, especially in running the government, she would not go wrong and would never regret her decision. She told me that she had received a similar report about Ghulam Ishaq Khan from Iftikhar Gillani, who was in some way related to Ghulam Ishaq Khan.

Dinner was served and we moved to the dining-room. Manna made me sit, as always, at the head of the table. Benazir was sitting on my right. After some time, she changed her seat and sat on my left as she has a problem with her left ear and could not hear me properly. Over dinner, she asked searching questions about Islamabad and the working of the federal government. She told me that she did not know the working of the bureaucracy and, unlike her father, hardly knew any of the senior civil servants or army generals. I told her that with Ghulam Ishaq Khan at the Presidency, she would have no problem in running the government or dealing with the bureaucracy. It was already past ten now and time for her to go home. Before leaving, she said she hoped to meet me again, but not, as before, at such long intervals. Two things struck me: she had grown into a very attractive, tall young woman, blissfully ignorant of the complexity of the problems lying ahead of her. But what struck me most was that tragedy had left no trace of bitterness in her. The impression I got was that she was breaking with the past and was looking forward to her immense responsibilities in the changing political situation. Throughout the evening, Asif scarcely participated in the conversation and just listened.

I had been out of office for about five years. I loved what I was doing. I knew from experience the tensions, the lack of privacy, the demands on time, energy, emotions that come with proximity to the President. I knew that a political storm was brewing and I was going to be in the eye of the storm. The job ahead was going to be the toughest, most demanding, and yet the most exhilarating of all jobs I had ever held. Working with Ghulam Ishaq Khan was something special, a great opportunity and a privilege and I was not going to miss it. After five years in the wilderness, I was back in business. I was reminded of Macarthur's famous comment in his farewell address to Congress in 1951, 'Old politicians sometimes die, but they seldom fade away'. In our country, this phenomenon is obviously not restricted to old politicians only.

This was the beginning of a completely new period in my life. When I entered the Presidency, I soon realized that my arrival on the scene was viewed with misgiving by some people close to the President. They were working for the Presidency, not for the man. Personal loyalty to Ghulam Ishaq Khan, an essential virtue in staff members, was given low priority. My position was clear: I was working for the man, not the Presidency.

Towards the end of July 1990, there were firm indications that the President had taken the fateful decision to dissolve the National Assembly and sack Prime Minister Benazir Bhutto and her Cabinet. The Chief of Army Staff, General Aslam Beg had been taken into confidence and his agreement secured. Logistics and other details were worked out in a series of meetings with Major General Asad Durrani, Director, Military Intelligence, who represented the COAS. The Dissolution Order was drafted by the President in consultation with his legal advisers including Sharifuddin Pirzada, Aziz Munshi, Rafi Raza, and Brigadier Zulfiqar.

While all this was happening and the President's advisers were burning the midnight oil in the Presidency, Benazir Bhutto was blissfully ignorant of the axe which was about to fall on her government and went about her business as if all was well. She was aware of widespread rumours of the impending dissolution of the Assembly but, like Stalin on the eve of the German invasion of the Soviet Union, she dismissed these rumours as a clumsy propaganda manoeuvre of the elements arrayed against her. But, in order to reassure herself, she sent Happy Minwala, her Special Assistant, to call on the President, to find out if there was any basis for these rumours, and what had led to the deterioration in her relations with the President. The President assured Happy that he had no intention of doing anything against the Constitution — which was perfectly consistent with the action he was about to take. Later in the day, Benazir herself called the President and got confirmation of the action the President was about to take. When she asked for his reasons, he advised her to listen to his six o'clock address to the nation. It reminded me of Molotov's memorable comments on 22 June 1941, the day Germany attacked the Soviet Union, and the statement read out to him by Ambassador Schulenburg of Germany: 'Do you believe that we deserved that?' Molotov asked. It was obvious that Benazir, like Stalin, had been caught napping and her intelligence agencies had not served her well.

On 6 August 1990, President Ghulam Ishaq Khan, in exercise of the powers conferred on him by clause (2) sub-clause (b) of Article 58 of the Constitution, dissolved the National Assembly. As a consequence thereof, the Prime Minister and the Cabinet ceased to hold office. There was no deception plan. No effort was made to conceal the operation. Between 1 August and 6 August, we were apprehending a pre-emptive move by the Prime Minister, but, with every passing day and with D-Day approaching and nothing happening, an eerie feeling gripped us all. Why was the Prime Minister not making any move? Was she going to spring a surprise? What if she went on air, addressed the nation, and disclosed that a plan was afoot to dissolve the National Assembly and dismiss the elected government? The element of surprise would be gone. How would the President then react? Would he call off the operation or go ahead and dissolve the Assembly? How would the country react? These were some of the questions agitating our minds. Keeping all this in view, it was suggested to the President to bring D-Day forward and dissolve the House on 4 August. The President did not agree. Subsequent events proved that all our apprehensions were unfounded. For a variety of reasons, Benazir had discounted the possibility of an imminent dissolution and had made no contingency plans. In his address to the nation, the President warned that 'undemocratic protest over this constitutional and democratic step will just not be tolerated. If someone acts irresponsibly and in order to escape public accountability, tries to misguide the people, he shall be strictly dealt with'.

The country reacted calmly. There were no protests and no demonstrations. A caretaker government was formed under Ghulam Mustafa Jatoi and, almost immediately, hectic preparations began for the election due in November 1990. As a result of this election, Mian Nawaz Sharif, Chief Minister of the Punjab emerged as the leader of the house in the National Assembly with a strong majority. I congratulated him when I called him from the President's office and told him that we all looked forward to his arrival in Islamabad. On that bright sunny day, with not a speck of dark cloud on the horizon, the future looked rosy. The President looked forward to a pleasant and good working relationship with Nawaz Sharif. Fate willed otherwise.

Chapter 7

Toward confrontation

For about one year, outwardly at least, relations between the President, Ghulam Ishaq Khan, and the Prime Minister, Mian Nawaz Sharif, remained cordial. The first indication that all was not well between the two came on the occasion of the President's address to the joint session of the two Houses of Parliament in December 1991, when the President was subjected to insults and humiliation and shouts of 'Go, Baba Go', by the entire opposition led by Benazir, in full view of the entire diplomatic corps, Service Chiefs, and the national and international media. I was shocked when Nawaz Sharif and his party, as if according to a pre-arranged plan, did not protest, made no move in defence of the President, and remained silent spectators throughout this disgusting spectacle, which they seemed to relish. Despite this, for a full half an hour, the President faced Benazir's onslaught all by himself and continued with his address. I met the President immediately thereafter and complimented him on the dignified manner in which he had handled the situation. I also told him how I viewed Nawaz Sharif's unresponsive, calculated silence on the occasion which, to say the least, was quite intriguing. The President just smiled and made no comment. From that day onward, I began to doubt Nawaz Sharif's loyalty to the President and it became clear to me that he had a different agenda and a different game plan. The President, however, continued to give him the benefit of the doubt.

President Ghulam Ishaq Khan administering oath of office to the Advisers to the Prime Minister at the Presidency, Islamabad, on 9 November 1990

Towards the end of 1992, however, there were clear indications that a rift had developed between the President and the Prime Minister, Mian Nawaz Sharif. A week before the sudden death of the Army Chief, Asif Nawaz Janjua, on 8 January 1993, Chaudhry Nisar Ali Khan, Minister for Petroleum and a member of Nawaz Sharif's kitchen cabinet, met me in my office and we discussed the matter threadbare for about three hours. We both agreed that the President and the Prime Minister must remain on the same wavelength and that the two of us would meet regularly to remove any misunderstanding that might develop between them. Addressing Nisar before he left my office, I said: 'I will do my best to keep the President and the Prime Minister together in the spirit of the discussion we have just had. I hope you will do the same. But if, in spite of our best efforts, we fail and they fall out, I will regard it as our joint failure, and I want to leave you in no doubt that in that case I will stand by the President'. Nisar responded by saying that he appreciated what I had just said and that he understood my position. When he left, I was relieved, felt very happy and confident that, with Nisar by my side, we would be able to take care of any problem that might arise between the President and the Prime Minister in the days to come, and foil the designs of their common political opponents. Subsequent events were to prove how wrong I was.

January 1993

Two important political developments indicated change in the air. One was a speech by Iftikhar Gillani, a former PPP Law Minister, in which he pleaded for a dialogue between the opposition and the government and termed those opposing such a dialogue as enemies of the country. The Prime Minister responded positively to Gillani's overture.

The other important development was Benazir's surprise election as Chairperson of the Foreign Affairs Committee proposed by no less a person than the Minister of State for Foreign Affairs and seconded by Shahbaz Sharif, the brother of the Prime Minister, without the knowledge of the President. Obviously, something was cooking and it caused eyebrows to be raised in the Presidency. It was clearly indicative of some sort of a compromise between the government and the opposition. This was the time when all of Benazir's moves had backfired. The long march had ended in failure. Her party was divided between the doves and hawks. The Punjab group, composed of Farooq Leghari, Salman Taseer, Ehsanul Haq Piracha, Tariq Rahim, and Aitzaz Ahsan, was complaining of persecution at the hands of the government and were all for taking a hard line. But the doves had their way and the party opted for dialogue with the government.

The most important development, however, which influenced the course of political events in the country and the fate of the President and the Prime Minister, was the sudden death on 8 January 1993 of General Asif Nawaz, the Chief of Army Staff and an important member of the troika. It was common knowledge that relations between the Prime Minister and the Army Chief were strained and there was no love lost between them. Who was going to succeed him? The Eighth Amendment imposes huge responsibilities on the President. It is the President and the President alone who appoints the Chief of Army Staff in his discretion. How was he going to exercise this power? The sudden death of Asif Nawaz had shocked the nation. Nobody had thought of who was going to succeed him. All these thoughts raced through my mind as I drove back to the Presidency after attending the *janaza* prayers for the late General. On arrival, I was summoned by the President. Without his telling me, I knew what was on his mind. Asif Nawaz's successor had to be appointed and appointed quickly, for the Army must know who their Chief was going to be. Together we scrutinized the dossiers of about half a dozen senior officers. We went over their records in order to know how they were assessed by their superiors, what their performance was in war and peace, and what their reputation was, ascertained on the basis of what others thought of them. As a result of this exercise, the Chief of General Staff, Lieutenant General Farrukh was selected to fill the vacuum. We thought we had made the best choice. As I was leaving the President's office, the President told me that although the Chief's appointment was made by the President in exercise of his discretionary power, he would, in the course of the day, discuss it with the Prime Minister and inform him of his decision. As I left the President's office, I felt relieved that a major decision had been made strictly on merit and I had no doubt in my mind that it would be welcomed by all concerned. After lunch, I accompanied the President in his helicopter to Chakri, the ancestral village of General Asif Nawaz, to attend the burial. The President was deep in thought throughout the flight and talked to nobody. After the burial, I saw Ghulam Ishaq Khan and Nawaz Sharif standing silently near the President's helicopter but I did not suspect anything amiss as they are both very shy and private persons and not very good conversationalists. On the way back to Islamabad, the President was again very quiet and kept his thoughts to himself. On landing, we shook hands and I drove back home.

It had been a very tiring day and I was looking forward to early dinner and sleep when, at about 9 p.m., Chaudhry Nisar, called to say that he had to meet me immediately to discuss a matter of supreme national importance. There was an air of urgency in his tone. We met in my study and, over a cup of green tea, Nisar told me that the President and the Prime Minister had had a very unpleasant meeting earlier in the day; that the President's nominee for the new Army Chief, General Farrukh, was not acceptable to the Prime Minister; and that if the President insisted on appointing Farrukh as Army Chief, a first-class political crisis would develop, leading to the resignation of the Prime Minister, because Nawaz Sharif just could not work with Farrukh. When I asked why Farrukh was not acceptable to the Prime Minister, Nisar told me that the Prime Minister was convinced that Farrukh was responsible for all his problems with the late General Asif Nawaz. I was stunned. Nisar asked me to intervene in the spirit of the arrangement worked out between the two of us a week earlier. Nisar told me that any general other than Farrukh would be acceptable to the Prime Minister. I thought if Farrukh's appointment was going to lead to a political crisis involving the two pillars of the state, the President should not insist on it and should accommodate the Prime Minister. I promised to speak to the President. Early next morning, I went to the Presidency and met the President. He confirmed that he and the Prime Minister had had an unsuccessful meeting and that the Prime Minister was threatening not to co-operate with General Farrukh if he were appointed as the new Army Chief. I advised the President against a showdown with the Prime Minister on this issue. Happily, in view of the Prime Minister's sharp reaction, his strong views on the subject, and my timely intervention, wiser counsels prevailed. The President dropped Farrukh and the search for another Chief of Army Staff began. We went over the dossiers again and the choice fell on Lieutenant General Abdul Waheed Kakar. I told the President that Waheed's appointment would be assailed on ethnic grounds and he would be criticized for appointing a fellow Pakhtun as the

Army Chief in order to bolster his own position against the other member of the troika. The President replied that he could take care of the ethnic charge as in his entire career, as his record would show, he had never made any decision on ethnic grounds. I felt relieved that the President had in his wisdom reconsidered the matter and avoided a head-on clash with the Prime Minister. A little later, the Prime Minister came to the Presidency and was apprised of the appointment of the new Army Chief. Lieutenant General Abdul Waheed was then called to the Presidency to hear the news of his appointment as the Chief of Army Staff. I was congratulated by Chaudhry Nisar and others in the Prime Minister's camp for averting a major political crisis. Nisar told me that, on his return from Switzerland, the Prime Minister would go straight from the airport to meet the President and express his gratitude for accommodating him in the matter of the appointment of the Army Chief. That day, I left the Presidency in an optimistic mood. Little did I know that it was not the end but the beginning of a serious confrontation between the President and the Prime Minister. For some inexplicable reason, Nisar never contacted me again. Would it have made any difference if he had? I wonder.

It soon became evident that Nawaz Sharif was not pleased with the appointment of General Waheed; he had others in mind. With the elimination of General Farrukh, he had been hoping that one of the others, and not General Waheed, would be the new army chief. When this did not happen, he stepped up his campaign for the repeal of Eighth Amendment, which is the source of the President's power of appointing Service Chiefs.

February 1993

The repeal of the Eighth Amendment now became a subject of heated discussion among political elements. While some favoured the removal of this sword of Damocles, hanging over the Parliament and the Prime Minister, others thought it might turn the Prime Minister into a dictator.

'Asif Zardari's release on bail and departure for London, Nawaz Sharif's sending of a bouquet to Benazir on the birth of her child, and Farooq Leghari's hint that his party was not opposed to "dialogue" with the government, were all pointers to a wind of change in the political field. Playing a shrewd political game from the comfortable distance of London, Benazir opened channels of communication with the Presidency, simultaneously allowing her party leader Iftikhar Gillani to keep talking to the Prime Minister's men. She now watched the on-going tussle between the Prime Minister and the President and determined to derive maximum advantage for herself.'[1]

Meanwhile, the Prime Minister came out openly for the scrapping of the Eighth Amendment. The battle lines had thus been drawn between the President and the Prime Minister. Public attention was now focused on the battle royal that was about to begin.

'Nawaz Sharif in his Senate speech took up the gauntlet against the Eighth Amendment and set up a Sub-Committee under Ghous Ali Shah to work out a consensus on the matter. This divided the Parliamentary Group into Ghulam Ishaq Khan Group and Nawaz Sharif Group.' Ghulam Mustafa Khar, a one-time PPP stalwart, now in the National Democratic Alliance, addressing a news conference in Rawalpindi on 21 February 1993 after a meeting with the President, opposed the undoing of the Eighth Amendment as long as the present government was in power. Linking the move to scrap the Eighth Amendment with Nawaz Sharif's ambitions to acquire absolute power, Khar came down heavily against the Prime Minister and his policies. 'Nawaz Sharif has gone "mad" Khar said "to acquire power and he wants to pave the way for One Party Government."'[2] Even within the Islamic Jamhuri Ittehad, opinions on the subject were divided.

In another development, Makhdoom Amin Fahim of Hala (Sindh) a PPP stalwart, came all the way to Islamabad to see the President on 14 February 1993. Close on his heels, the very next day, two other PPP MNAs, Faisal Saleh Hayat and Nazir Sultan, met the President. In order to keep everybody guessing, at a press conference in Islamabad on 18 February 1993, Farooq Leghari said that the MNAs had met the President in their private capacity and that it signified no change in the attitude of the Party.

March 1993

The death of the Pakistan Muslim League President, Muhammad Khan Junejo on 21 March 1993, and the impatience shown by Nawaz Sharif in getting himself nominated for the post of the President of Pakistan Muslim League through 'party elders', resulted in a full-blooded rebellion within the party led by Hamid Nasir

Chattha, and to the resignation of four cabinet ministers. Contrary to popular belief, the resignation of the cabinet ministers did not have the support of the President. I was present when the issue was raised by a group of rebel MNAs, which included Anwar Saifullah, the President's son-in-law, and was led by Hamid Nasir Chattha. When they called on the President to seek his blessings for the proposed move, the President advised against it. Chattha was the first to raise the banner of revolt against Prime Minister Mian Nawaz Sharif. He was now on the warpath and all anti-Nawaz elements in the party were rallying round him. The emergence of the King's Party within the PML had the tacit support of President Ghulam Ishaq Khan. The high-tension relationship between the two manifested itself even in purely social settings. At the funeral of the President's brother-in-law, Nadir Durrani, on 8 March 1993, the Prime Minister was conspicuous by his absence. The President stayed in Peshawar for two days and received visitors who came to condole with him. One of these visitors was General Abdul Waheed, the new Army Chief. People were wondering why the Prime Minister was not there. This significant omission on the part of Nawaz Sharif was a clear indication that all was not well and difficult days were ahead. The Prime Minister was also not there at the *iftar* party hosted for the Service Chiefs in the Presidency on 18 March, nor was the President present at the party hosted by the Prime Minister on 19 March. Even at the burial of Mr M. K. Junejo on 21 March 1993, the two managed to keep their distance, using different aircraft, reaching at different times, sitting in different rooms, and shaking hands formally and reluctantly when they could not avoid it.

In the background of the high tension between the two top pillars of the state, locked in an epic test of wills, Benazir sitting in London devised a strategy of widening the gulf between the two, maintaining a dialogue with both sides, and fully exploiting her unique position of tilting the balance in favour of whichever side was likely to win. In a desperate bid to secure support against the President, Iftikhar Gillani and Mahmud Khan Achakzai were sent on a mission to London with what was described as an attractive package deal. Benazir did not rise to the bait. At about the same time, Ghulam Mustafa Jatoi went on a similar mission of wooing Benazir, with the knowledge and tacit approval of President Ghulam Ishaq Khan. After the unsuccessful mission of Gillani and Achakzai, we noticed a definite Benazir tilt in favour of the President. This was reminiscent of the British military mission dispatched to Moscow on the eve of the Second World War by Chamberlain on a slow passenger-cargo vessel to work out a treaty of mutual assistance with the Soviet Union, and Ribbentrop's dash to Moscow with full powers from the Fuhrer, authorizing him to settle fully and conclusively the total complex of problems between the Reich and the Soviet Union. Of course, there were marked dissimilarities between the two situations. Ghulam Ishaq Khan was no Fuhrer and Nawaz Sharif was no Chamberlain. Benazir was no Stalin either. G. M. Jatoi carried no package deal nor did he have powers from the 'Fuhrer', authorizing him to settle fully and conclusively the total complex of problems. In the end, Benazir decided to throw in her lot with the President. Ghulam Ishaq Khan had beaten Nawaz Sharif to it.

Manhattan project

Towards the end of 1992, I noticed a significant change in the attitude of the PPP when a number of top PPP leaders from the Punjab, the so-called hawks who were dead against a rapprochement with Prime Minister Nawaz Sharif, established contact with me and started frequenting my house. The first to meet me was the late Chaudhry Altaf Hussain, who later became Governor Punjab. Chaudhry Altaf was a soft-spoken, pleasant man, with a very disarming personality. He was all for a rapprochement between Benazir and President Ghulam Ishaq Khan, and was dead against Nawaz Sharif. 'It was unfortunate', Chaudhry Altaf told me, 'that Benazir Bhutto and Ghulam Ishaq Khan had fallen out; that she had been led astray by some of her advisers; she was willing to make amends.' He sought my help in bringing the two together. I made no commitment and reported the conversation to the President who told me that he too had been contacted indirectly. This was the first of a series of visits by Chaudhry Altaf for whom, over a period of time, I developed great respect and affection. He was followed by Tariq Rahim, Salman Taseer, Ehsanul Haq Piracha, and Faisal Saleh Hayat. The gist of their message was that they were all for reconciliation with the President and dead against Nawaz Sharif and would resist all attempts to bring Benazir and Nawaz Sharif together. They told me that the Punjab PPP in particular would resist all such attempts. It was obvious that there was a deep division within the PPP high command on this issue. I conveyed all this verbatim to the President.

The pace of events quickened when I was told that Farooq Leghari, one of the top PPP leaders and a close confidant of Benazir Bhutto, wanted to meet me. With the permission of the President, I met Farooq at the residence of a common friend, Habibullah Kundi. Others present were Mir Afzal Khan, Chief Minister NWFP, who drove me to Kundi's house, and Aftab Ahmad Khan Sherpao, the future PPP Chief Minister of the NWFP. This was the first in a series of meetings with Farooq and Sherpao, who obviously spoke with the full authority of Benazir. The venue was later shifted to my house in Islamabad. Farooq wanted me to convey to the President that the mission of Iftikhar Gillani and Mahmud Achakzai to London had failed; that Benazir had opted for a genuine recon- ciliation with the President; that Nawaz Sharif was seeking repeal of the Eighth Amendment so that the President was stripped of all powers; that they would resist all such attempts on the part of Nawaz Sharif to weaken the President and acquire dictatorial powers for himself. He wanted me to convey to the President that the time had come for the President and Benazir to join hands and remove Nawaz Sharif from power before it was too late. I reported all this to the President. The President reacted positively and authorized me to tell Farooq and Sherpao that he agreed with this assessment and suggested a no-confidence motion against Nawaz Sharif. Farooq did not agree. He told me that past experi- ence had shown that, in our circumstances, it was almost impossi- ble to bring about an in-house change and all such attempts had, therefore, failed.

Ghulam Ishaq Khan, on his part, was averse to the dissolution of the National Assembly by him for the second time within three years. Dissolution, he said, was considered anti-democratic and frowned upon by the superior judiciary. His experience was that the people who had urged him in the name of Pakistan to dismiss a corrupt government and dissolve the National Assembly, were nowhere to be seen after the dissolution and dismissal of the government in 1990, and he was left holding the baby. When I mentioned this to Farooq, he told me that the President's action this time to dissolve the National Assembly and dismiss the government would, unlike the past, have the full support of the PPP, a party which enjoyed mass support throughout the length and breadth of the country, and that the objective situation on the ground would have to be taken into consideration by the Courts. He thought there would, therefore, be no difficulty in defending the President's action, if it was challenged in the Court. In order to strengthen the President's hands, they offered to secure the resignations of more than half the total membership of the National Assembly and submit them to the President. This and other connected issues were discussed in a series of meetings which followed. At one of these meetings, in view of the delicate nature of the operation, I suggested we give it a code name. I had been reading Richard Rhodes' *The Making of the Atomic Bomb* and suggested we call it the Manhattan Project. Farooq liked the idea and so did others.

We started as adversaries but, with the passage of time, we got to know each other very well. I developed great respect for Farooq, the future President of Pakistan, and Aftab Sherpao, the future Chief Minister of NWFP.

April 1993

On 17 April, a fateful day in the history of our country, I drove to the Army House, accompanied by my son Javed Khan for a dinner engagement at 7.30 p.m. with General Waheed, the Chief of Army Staff and his gracious wife Yasmeen. We got there at 7.25 p.m. General Waheed and his wife were strolling on the lawn when we drove into the porch. As the Prime Minister was going to address the nation on television at 7.30 p.m., General Waheed suggested we watch the address first and have dinner afterwards. We all gathered in front of a television set. What we heard stunned us: Nawaz Sharif directly accused the Presidency and alleged that, 'hurdles are being placed in my way to serve the nation and that all efforts to help the country are being subverted by unscrupulous and dirty politics of those who are supposed to be guardians of democracy and symbol of Federation and that a lot of pressure, threats, intimidation, and blackmail all of which aimed at forcing me to step down was being exercised.' Nawaz Sharif declared that he 'would not resign', 'would not dissolve the National Assembly', and 'would not take dictation'.

When the Prime Minister finished speaking, General Waheed said 'Good God! We are in serious trouble'. He asked me what would happen next. I was stunned but quickly recovered my wits and said, 'This is tantamount to a declaration of war by the Prime

Minister against the President'. After this open declaration of war, how could the two work together and how could the affairs of the Federation be run in accordance with the Constitution? I told General Waheed that in the past his predecessors had imposed martial law on much weaker grounds, but, thanks to the Eighth Amendment, this was perhaps not necessary as the Amendment gave powers to the President to resolve the crisis constitutionally by dissolving the National Assembly, dismissing the government, and referring the matter to the electorate for its verdict. At dinner, this was the sole subject of discussion. General Waheed was visibly relieved to hear that there was a constitutional way to resolve the crisis. At the mention of martial law, he threw up his hands and said that martial law was out of the question, but he asked me to convey a message to the President, on his behalf, that very night, that though martial law was out of the question, anything the President did in accordance with the Constitution would have his support. He said he would have conveyed the message himself but in the delicate situation which had arisen, it might be misunderstood. I was left in no doubt that if the President did not exercise his power under article 58 (2) (b), imposition of martial law would become unavoidable. Dinner over, I drove straight to the house of Anwar Saifullah, the President's son-in-law, and asked him to get me an immediate appointment with the President. Within minutes, I was told that the President was waiting to receive me. At the Presidency, I conveyed General Waheed's message and briefed the President on my conversation with the Chief. The President was calm. He said, 'Let us sleep over it. We will talk about it in the morning.'

Next morning about lunch-time, the President called me and asked me to go to Rawalpindi, meet General Waheed, and inform him that he had decided to dissolve the National Assembly and dismiss the government in exercise of his powers under the Constitution. General Waheed received me at the Army House at about 3 p.m. This was my second visit to the Army House within twenty-four hours. When I got there, General Waheed told me that Fazlur Rahman, the President's Secretary had called after I had left the Presidency to tell me to await his telephone call before delivering the President's message to him. Fazal called a few minutes later and I was allowed to deliver the President's message to the Army Chief. When he heard the message, he showed no surprise and told me that he would take all necessary security measures. He wanted to know who should be contacted in the Presidency for co-ordination. I told him that Brigadier Zulfiqar would be the contact man in the Presidency. I took leave of the General and drove back to the Presidency.

The second act in the unfolding drama began on 18 April: President Ghulam Ishaq Khan exercised the powers conferred on him under Article 58(2)(b) of the Constitution, dismissed Nawaz Sharif's government, dissolved the National Assembly, and brought the political process back to square one. The event came as no surprise to those watching the national scene. It was unheard of in any political system that two pillars of the state should avoid each other and abjure even normal social intercourse. The abrupt announcement made by Sharif on 24 February in the Senate of his decision to undo the Eighth Amendment was a watershed in the relations between the two dignitaries. The move was premature as Nawaz Sharif could not expect the necessary two-thirds majority to steer the constitutional amendment through. This fact alone became the *casus belli* between the two pillars of the State.

Nawaz Sharif's meeting with the President on 14 April for a rapprochement was unfortunately followed by a Press Note from the Presidency, saying what the Prime Minister had been asked to do. This, in my opinion, was unnecessary and, in the charged atmosphere prevailing at the time, was misconstrued and produced unintended results. Nawaz Sharif, too, overreacted. His address to the nation on radio and television was nothing short of a declaration of war against the President. The irony is that until that time Ghulam Ishaq Khan had had no intention of dissolving the National Assembly or of dismissing the government, and was resisting all attempts on the part of hardliners in his camp to act against Nawaz Sharif. When the requisite number of resignations of MNAs had been secured, Sharifuddin Pirzada, Rafi Raza, Aziz Munshi, Fazlur Rahman, and myself met the President. When the legal luminaries told him that in view of these resignations, the President could dissolve the National Assembly in exercise of his power under Article 58(2)(b) and his action, if challenged, could be successfully defended in Court, the President reacted sharply. He said he had no intention of using the hatchet a second time and that resignations alone did not justify dissolution. He went red in the face and started doing his file work which was a polite way of telling us that the meeting was over.

red in the face and started doing his file work which was a polite
way of telling us that the meeting was over.

Nawaz Sharif, through his speech of 17 April, achieved what a
whole battery of legal luminaries and hardliners in the President's
camp had failed to achieve. The speech broke the President's
resistance and left him with no choice but to dissolve the National
Assembly. Was this the result Nawaz Sharif intended? I wonder.

May 1993

On 26 May, the Supreme Court overturned the action of the President under Article 58(2)(b) of the Constitution. In his dissenting
judgment, Justice Sajjad Ali Shah (currently Chief Justice) Supreme
Court of Pakistan observed:

1. I have gone through very carefully, elaborate leading judgment proposed to be delivered by my learned brother
   Shafiur Rahman, J. for whom I have great regard and whose
   profound learning I always keenly admire but with opti-
   mum respect I say that I find myself unable to agree with
   his views and resultantly I venture to write dissenting judgment. Facts in great detail are described in the main judgment but for the purpose of brief recapitulation it is necessary and proper to state that on account of differences, which
   arose between petitioner as Prime Minister and respondent
   No. 1 as President of Pakistan, erosion crept in the working
   relationship of the two and in that context and on that subject, in order to avert complete breakdown, meeting took
   place between the two at Presidency on 14.4.1993, which
   later turned out to be the last meeting. For the sake of brev-
   ity, petitioner and respondent No.1 would be referred here-
   after as the Prime Minister and the President respectively.

2. In my humble opinion in this regard the most important
   and pivotal point is the making of speech by the Prime
   Minister and its tenor and purport which is not disputed
   but on the contrary is being defended vociferously on the
   ground that the Prime Minister acted within his powers in
   the Constitution and the President had no business to
   advise the Prime Minister in the Parliamentary form of
   Government. The tenor of the speech of the Prime Minister shows clearly that he endeavoured to take into confi-

accordance with the provisions of the Constitution and for such situation he was not to be blamed and the blame in its entirety lay on the door of the Presidency and the person of the President who colluded with elements inside the ruling party and outside who were hell-bent to destabilise the Government.

3. In my opinion the question of apportionment of blame for creating such a situation is relegated in the background and the fact that such a situation is created bringing about deadlock and stalemate in the working relationship of two pillars of the Government of Federation has become a fait accompli which enables the President to exercise his discretionary power under Article 58(2)(b). There is no dispute about the fact that after the speech of the Prime Minister to the nation on T.V. on 17.4.1993 tone of defiance and confrontation was set by the Prime Minister and not reconciliation and this in fact is more than sufficient to say that situation is created spelling out in clear and unambiguous terms breakdown of working relationship between the President and the Prime Minister, hence Government of Federation could not be carried on in accordance with the provisions of the Constitution and appeal to the electorate was necessary. There is no gainsaying that problem would be solved by the unilateral offer made by the Court to the Prime Minister for assurance that if the Government was restored he would work hand in hand with the President. Such offer was not made to the President. Action and reaction are equal and opposite. By the tenor of the speech the President could feel hurt and humiliated. No such compromise took place between the two to say that they had patched up the differences and were reconciled with all sincerity considering bygones as bygones.

4. Scheme of the Constitution is such that both the Prime Minister and the President are king-pins in the machinery of Government of Federation and have to work hand-in-hand in atmosphere of congeniality to carry out day to day government and executive acts which are to be taken in the name of the President on the advice of the Prime Minister and in that connection the summaries have to go for approval of the President. What would happen if the President does not cooperate.

5. I would like to point out here that in the case of Tariq Rahim the situation was not so bad and Prime Minister Ms Benazir Bhutto had not made any speech to the nation criticising openly and in public the person and office of the President. In the absence of such speech apparently situation of open confrontation had not arisen as in the present case, which means that grounds for dissolution in that case were to be considered on their merits. Although the grounds were fewer in number than grounds in the present case and material in support of grounds quantity and qualitywise was far inferior but even then order of dissolution passed in that case was upheld and not in the present case.

6. In my humble opinion when Constitutional petition was entertained in this case in this Court straight-away without allowing it to be heard in the High Court and since there is no other forum of appeal after this Court, it was the bounden duty of this Court to have scrutinised the material produced in support of grounds of dissolution with more care and caution in conformity with guidelines laid down in the cases of Haji Saifullah Khan and Khawaja Ahmad Tariq Rahim decided by this Court earlier in point of time.

7. In my humble opinion Article 58(2)(b) of the Constitution has come to stay in the Constitution whether it is liked or abhorred. Constitutions of two countries are not alike because Constitution of each country is framed keeping in view the objective conditions, historical and cultural background with pronounced customs and religious ethos. If Article 58(2)(b) has come into existence and forms part of the Constitution on account of some compromise and it is disapproved now it can be removed or diluted or amended in the manner prescribed in the Constitution. It is the function of the legislature to legislate and of the Court to interpret the law. The Court cannot and should not take upon itself the duty of entering into the field of legislature but should confine itself to its original function of interpreting the provisions of the Constitution as they are and other laws. While interpreting the provisions of the Constitution, it becomes the duty of the Court to see that interpretation is done in such a manner which advances the noble object of workability of the Constitution. The provisions of the Constitution cannot be interpreted by the Court in such narrow

form to make that provision almost redundant and meaningless.

8. By rejecting the material in support of grounds of dissolution in instant case, interpretation of Article 58(2)(b) is rendered by this Court narrowing down its scope to almost zero point which amounts to declaring that no President would be able to ever dissolve the National Assembly and dismiss the Government of the Prime Minister in spite of the fact that he has substantial material in his possession because the Court is not satisfied with intrinsic value of the material. In other words Article 58(2)(b) is rendered almost redundant which can be done by the legislature only.

9. I see no reason to justify departure from the guidelines laid down in the cases of Haji Saifullah Khan and Khawaja Ahmad Tariq Rahim for consideration of material in support of grounds of dissolution. I see no difference in the material produced in support of grounds of dissolution in the case of Tariq Rahim and in the present case. The present line of reasoning in the majority judgment can be accepted only when positive assertion is made that case of Khawaja Ahmad Tariq Rahim was wrongly decided.

10. I am of the opinion that in view of the relevant case-law mentioned above, this Court as highest Court of the country has to act within the limitations prescribed by the law while in the process of interpretation of the Constitution and the law. This Court can interpret but not legislate and while interpreting can narrow down the scope but not so much that the provision under comment is rendered almost redundant. So far Article 58(2)(b) of the Constitution is concerned, it is already interpreted and construed very ably in the cases of Haji Saifullah Khan and Khawaja Ahmad Tariq Rahim as mentioned above. Power under Article 58(2)(b) can be exercised by the President when there is actually an imminent breakdown of the Constitutional machinery and there is failure of not one, but many provisions of the Constitution giving impression that country is being run by methods extra-Constitutional. The President must form his opinion on the basis of material before him. From the Full Bench of 11 Judges, which has heard the present case, 7 Judges are same who heard the previous case of Ahmad Tariq Rahim in the Full Bench of 12 Judges of this Court.

From those 7 Judges, six upheld the order of dissolution passed by the same President dismissing Government of the Prime Minister Ms Benazir Bhutto dissolving National Assembly. Three more Judges of the present Bench maintained order of dismissal of the Government and dissolution of the National Assembly while hearing Constitutional petitions in the High Courts at Lahore and Karachi. So from the present Bench of 11 Judges, 9 Judges having upheld order of dissolution in the previous case of Tariq Rahim are now of the view that in the present case material in support of grounds of dissolution is not sufficient and order of dissolution is without lawful authority and of legal effect.

11. With respect I say that I do not feel inclined to agree with the majority view. I am of the opinion that Article 17(2) of the Constitution does not give Fundamental Right to the political party to conclude its tenure of office. Further I do not agree that by mentioning subversion of the Constitution in the order of dissolution, Fundamental Right of the Prime Minister under Article 14 of the Constitution is violated nor there is any justification to conclude that the Prime Minister was being prevented by the President from extending political activity of the executive government of Federation to the Federally Administered Tribal Areas.

12. Somehow or the other I regret to say that I have not been able to reconcile myself to agree with the reasoning advanced for taking the different view now in this case than from the view previously taken in the case of Khawaja Ahmad Tariq Rahim when in both the cases the allegations were more or less the same and material produced in support of grounds of dissolution is much more in the present case than in the previous case. One extraordinary feature of the present case is that the Prime Minister made public address on television criticising the President openly declaring confrontation resulting in situation in which Government of Federation cannot be carried on in accordance with provisions of the Constitution justifying fully well appeal to the electorate. It could have been left to political sovereign to decide the matter. I am also of the view that Article 58(2)(b) is an independent provision under which the President is empowered to dissolve the National Assembly in his discretion if he is satisfied that a situation has arisen in which the

Government of Federation cannot be carried on in accordance with the provisions of the Constitution and an appeal
to the electorate is necessary. Opinion of the President
cannot be substituted by the Court. If he has formed such
opinion and the grounds of dissolution are supported by
material which was available before him at the time of formation of such opinion, the Court should allow order to
stand and political sovereign to give final decision.

13. It is understandable that in the case of Haji Saifullah Khan
even if order of dissolution was found to be invalid, restoration of the National Assembly and the Government was not
allowed for the reasons that administrative machinery was
fully geared up for election which could provide opportunity to all political parties to participate as previous
elections were held on non-party basis. Another reason was
that writ jurisdiction was discretionary and that discretion
could be validly refused because greater harm could have
been caused, if relief had been allowed and national interest
had to be given precedence over right of individuals. In Tariq
Rahim's case the Federal Government of Ms Benazir Bhutto
was dismissed and National Assembly was dissolved. There
was material in support of grounds of dissolution and the
same was considered to be sufficient to justify action of dissolution. In the instant case there is complete deviation from
the guidelines laid down in the case of Tariq Rahim. So far
consideration and availability of material in support of
grounds of dissolution is concerned although more grounds
exist in the present case as alleged in the order of dissolution for which voluminous material is produced but the same
is rejected for reasons which to me appear to be insufficient.

14. Maybe I am wrong and am imagining the things unneces-
sarily and I hope that I am wrong but from what it appears
to me that there is no difference in the case of Khawaja
Ahmad Tariq Rahim and in the present case, so far allegations, grounds for dissolution and material produced in support thereof are concerned. In the present case departure is
made and same yardstick of evaluation of material is not
applied. Seemingly it so appears that two Prime Ministers
from Sindh were sacrificed at the altar of Article 58(2)(b) of
the Constitution but when turn of Prime Minister from
Punjab came the tables were turned. Indisputably right at

the very outset of the proceedings indications were given that decision of the Court would be such which would please the nation. It remains to be seen whether what would please the nation would be strictly according to law or not. In my humble opinion decision of the Court should be strictly in accordance with law and not to please the nation. What may please the nation, may turn out to be against the letter and spirit of the law and the Constitution.

15. In my opinion for the present crisis in the country the solution is not restoration of the Government and the National Assembly but appeal to the political sovereign which is a Constitutional remedy. At the time when order of dissolution was passed, two pillars of the Government of Federation had already reached point of no return and reconciliation between them does not appear to be likely. In such circumstances it would be futile to hope that chapter of bitterness in the past would be forgotten and they would work hand in hand for smooth sailing and success. In such circumstances restoration would do more harm than good and political situation would deteriorate further giving open licence to horse-trading to both sides for winning support of the members of the Assemblies by fair means or foul, which would most certainly be inconsistent with running of the Government and flourishing of the democratic institution in accordance with the provisions of the Constitution. I have written this dissenting judgment just to keep the record straight and to say that in my humble opinion it was a fit case in which same result should have been announced as in the previous case of Tariq Rahim. I would, therefore, dismiss this petition.

The Supreme Court decision should have brought the tussle between the President and the Prime Minister to an end, but this was not to be. Many thought the party was over but, 'the party ain't over until the fat lady sings. And she's not in the stadium yet'. The battle scene shifted from the Centre to the Punjab. After a marathon session at my house lasting till the early hours of the morning, Benazir was able to persuade Manzoor Wattoo, Chief Minister of the Punjab to dissolve the Provincial Assembly, as his position had become shaky. Wattoo hemmed and hawed but, in the end, he agreed. On his return to Lahore, he advised the

Governor, Chaudhry Altaf Hussain to dissolve the House. Whether the advice was validly tendered under Article 112 of the Constitution became an issue before the Lahore High Court.

The pattern was repeated in the NWFP. Mir Afzal Khan, the Chief Minister, got the Assembly dissolved on 30 May. Nawaz Sharif, although restored to power in the Centre, now found himself in a state of confrontation with the provinces of the Punjab and the NWFP.

June 1993

On 28 June, when the Lahore High Court ordered the restoration of the Provincial Assembly, the Chief Minister, Manzoor Wattoo advised the Governor to dissolve the Assembly within seven minutes of the order of the High Court. Contrary to popular belief, the second dissolution did not have the approval of the President who was opposed to it. The credit or discredit for this decision goes entirely to Chaudhry Altaf, the Governor, and Manzoor Wattoo, the Chief Minister.

Nawaz Sharif met the President on 29 June and demanded the removal of the Punjab Governor but drew a blank. The President reacted very sharply when some of the people around him advised him to sack the Governor in a spirit of accommodation with Nawaz Sharif, who was riding high after the Supreme Court judgment.

In a desperate bid to sort out the Punjab impasse, Nawaz Sharif resorted to the extreme measure of getting a Resolution adopted by the Parliament on 29 June to take over the provincial administration under Article 234 of the Constitution. 'The Nawaz Government armed with the Resolution of the Parliament and treating it as self-executary did not consider it necessary to obtain President's approval and proceeded unilaterally to enforce it. Orders signed by the Cabinet Secretary were faxed to the Provincial Government, IG/Chief Secretary were posted to replace the incumbents and Mian Azhar was named as Administrator-designate of the Province, as part of the exercise to take over the Province. The Provincial Government, far from yielding to the measures chose to confront the Centre. Chief Minister Manzoor Wattoo dubbed the Centre's orders as fake, not being signed by the President and refused to take notice of them.'[3] Sharif's attempt to use the Rangers to enforce his orders was foiled by the timely intervention of the COAS.

As the crisis seemed to be deepening every day with no sign of a patch up, I decided to get away from it all and go to Nathiagali, a hill station about two hours drive from Islamabad. It was at Nathiagali in the first week of July 1993 that I received an urgent message from the Army Chief, General Abdul Waheed, asking me to meet him at the Army House, Rawalpindi at 5 p.m. At 4.50 p.m. as my car was approaching the Army House, it was stopped and the PSO to the Chief, instead of taking me to the Army House, took me to his own house. I was quite intrigued. It was explained to me that the Chief was in a conference with his Corps Commanders and would receive me as soon as the conference was over. Why couldn't I be made to wait at the Army House? Why was I taken to the PSO's House? Was it because my meeting with the Chief was to be kept a secret from the Corps Commanders? I still do not know. After about ten minutes, the all clear was given and I was taken to the Army House. The Chief told me that he and his Corps Commanders had discussed the political crisis and, in their opinion, the only way out was to ask Nawaz to advise the President to dissolve the National Assembly and the Provincial Assemblies, sack the government, and hold fresh elections with Nawaz as the head of the caretaker government. He and I, according to this plan, were then to go to the Presidency to seek the President's approval. The Chief told me that in the meeting with the President, he would keep quiet and I would do all the talking. I raised some objections but the Chief told me that all would be taken care of. He told me that he would get an appointment with the President for 8 p.m. and that he would pick me up on his way to the Presidency. Instead, he turned up at my house at midnight and told me that he had gone to the Prime Minister's House to meet Nawaz Sharif to secure his agreement first. This he did not get because Nawaz Sharif wanted to consult his father in Lahore. The scheduled meeting with the President did not take place. The Waheed Formula was therefore a non-starter.

The final solution — July 1993

With no signs of an end to the political impasse, a delegation of the Islamic Deeni Ittihad (IDI), led by Senator Maulana Samiul Haque, met the President in the hope of getting the President and the Prime Minister to agree to a dialogue to devise ways and means for defusing the political crisis. The President told them that, as

far as he was concerned, he had no problem with the Prime Minister but it was the view of the Opposition that the only way to end
the crisis was to hold immediate general elections. Nawaz Sharif
should, the President suggested, discuss this with the Opposition.
Maulana Samiul Haque told the President that Nawaz Sharif was
not in favour of holding elections while he (Ghulam Ishaq Khan)
continued as President. The President told the Maulana that he
was prepared to step aside if this would clear the way for early
elections; but also that Nawaz Sharif must simultaneouly advise
the immediate dissolution of the National Assembly, resign, and
make room for a neutral government to supervise the elections.
This was accepted by Nawaz Sharif in his meetings with the President on 12 and 15 July. I was not present at these meetings but
was called by the President after Nawaz Sharif had left and briefed
on the latest developments. He said, 'I do not know if I have done
the right thing by agreeing to this arrangement.' With this, the
drama that was shattering everybody's nerves came to an end.
Contrary to popular belief, the COAS was nowhere in the picture
at this stage. The credit for this arrangement goes to the President
and the Prime Minister and Maulana Samiul Haque who brokered
it. The COAS came in later to work out the modalities.

I was asked by the President to contact Benazir and brief her
on this development. She was in Lahore and when I telephoned
her, I was told that she was asleep. I called again after an hour and
when she came on the line I briefed her on the latest situation. I
told her I had some good news and some bad news for her. The
good news was first that the election would be held in October
1993 and she would not have to wait till 1995; second, that Nawaz
Sharif would not be the prime minister at the time of election,
which would be held under a neutral government; and third, that
the provincial assemblies would be dissolved and neutral governments formed to supervise the election in the provinces as well.

Benazir asked me what the bad news was. I told her that President Ghulam Ishaq Khan had agreed to resign simultaneously
with the dissolution of the National Assembly. She said, 'Why should
the President resign? Nobody other than Nawaz Sharif wants him
to resign.' I told her that it was part of the package deal which had
made early elections possible. Benazir said that the President was
making a big personal sacrifice and that she would go along with
this arrangement only if he would agree to become her presidential candidate; she asked me to convey this to the President. I said

I would, but added that she should make the offer herself, to which she agreed.

The President asked me to brief General Waheed on the latest developments. On reconsideration, he said he would send for him and brief him himself. The next day when the COAS came to the Presidency to meet the President, he did not come alone: he was accompanied by the Prime Minister. That is when discussion on modalities began. The decision to quit had already been taken.

The final episode

'18 July 1993 was a sad and a tragic day in the turbulent political history of our country. On that day, the chess game for power which had bedevilled the nation and cast shadows on its future ultimately came to a close.'[4] I witnessed the drop-scene of this sordid drama. The country stood on the edge of a precipice. The President and the Prime Minister — the main characters of the tragic drama — who had been in a state of total confrontation since the beginning of the year, were about to take their last bows. When I entered the President's office, it appeared as if two heads of hostile countries were meeting with each other in an atmos- phere charged with high tension and filled with recrimination, and, what is worse, in the presence of their subordinates, the COAS General Abdul Waheed, Corps Commander Lieutenant Generals Ghulam Muhammad, and Javed Ashraf Qazi, DG ISI. The Prime Minister was assisted by Lieutenant General (retd.) Abdul Majid Malik, who was doing most of the talking. The President, who was also the Supreme Commander of the Armed Forces of Pakistan, and the Prime Minister, the two civilian pillars of the state, were at each other's throats. It was disgusting. I felt very depressed and remained silent, except on a couple of occasions when I thought intervention was necessary. The thought that raced through my mind over and over was, to quote Nixon: 'How was it possible to have been so high and now to be so low?' How did these two former allies, their course set by the hand of Fate, drift apart and become such implacable enemies? Why had Nawaz Sharif, who owed so much to Ghulam Ishaq Khan, his benefactor, his guide and philosopher, now become his sworn enemy? What powerful forces drove them both into this abyss, from which neither benefited and which did incalculable damage to both of them and to the coun- try? What sequence of events led to this Greek tragedy? Was it

unavoidable or did we stumble into it? Why did it become so difficult to pull back before we went over the precipice? Why did the
'best' and the 'brightest' on both sides lead us into this tragedy?

Did it have to end in such an ignominious manner? Was the
clash between Ghulam Ishaq Khan and Nawaz Sharif inevitable?
My answer is it was not. Could it have been prevented? My answer
is that perhaps it could. It could have been prevented before
Nawaz's declaration of war against the President on 17 April 1993
but not afterwards. In spite of all Nawaz Sharif's acts of omission
and commission, Ghulam Ishaq Khan had no intention of sacking
him before 17 April 1993. Unknown to Nawaz Sharif and his associates, Ghulam Ishaq Khan always gave him the benefit of doubt.
Until 17 April 1993, between Benazir and Nawaz Sharif, Ghulam
Ishaq Khan's preference was always for Nawaz Sharif. Against
Benazir, his main political opponent, Nawaz Sharif could not have
found a more dependable, more steadfast, and more committed
ally than Ghulam Ishaq Khan. It is a great tragedy that Nawaz
Sharif completely misunderstood the man and unwittingly drove
a reluctant Ghulam Ishaq Khan into the arms of Benazir.

Circumstances had brought together this austere mandarin and
Nawaz Sharif, a young man in a hurry — basically a decent, well-
meaning person, action-oriented, with a great deal of contempt
for the bureaucracy, established methods, and regular procedure,
with little or no political or administrative experience, no intellectual pretensions, unconcerned with rules or regulations, shy, wary
in speech, and difficult of approach. Is it therefore surprising that
there was no meeting of minds between them and very little inter-
action? In a parliamentary democracy, the prime minister by
convention meets the president every week to discuss state affairs.
These two never met more than once a month, if that. In the
absence of direct communication, they soon drifted apart. Communication through intermediaries with their own agenda did more
harm than good and led to misunderstandings and distrust. The
only thing in common between these two strangers was their
hostility to Benazir Bhutto.

As President, Ghulam Ishaq Khan dissolved two National
Assemblies, sacked two successive governments headed respectively
by Benazir and Nawaz Sharif in exercise of his power under
Article 58(2)(b) of the Constitution, mainly on the grounds of
corruption and abuse of power and authority for personal benefit.
The first order was upheld by the Court. The second order of

dissolution was reversed. Both orders were hailed by the opposition but denounced by the party in power. It is too early to sit in judgment on Ghulam Ishaq Khan's role as President of Pakistan. We should await the verdict of history. One can, however, assess his personality.

Ghulam Ishaq Khan was brilliantly intelligent. No one met him without realizing that he possessed a powerful mind, quick to grasp facts. He had a memory that was remarkable not only for the huge amount of data it contained but for the astonishing speed and accuracy with which he was able to retrieve the facts he wanted. He was a living data bank regarding agriculture, animal husbandry, forests, irrigation, energy, dams for hydroelectric power, finance, and every aspect of the economy of Pakistan. In these fields, he had no equal. His mastery of facts was dazzling. In all his meetings with civil servants or foreign dignitaries, he was the best-informed, best-prepared, and most articulate person. Here was a man who did not merely respond to the system: he dominated it. Another facet of his personality which one did not fail to notice was that he was very shy. He loved debate and intellectual confrontation, but he never bullied or humiliated anyone.

Ghulam Ishaq Khan never liked the Press and stayed away from it. He was insensitive to the news media and had nothing but contempt for them. Naturally, he was not very popular with the Press. Till the end, he did not know how to conduct himself with journalists. He paid dearly for it. Ghulam Ishaq Khan, like Eisenhower, downplayed the importance of the Press. In January 1961, Robert Spivack asked Eisenhower if he felt the reporters had been fair to him over the years. 'Well,' Eisenhower replied, 'when you come down to it, I don't see that a reporter could do much to a President, do you?' Ghulam Ishaq Khan's answer would have been no different. His main concern was always substance, not image.

Shy and sensitive, GIK considered political polemics alien to the dignity of his office. Like Herbert Hoover, he would say, 'This is not a showman's job. I will not step out of character'. No wonder, GIK's term was a monumental failure in public relations.

In his dealings with his staff, he was very polite. He never addressed anybody formally. He never indulged in small talk except with very close friends.

Ghulam Ishaq Khan wanted his staff to present him with drafts of his speeches but he would then cross out, insert, rephrase, and revise the draft until he had what he wanted. He took the English language, as he took most things, very seriously.

Unlike the more ambitious mandarins in Pakistan, Ghulam Ishaq Khan abhorred publicity and never sought to enhance his role for popular consumption. He shies away from self-promotion and must have his personal history dragged out of him.

Like Gerald Ford, Ghulam Ishaq Khan became President not because he was popular with the people, not because he campaigned for the job, but because of his character, his ability, his experience, his integrity, and his trustworthiness.[5] He was undeniably the right man in the right place at the right time to fill the vacuum created by the sudden death of Ziaul Haq.

Like Gerald Ford, his greatest asset was the courage to do what he thought was right, despite the political consequences. To that, I would add incorruptibility. Ghulam Ishaq Khan did not know how to make himself a popular president: he was bereft of showmanship.

In his view, the first responsibility of every president is to protect Pakistan's national security. Even his worst enemies would admit that Ghulam Ishaq Khan never compromised on national security. This is evident from the minutes of the call on the President by Mr Reginald Bartholomew, US Under-Secretary of State for International Security Affairs on 20 November 1991. After this fateful meeting, I knew Ghulam Ishaq Khan's fate was sealed.

'Big men', observed Peggy Noonan, 'when they leave the Presidency are often dismissed and derided for years before we see their true dimensions. As I say, this is inevitable. You need distance before you can see how big the mountain is; up close, a mountain is just a mass, but take some time and travel away from it and you can turn back and see how big it was.'[6] It is too early to sit in judgement on Ghulam Ishaq Khan. Meanwhile, he does not lose sleep over what his detractors say about his record. He is more than willing to submit his actions to the judgement of time.

'Character counts in the Presidency more than any other single quality. It is more important than how much the President knows of foreign policy or economics or even about politics. When the chips are down — and the chips are always down in the Presidency — how do you decide? Which way do you go? What kind of courage is called upon? Talking of his hero Andrew Jackson, Truman once said, "It takes one kind of courage to face a duellist, but it is nothing like the courage it takes to tell a friend no.'"[7] Ghulam Ishaq Khan had that kind of courage.

No one was as well prepared for the presidency as Ghulam Ishaq Khan was. He knew the establishment, both civil and military. He knew better than anybody else how the system worked.

Like Truman's decision to fire General Douglas MacArthur, Ghulam Ishaq Khan's decision to sack Nawaz Sharif was by far the most unpopular and controversial decision of his presidency. Like Truman, while he was attacked on all sides, torn to shreds in newspaper editorials, Ghulam Ishaq Khan went on with his work as usual, just riding it out. Those around him wondered how it was possible for him to do so. He said he was sure that in the long run the country would judge him to have done the right thing. Besides, he had only done his duty. The Constitution stated clearly what he was required to do and he had taken an oath to uphold the Constitution. Like Truman, it was not difficult for him at all. Ghulam Ishaq Khan always said that history would be the final judge of his performance and that what he had done must stand the test of time. If he was blasted by the Press or his decision overturned by the Supreme Court, these were not his main concerns: what matters — or ought to matter according to him — is what is best for the country.

I know of no one who was on the presidency staff or the domestic staff or among the civil servants who had worked with him who did not like him. He had a remarkable quality, greatly needed in our rulers: he put people at ease. He treated them as human beings. He showed them a lot of respect and never tried to overawe them with his authority.

Ghulam Ishaq Khan put on no airs, he wore no masks: what you saw was what you got. He spoke his mind and, in the process, made many enemies but also some friends. He always knew where he was going and did not much care what anyone else thought. In that sense he was not a politician, because politicians hide their inner personalities. Ghulam Ishaq Khan never wanted nor even made any effort for people to like him.

He was a loner from the start. Contemptuous of politicians, he always remained aloof from them. He was not cut out for the manoeuvres and cut and thrust of parliamentary democracy. The simplicity and austerity of his personal life and living habits, the lack of pleasure or diversion or humour, made communication with him difficult. He never permitted any intimacy, friendship, or informality, except with very few of whom I am proud to say I was one. Ghulam Ishaq Khan was at times too forgiving of the ambitions and game-playing of some of the people around him and was loyal to some who did not deserve it and who did not return that loyalty.

By 1977, when Ghulam Ishaq Khan ended his career as a civil servant, he was almost a paragon of virtue. The salient features of his character included patriotism, devotion to duty, financial and moral integrity, intellectual honesty, modesty, and humility. Did these virtues survive the poundings, the rough and tumble of politics and the temptations of power? In the eyes of many, including some of his admirers and not all his detractors, he began compromising his principles. According to them, it cannot be said that during his presidency, virtue was always rewarded and the corrupt and dishonest ignored, if not punished. The first deviation from principle, in public perception, came when he included Asif Zardari in the caretaker cabinet headed by Mir Balakh Sher Mazari. Asif had developed a reputation for corruption and was facing several criminal cases under the Banking Act. How could he be sworn in by Ghulam Ishaq Khan? It was easy to be virtuous when virtue was rewarded as it was when Ghulam Ishaq Khan was a civil servant. Not so easy in the game of politics, in which virtue is ignored, partisanship is rewarded, and principle sacrificed. This, I know, was the most difficult of all his decisions, but he was left with no choice. He was willing to pay this price to win his battle against Nawaz Sharif.

In public perception, another act of indiscretion on the part of Ghulam Ishaq Khan was to shield some of his sons-in-law, his Achilles heel, the only chink in his armour which his enemies fully exploited. It is disastrous for a President to protect his relatives or turn a blind eye to their acts of omission and commission. I was therefore distressed to hear when the President told me about his spirited defence in a GHQ meeting of his son-in-law. A man of Ghulam Ishaq Khan's unimpeachable integrity was expected to set a higher standard for the conduct of his relatives. Whatever the merits of the case, it was unwise to spring to the defence of his son-in-law in the presence of top army brass. He could have established a moral tone that would have made any deviation from the straight and narrow on the part of his relatives impossible while he was the head of state. Ghulam Ishaq Khan should have known that leaders like himself, with spotlessly clean records, who have great achievements to their credit, must be on guard against stumbling on the little things.

Ghulam Ishaq Khan's departure from the bureaucratic and political stage after almost fifty years marked the end of an epoch. Speaking from long and close personal association, I can testify that, behind his stern and forbidding appearance, was a rather kind-hearted person, loyal to his friends and fellow workers, devoted to his work, and with great professional competence. He earned the respect of his associates and foreign counterparts. His chief priority always was the defence of our national interests as he saw them.

Chapter 8

Making the rulers accountable

A Wizard told him in these words our fate:
At length Corruption, like a general Flood.
(so long by watchful ministers withstood),
Shall deluge all;
Pope

After Nigeria, Pakistan is the most corrupt country in the world.
Transparency International Berlin
June 1996

The Ruler must first be careful about his own virtue. Possessing the virtue will give him the people. Possessing the people will give him territory. Possessing the territory will give him wealth. Possessing the wealth, he will have resources for his expenditure. Virtue is the root, wealth is its branches. If he makes the root his secondary object and the branches his first, he will only anger the people and teach them dishonesty. Hence the accumulation of wealth is the way to disintegrate the people, and the distribution of wealth is the way to consolidate the people. Likewise, when his words are not in accord with that which is right, they will come back to him in the same way, and wealth got by improper means will leave him by the same road.
Confucius

I was sworn in as a federal minister on 11 August 1990. A few days later, I was allocated the portfolio of accountability to which President Ghulam Ishaq Khan attached the highest priority. One of the reasons incorporated in the dissolution order on which the President based his opinion that the government of the federation could not be carried on in accordance with the Constitution and an appeal to the electorate was necessary referred to corruption and nepotism in the federal government, its functionaries, authorities, and agencies, statutory and other corporations, including banks working under its supervision and control, and the holders of representative offices; corruption which had reached such proportions that the orderly functioning of the government in accordance with the provisions of the Constitution (including the requirements of the oath prescribed therein), and the law, no longer carried credibility and, despite being subject to wide public condemnation, the government had failed to take appropriate actions in this behalf.

In his address to the nation on 6 August 1990, the President had said, 'Side by side with these agonizing conditions, innumerable stories were circulating among the people of the misuse of power to accumulate and multiply personal fortunes and dole out favours. Bribery, dishonesty, and corruption were burning topics. Big scandals appeared frequently in the national and international Press. It was being openly said that financial irregularities had crossed all limits and corruption has broken all records. The treatment of the public exchequer like hereditary *jagirs* and the plunder of national wealth as booty were so widely reported that the word 'corruption' became the trade mark of policies in Pakistan.

'It was also said that, with a view to paving the way for receiving and distributing unlawful concessions from the commercial banks and other financial institutions, such as the Agricultural Development Bank, NDFC, and PICIC, hand-picked persons were appointed in key positions, without proper qualifications and experience. Then, loans worth billions of rupees were given to favourites for political reasons, without the requisite documents, collateral securities, or proper processing. Repayable loans of millions of rupees were also written off or the terms and period of their repayment were unconscionably relaxed. Consequently, there were speculations about a few banks becoming insolvent.

'Newspapers also raised a hue and cry about similar wrong-doings in commercial deals. According to them, millions of rupees were made in commissions on the sale of huge quantities of cotton and rice to firms with doubtful credentials at prices much lower than those on the world market. Similarly, it was reported that purchases worth billions of rupees were made in various sectors, including energy, aviation, and communications, on considerations of personal gain rather than of genuine need, better quality, and lower prices.

'Stories of huge bribes and of political favouritism were also rife in relation to government contracts, import and export licences, permits of various types, and industrial sanctions. The allotment of residential and commercial plots and valuable state land at nominal rates was also widely reported. It was not only the Press which levelled serious charges of corruption, political circles also claimed to have — and published in quite a few cases — alleged documentary evidence in support of such charges.

'In the face of such a blitz of corruption charges, it was incumbent upon a responsible government to order investigations, instead of dismissing them as conspiracies to malign the government, political propaganda, or mudslinging. It is possible that the allegations would have been proved wrong. But the chances of their being correct could also not be ruled out. The basic point is that they should have been investigated by an impartial and independent agency so that the facts could have come before the people, whose trust in the elected representatives could have been restored. There were loud demands to this effect but they were ignored. However, when the pressure of public opinion mounted, investigations were assigned to a hand-picked person with no legal authority. He could neither claim acceptance in political circles nor inspire public trust.

'Those who complained of corruption were repeatedly advised to go to Court. Apart from the fact that, in a democracy, it is the people and not the Courts who are approached to vindicate one's position, the advice was not wrong in principle. However, in a court case, it is necessary to investigate the charges, which is not possible without the co-operation of official agencies. Relevant documents and files are also in official custody and no outsider can have access to them without the permission of the government. That being the case, the suggestion of going to Court would have proved futile.

'Then, at least in one instance, the court had upheld the charges of nepotism and abuse of authority. But to what avail? How far was the court's verdict honoured? In democratic countries, even on minor charges of corruption, resignations are either voluntarily tendered or are asked for, without waiting for proof, so that impartial and conducive conditions for free investigations are ensured. How far was this tradition followed? One only regrets that a tradition of accountability was not created.'

On the basis of documents supplied by Mr Fazlur Rahman Khan, Secretary to the President, the FIA investigated a large number of allegations of corruption, nepotism, favouritism, abuse of power, and authority against the former Prime Minister Ms Benazir Bhutto and her ministers. The inquiry reports submitted by the FIA were closely scrutinized by the Attorney General, Mr Aziz Munshi, Mr Sharifuddin Pirzada, Mr Rafi Raza, and myself. Of a large number of cases of misconduct within the meaning of Article 4 of PPO No. 17 of 1977 reported by the FIA, six glaring cases against the ex-prime minister were selected for further processing. Another nine cases selected for further processing pertained to ex-federal ministers and members of the National Assembly. With the approval of the Law Division, the cases were then submitted to the Caretaker Prime Minister, Mr Ghulam Mustafa Jatoi, through his Special Assistant, Mr Kamal Azfar. The Prime Minister, after satisfying himself that there were reasonable grounds for believing that the ex-prime minister and other ex-ministers and holders of public office had committed acts of misconduct, advised the President to refer the cases to Special Courts, with the request that the Courts should decide the cases, record their findings, and pass appropriate orders in accordance with the law. In accordance with the advice of the Prime Minister, after satisfying himself that reasonable grounds existed for believing that acts of misconduct had been committed, the President referred the cases (Appendix 2) to Special Courts established under the law. The entire operation was completed within less than three months.

The President was advised by his legal experts that the Special Court, on receiving the reference, would scrutinize the necessary records relating to the charge mentioned in the reference and issue notice to the respondents, requiring them to show cause why it should not proceed further against them; and after such further scrutiny of records and such inquiry as it thought fit and after giving the respondents an opportunity of being heard, record its findings. The President was assured that the court proceedings which, we were told, would be of a summary nature, would not take more than two months. We had no doubt whatsoever about the outcome, as all the references were supported by unimpeachable documentary evidence.

However, once the references were filed in the Courts, the entire process of accountability, the laws governing this process, the Special Courts established under this law, came under a blistering attack by the Opposition led by the ex-prime minister. It was said that these were dead laws; that these laws were unconstitutional; that they reversed the presumption of innocence; and that the references were made to Special and not Ordinary Courts. This created a lot of confusion and an official spokesman had to clarify the fact that the process of accountability was being carried out under the existing laws of the land which basically dated back to the days of the former prime minister, late Mr Zulfikar Ali Bhutto.

Commenting on reports describing the said laws as 'dead laws', a government spokesman pointed out that the two laws under which special courts for accountability were to be constituted had existed on the statute book since 1973 without ever having been questioned. Explaining the genesis of the two laws, the spokesman said that it was during Mr Bhutto's days that the Holders of Representative Offices (Prevention of Misconduct) Act, 1976, and the Parliament and Provincial Assembles (Disqualification of Members) Act, 1976, had been promulgated. These were passed during the last days of the first Parliament under the 1973 Constitution and promulgated on 9 January 1977. Subsequently, the contents of these two Acts were adopted with some modifications by the then President, Chaudhry Fazal Elahi, and promulgated as President's Orders 16 and 17 later in 1977. President Fazal Elahi had taken care to bring the original Acts in closer conformity with the demands of justice by removing certain provisions which were discriminatory and which fell short of the standards of natural justice followed in all civilized countries.

The original Acts as passed by the Parliament in January 1977 exempted the prime minister and the chief ministers from the process of accountability. Moreover, they did not even allow the accused to be heard in person by the court, nor did they provide for any legal assistance to him. These undemocratic flaws were removed when the equivalent of the two Acts were promulgated as President's Orders 16 and 17 of 1977. They left no one above the law, bringing even the prime minister and the chief minister within their purview. They also provided for the right to appeal in no less a forum than the Supreme Court of Pakistan. Further, they gave the accused the right to be heard in person and to have recourse to legal advice and assistance.

That President's Orders 16 and 17 did not provide for disqualifications outside of Articles 62 and 63 of the Constitution, and were therefore not unconstitutional is evident from the fact that Article 63 provided, *inter alia*, for a person to be disqualified if 'he is found guilty of corrupt or illegal practice under any law for the time being in force', and also if 'he is for the time being disqualified from being chosen as a member of Parliament or of a Provincial Assembly under any law for the time being force.' These provisions of the Constitution had been there from 1973 onwards and the Act promulgated by Mr Bhutto's Parliament and the President's Orders issued by President Fazal Elahi came subsequently to give effect to their real spirit.

A wrong impression was created that PO 17 reversed presumption of innocence. The sub-rule referred to in this context was exactly the same as in Act V of 1977. The proviso related only to facts which the respondent failed or refused to answer or explain. In that event, the Court might draw an adverse presumption against him. This was a standard provision under the law of evidence.

A close comparative study made it absolutely clear that the spirit and essence of the laws under which the caretaker government was to proceed had essentially been borrowed from Mr Bhutto's laws. The amendments were intended only to make them more just and democratic.

Instead of initiating action under the law against corrupt public representatives, the ex-prime minister advised the people to approach the Courts. But the legal position was that the Courts could not proceed against public representatives without the prior sanction of the prime minister or the chief minister as the case might be. The ex-prime minister was suggesting a course which was impossible to follow.

The confusion sought to be created in the public mind with regard to the rationale of having special laws calls for some clarification. There were numerous instances of 'Special Laws' dealing with special situations, ranging from Service Tribunals, Special Custom Courts, Banking Courts, and the Hoarding and Blackmarketing law. This rationale is to be found in the general practice that special types of offences have to be dealt with under special laws. Corrupt practices and misconduct of elected representatives, who are the custodians of public trust and are vested with the responsibility of making laws, deserve to be dealt with under special laws and at forums other than those meant for citizens in general. An additional rationale was the need for speedy justice. It is common knowledge that ordinary courts are too heavily burdened to be expected to decide cases as speedily as is required in the interests of justice and democracy.

We felt confident that we were on strong legal ground and looked forward to the early disposal of the cases with some optimism. Then came the first bombshell from Lahore. The Special Court of Mr Justice Munir A. Sheikh, after scrutinizing the record relating to the charge mentioned in the reference against Jehangir Badr, a federal minister in Benazir Bhutto's Cabinet, returned the reference to the President, the referring authority, under Article 4(3)(a) PPO 17 of 1977 because, in its opinion, based on the scrutiny of the record alone and without hearing the parties, no charge could be established. Nobody expected a presidential reference, prepared by some of the best legal experts in the country after a good deal of care and deliberation, to be dismissed in such a summary fashion, without hearing the referring authority and without an opportunity having been given to produce evidence in support of the charge. This gave us a foretaste of what was to follow.

In spite of our best efforts to expedite the proceedings, none of the six references against the former prime minister, Ms Benazir Bhutto, could be decided one way or the other for more than two years. Adjournments were frequently asked for and freely given. No opportunity was missed to delay the proceedings. Even in ordinary civil and criminal cases, delays benefit the defendants. Why should the respondents, all holders of public offices, have expedited the proceedings when they knew that time was on their side, 'that witnesses who could prove the case against them may forget, or lose interest out of sheer disgust, or be won over, or — most important of all — the political situation may undergo a favourable change'? Because delays yield such rich dividends, it pays to seek adjournments, to involve the courts in tangential inquiries unrelated to the core issue, i.e., finding out whether the respondent abused his or her power or authority. We soon realized that we had gotten off the main track. No wonder there is a widespread popular belief that people who loot and plunder can get away with anything and that our law is neither swift, nor sure, nor powerful, nor just, but only a paper tiger.

It is standard practice to allow at least one appeal on the final order or judgment; but we were horrified to realize that every interim order passed by the Special Court in the course of the inquiry or scrutiny of the record relating to the reference could be appealed against, resulting in considerable delay. The proceedings in the Special Court could thus be brought to a standstill, pending disposal of the appeal. For this, we had only ourselves to blame. The law was amended by us so that we could appeal against the order passed in the reference against Jehangir Badr. We were paying a heavy price for this amendment of dubious value.

We soon realized that, under our existing judicial system, it takes longer to get an answer from a respondent in a reference case than it takes to send a man to the moon and bring him back. There are so many loopholes in the system that the final judgment could easily be avoided for years. On one pretext or another, the respondent, Ms Benazir Bhutto, successfully evaded submitting her reply to the prosecution case made out against her after a long, tortuous, and dilatory process in which some witnesses were cross-examined for months. No wonder some of them became nervous wrecks.

Once Benazir Bhutto came back to power, all references were, decided in her favour with lightning speed. This did not come as a surprise, as the objective situation had changed. Benazir Bhutto was now occupying the Prime Minister's House once again and Ghulam Ishaq Khan, the referring authority, had ceased to be the President and the referring authority.

In the midst of all this, our difficulties were further compounded when Mian Muhammad Nawaz Sharif, who had been elected as Prime Minister in October 1990, took a fateful political decision not to associate himself with the process of accountability initiated by his predecessor, the caretaker Prime Minister Ghulam Mustafa Jatoi. I used to send a weekly report to the Prime Minister, explaining the progress, or lack of it, in each case, and the problems we were facing both within and outside the courts. Not once did the Prime Minister show any interest in these cases. Not once did he ask me what I was doing or why the references were not moving forward. He did hold one meeting but that was on the initiative of Chaudhry Shujaat Hussain, the Interior Minister, who called me after a meeting with the President and invited me to his house for a breakfast session. The President had drawn his attention to the lack of interest in the references on the part of the government and the supreme indifference shown by the Prime Minister in particular to the fate of these cases. After his meeting with the President, reality suddenly hit Shujaat; he realized the political implications of the references and, with a rare clarity of vision and in almost prophetic words, gave expression to his worst fears: 'If Benazir Bhutto went scot-free and returned to power,' Shujaat told me in Punjabi, 'BB would hang us upside down. This calamity has to be averted at all costs.' Within twenty-four hours, the Prime Minister called a meeting in his chamber to discuss accountability. Those present were Chaudhry Nisar, Aziz Munshi, the Attorney General, the Law Secretary, Chaudhry Shujaat, and myself. Each case was reviewed in depth. Certain decisions were taken to expedite the cases. I felt better. At last, things were moving. Not long after, I realized how I had misjudged Nawaz Sharif. Little did I know that this was destined to be our first and last meeting on accountability. The word 'accountability' was not uttered or heard again in the corridors of power — as if it were a dirty word. President Ghulam Ishaq Khan was left to fight the battle all by himself. With no support from the federal government, with an indifferent prime minister who showed little interest in the Court battles, everybody got the message loud and clear. The fate of the references was sealed and the result was a foregone conclusion. Nawaz Sharif thought he could some day offer to withdraw the references to win over Benazir to his side and enlist her support against the President. Fate willed otherwise. But I am anticipating.

What conclusions should be drawn from this failed experiment in accountability of the holders of public office in Pakistan? Is the concept itself basically unsound, unworkable, or unrealistic? The problem in my opinion is not conceptual. Every person in a position of authority, from the President downwards, is answerable to the people in accordance with law. Without accountability, the functionaries of the state are likely to make a mockery of the law and of the norms of responsible conduct. Holders of public office are trustees and are, therefore, expected to set a much higher standard of financial and moral integrity. If they betray the trust reposed in them, the electorate, the ultimate political sovereign in a genuine democratic country will throw them out at the time of elections; but in between elections, they can and must be taken to a court of law and punished and disqualified from holding any public office for any act of misconduct. Accountability of people known to be corrupt, who have already betrayed the trust reposed in them by their constituents, in order to be meaningful and serve as a deterrent, must precede and not follow elections. This is a universally recognized principle in all democratic countries and there is no reason why holders of public office in Pakistan should be exempt from it. The laws governing accountability in Pakistan are based on this principle and, with some minor modifications, should be acceptable to all.

Article 58(2)(b) of the Constitution empowered the President to dissolve the National Assembly and sack the prime minister and the cabinet under certain conditions. President Ghulam Ishaq Khan exercised this power twice, once against Benazir Bhutto in August 1990, and the second time against Nawaz Sharif, in April 1993: two prime ministers belonging to two different political parties. Both orders were challenged in Court. The action against Benazir Bhutto was upheld, while the subsequent action against Nawaz Sharif was held illegal and reversed. Ghulam Ishaq Khan came under vicious attack by the aggrieved prime ministers and parliamentarians and he continues to be criticized for dissolving elected Assemblies and dismissing elected governments, in the name of accountability. The superior judiciary has not escaped criticism either. The judgments in both cases have been subjected to severe criticism and all sorts of motives have been publicly attributed to the judges.

So what lessons might be learnt from this experiment in accountability? First and foremost, that people have lost faith in the objectivity and impartiality of the two most important pillars of the state, the Presidency and the Judiciary, the two watchdogs charged under the Constitution with the responsibility of keeping a strict watch on the excesses and arbitrariness of the executive and the conduct of the holders of public office. Secondly, accountability has been reduced to a farce. In the name of accountability, successive governments have hounded, harassed, and persecuted their political opponents with the connivance of a corrupt administration. On the other hand, acts of gross misconduct, abuse of office, betrayal of trust, rampant corruption, and violation of oath of office by holders of public office go unpunished. Nobody in this country, neither the government, nor the opposition, nor the judiciary, is interested in accountability as it is understood in the West.

Thirdly, no matter how honest, upright, and well-intentioned you may be, your chances of bringing the guilty — be they holders of public office or civil servants — to justice under the existing judicial system and in the prevailing political environment are almost nil. It is, therefore, an exercise in futility and a total waste of time, energy, and public funds.

Fourthly, people have lost faith in the holders of public office and the institution of Parliament which no longer represents the general will or the hopes and aspirations of the people, and nobody sheds any tears when the Assembly is dissolved.

In South Korea, two former presidents, both military men, one a coup-maker and the other an elected president, are in jail and being prosecuted on charges of human rights violations and corruption respectively. A senior Republican Senator in the United States, Bob Packwood, who was accused of involvement in a sex scandal, was told by his colleagues to pack his bags and go home, otherwise he would face censure from the body of which he was a member. Other holders of high office have been forced to resign on corruption charges as has happened in Japan and Italy, and in the United States in the case of Vice President Spiro Agnew, who was alleged to have taken bribes. Also, the former US Congressman Rostenkowski, Chairman of the House Ways and Means Committee, was sentenced to seventeen months in prison for abusing his office and using employees to mow the grass at his summer house and to take photographs at the wedding of his daughter. He was also accused of using his house office account to buy stamps which he then converted to cash. As the former Congressman, the once powerful lawmaker and Chairman of the influential Ways and Means Committee stood up to hear the sentence, US District Judge Norma Halloway rebuked him for he had violated the faith of his constituents who had elected him from 1959 until 1994. 'You shamelessly abused your position,' Judge Norma said. She said his burden would be to know his term in office would be remembered as a disgrace.

'Pretty petty stuff, people thought and pretty unlikely behaviour for a figure as powerful and as capable of commanding support as Mr Rostenkowski. But the case against him turned out not to be petty. He goes to jail for having abused his office. That is a flashing yellow light for every office-holder', the *New York Times* commented.

Recently, Mr Gingrich, the powerful House Speaker in the US was reprimanded and fined US$ 300,000 for bringing discredit to the House by filing false information with the ethics panel and failing to get proper legal advice on whether his use of charitable funds for a college course he taught might violate the laws. The financial penalty was described as a reimbursement for extra work that the ethics committee performed because of inaccurate statements under the Speaker's name.

In Israel, Prime Minister Benjamin Netanyahu has had to face allegations of fraud and breach of trust, allegations contained in an eight hundred-page document, brought against him by the police. The main allegation against the Prime Minister was that his appointment of an attorney-general was part of a deal to win favourable treatment for his coalition partner, Aeich Deri, who faced trial on corruption charges.

'The fish', according to a Chinese saying 'begins to rot from the head first.' Accountability must therefore start from the top and apply first to the rulers, who should no longer feel they can get away with impunity. South Korea, Italy, and the United States have demonstrated that if there is a will, it can be done. The tragedy of Pakistan is that corruption at the summit of power is not hidden from public view — it is brazen, simply because those in power know by experience they will get away with it. For good governance, for politics to be conducted in a clean manner, for making the corrupt rulers, past and present, accountable, I sent to the government of Nawaz Sharif the draft of a Permanent Accountability Commission to take *suo moto* cognizance, independently of the President and the Prime Minister, of corruption and of abuse of power and authority by holders of public office. No action was taken. I raised the matter again in the caretaker cabinet headed by Mir Balakh Sher Mazari, but no decision was taken. It finally dawned on Mian Nawaz Sharif that holders of public office must be made accountable if they abuse their office or authority.

Responding to Nawaz Sharif's letter, President Leghari said: 'Please refer to your letter dated 1st June 1996 regarding your proposal that I seek the verdict of the people of Pakistan on the setting up of a permanent Judicial Commission for probing corruption charges against the rulers, public representatives and public servants.

'According to the Government, it is alive to and conscious of the menace of corruption and places it high on its priorities for its eradication. The Government is of the view that the Constitution and the law provide adequate mechanism for the process of accountability and that the proposed Judicial Commission would hinder, and not aid, the fight against corruption.

'In view of the foregoing, I am sure that you will agree that corruption is a national problem and the fight against corruption requires a non-partisan approach. If, therefore, I were to refer your proposal to a referendum, it would politicise an issue which requires for its resolution the united efforts of not only the Government and the opposition but of all the citizens of Pakistan.

'We must not allow artificial politicisation of the issue of corruption. Neither will any meaningful resolution emerge from accusations and counter-accusations. But we, the public representatives, will be failing in our duty if we try to ignore the issue or obfuscate it.

'The trust reposed by the people of Pakistan in their elected representatives must be honoured. The people want an end to corruption. Their representatives must respond. This they can do through Parliament. I, therefore, call upon the leadership of the majority ruling parties and the opposition, as indeed all members of the Parliament to cooperate to set up Select Committees of the National Assembly and Senate to probe into the issue of corruption and find remedies to eradicate this evil from our society. As I write to you, I am simultaneously asking the Prime Minister to agree to set up select committees of the National Assembly and the Senate as proposed above. I hope the majority coalition and the opposition alongwith all other members of the Parliament will cooperate in setting up the select committees and agree to suitable terms of reference and working of such committees.'

I find it difficult to believe that these were the President's own views on the subject and he was not toeing the government's line. Was it not within his knowledge that, in public perception, members of Parliament themselves, with a few exceptions, are participants in loot and plunder? How can they be expected to sit in judgement on themselves when they are a part of the problem? Do we need a select committee of the Parliament to tell us how to eradicate corruption at any level? There are half a dozen voluminous reports on eradication of corruption gathering dust in the Ministry of Interior. Why are holders of public office so allergic to subjecting themselves to judicial scrutiny on the eve of elections by a high-powered permanent judicial commission, deriving its authority from the Constitution, as I had suggested? The country needs, and unless I mistake its temper, the country demands ruthless accountability.

When will a holder of public office in Pakistan go to jail for having abused his office? And when will one of our judges rebuke a powerful holder of public office for 'betrayal of trust' and call his conduct 'reprehensible', while sentencing him to prison, as Judge Norma did Senator Rostenkowski? That will be the finest hour of our superior judiciary.

It is the duty of the nation to arrange for the accountability of those who betray the people's faith, who barter away the nation's trust, who plunder the country's wealth. Unless the people's representatives are strictly called to account now and those found guilty among them disqualified and prevented from capturing the Parliament, the entire democratic process will be reduced to a farce; clean politics and an honest democratic government according to the Constitution and the law will remain an illusion. All attempts on the part of these corrupt elements and robber barons to delay or postpone accountability in the name of early elections must, therefore, be resisted because, once elected, they will never be subjected to accountability.

Chapter 9

Farooq Leghari

With the election of Benazir Bhutto on 19 November 1993 as the Leader of the House by the newly elected National Assembly, attention was focused on the election of the President. As many as twenty-seven contestants were in the field. The candidates included:

1. Mr Ghulam Ishaq Khan, former President.
2. Mr Wasim Sajjad, Acting President, Pakistan Muslim League (Nawaz Sharif Group).
3. Nawabzada Nasrullah Khan, National Democratic Alliance.
4. Mr Akbar Bugti, Jamhoori Watan Party.
5. Sardar Farooq Ahmed Khan Leghari, Pakistan People's Party.
6. Mr Aftab Ahmad Sherpao, Pakistan People's Party.
7. Aftab Shaban Mirani, Pakistan People's Party.
8. Sartaj Aziz, Pakistan Muslim League (Nawaz Sharif Group).
9. Mr Gohar Ayub Khan, Pakistan Muslim League (Nawaz Sharif Group).
10. Syed Iftikhar Hussain Gillani, Pakistan Muslim League (Nawaz Sharif Group).
11. Mr Abdul Majid Malik, Pakistan Muslim League (Nawaz Sharif Group).
12. Mr Asghar Khan, Tehrik-i-Istiqlal Pakistan.
13. Mir Balakh Sher Mazari, independent.

President Farooq Ahmed Khan Leghari

14. Haji N. A. Zairian, independent.
15. Yahya Bakhtiar, independent.
16. Mir Mohammad Umar, independent.
17. Mr Saghir Hussain Sufi, independent.
18. Haji Moizzuddin, independent.
19. Pir Azizullah Haqqani, independent.
20. Pirzada Mukhtar Saeed, independent.
21. Mr Bashir Ahmad Meo, independent.
22. Syed Nazar Hussain Shah Gilani, independent.
23. Ghazi Shafiqur Rehman Siddiqui, independent.
24. M. P. Khan, independent.

About half the number were obscure persons and political non-entities. The Chief Election Commissioner rejected the papers of fourteen on technical grounds. The race then started for making it a one-to-one contest. The PPP and PML (N) withdrew their supporting candidates. The decks were being cleared for Wasim Sajjad of PML (N) and Farooq Leghari of PPP. On 12 November 1993, Akbar Bugti, Nawabzada Nasrullah, and Asghar Khan announced their withdrawal and announced the support of their parties for Farooq Leghari.

Ghulam Ishaq Khan, however, was still in the field and Benazir Bhutto soon realized that if he remained in the field, Farooq Leghari's chances would diminish. Benazir Bhutto was not going to leave anything to chance. One day, at 7.30 in the morning, Anwar Saifullah, Ishaq's son-in-law, called me to say that Benazir Bhutto would be meeting Ghulam Ishaq Khan, the former President, with her entire entourage in half an hour; Ghulam Ishaq Khan desired that I should be present. I quickly dressed and left for Anwar's house. Within minutes, the Prime Minister arrived, accompanied by her husband Asif Zardari, and also Farooq Leghari, Aftab Sherpao, Nawabzada Nasrullah Khan, and a number of others. A little later, Ghulam Ishaq Khan entered the drawing-room to hear what Benazir had to say. The two had not met since her farewell call on him at the Presidency after his resignation in July 1993. Ghulam Ishaq Khan was deeply hurt, and justifiably so, as Benazir Bhutto had not only reneged on her promise to sponsor him as her Presidential candidate, she had also not contacted him at all and had not bothered to tell him why she could not sponsor him. We had taken her promise at its face value, little realizing that such promises are made to be broken. There was, therefore, a great

deal of tension in the air. Benazir told Ghulam Ishaq Khan that
after much deliberation and discussion with her party stalwarts,
she had decided to sponsor Farooq Leghari as her presidential
candidate and she sought Ghulam Ishaq Khan's help in getting
him elected. What she did not tell him was that she had arrived at
this conclusion after ditching him and after the search for a consensus candidate had produced no result. Ghulam Ishaq Khan
enquired as to why he had been excluded from this exercise and
why he had been kept in the dark. Benazir Bhutto responded by
saying that the matter had been discussed in the presence of Ijlal
Haider Zaidi and, his son-in-law, Anwar Saifullah, and she had
asked them to convey her views to him. She then turned to me
and said that she tried to contact me also but I was not available
and could not be contacted. Ghulam Ishaq Khan told Benazir
Bhutto that nobody had reported anything to him. At this stage,
Benazir Bhutto told Ghulam Ishaq Khan that his decision whether
or not to withdraw could not be delayed because she had to report
the matter, and, in the event of non-withdrawal by Ghulam Ishaq
Khan, some other decisions would have to be taken. Ghulam Ishaq
Khan flared up and said, 'I know you are referring to the GHQ.
What have they got to do with it? I thought we are a parliamentary democracy. God help this country if such momentous decisions are going to be taken by the GHQ.' Ghulam Ishaq Khan and
Benazir Bhutto were locked in this futile discussion for quite some
time. At this stage, realizing that neither Benazir Bhutto nor Hamid
Nasir Chattha, head of his faction of PML, was going to support
him, I intervened and suggested to Ghulam Ishaq Khan that he
might consider withdrawing to ensure Farooq's success. Nothing
was decided and Benazir Bhutto and her party left empty-handed.
After they had left and we were alone, Ghulam Ishaq Khan asked
me how good his chances were. I replied, 'Under the circumstances,
not good at all.' He kept quiet. I think it was at this point that he
mentally decided to withdraw and leave the field to Farooq Leghari
and Wasim Sajjad.

According to the daily *Frontier Post*, 'In Benazir's search for a
consensus candidate, Wasim Sajjad . . . was contacted by Syed Ijlal
Haider Zaidi, the-once-upon-a-time Ghulam Ishaq Khan loyalist,
who literally offered the Presidency to him on a silver platter. It
was to be a single transaction, with Wasim handing over post-dated
appointment orders of Governors, Judges and a few others and he
would be adopted as a consensus candidate by the Pakistan

Democratic Front. Speaking strictly in terms of principle and integrity, Mr Zaidi should have been shown the door by the Acting President for even suggesting such incredulous bartering over the highest office of the land but he was not. Instead, Mr Wasim Sajjad made a counter-offer of providing all necessary guarantees of his future cooperation and took pains to emphasize that he would not block any such appointments or interfere in the working of the government, yet stopped a step short of agreeing to sign orders at a time when he had no legal authority to do so. And so the move fizzled out like his ambitions. A top-notch PPP leader denied making this offer, raising a fresh question about whether Mr Zaidi had made this offer on his own because the fact that this offer had been made was also confirmed by Wasim Sajjad to the author on the condition that the information would not be used prior to Nov. 13, 1993, [the following day]. But whatever the result of the aborted move, the ugly episode revealed the kind of politics that was being carried out in the filling of the office which is supposed to be the custodian of the Constitution but was turned into a commodity of political barter.'

The end result was that Farooq Leghari won by securing 274 votes against 168 secured by Mr Wasim Sajjad: a margin of 106 votes. The induction of Farooq Leghari marked the conclusion of the process that had started on 19 July 1993, with the simultaneous resignations of both Ghulam Ishaq Khan and Nawaz Sharif.

On the evening of the day that Leghari was elected as President, Aftab Sherpao came to my house and took me along to the Prime Minister's House. Benazir Bhutto was beaming with joy. Her party had for the first time captured the two commanding peaks, the office of the President and that of the Prime Minister. It was a comeback for her on a triumphant note. She had played her cards with skill and she had won. The real battle was about to begin: now she had to govern and not criticize. As Prime Minister, she did not have that luxury.

Political genius, said Bismarck, consists of hearing the distant hoofbeat of the horse of history and leaning to catch the passing horseman by the coattails. Nobody not endowed with this kind of genius could have accomplished what Benazir did. She was prepared to sup with the Devil if it could help her make a comeback. This is exactly what she did. She bounced back, returned from the political wilderness, out-manoeuvred both Ghulam Ishaq Khan and Nawaz Sharif, and captured the commanding peaks. That was undoubtedly her finest hour.

At her darkest hour in 1988, a miracle had come to pass. When everything looked so bleak and she was beginning to feel that she must doubt her lucky star, Providence intervened and struck down her greatest enemy. This reminded me of the historical parallel and the turning point in the Seven Years War when Frederick the Great faced overwhelming odds against an alliance of Russia, Austria, and France. Frederick said he would give up the fight and commit suicide; addressing Frederick, Carlyle wrote his apt and dramatic words in his *History of Frederick the Great* 'Brave King! wait yet a little while, and the days of your suffering will be over. Already the sun of your good fortune stands behind the clouds, and soon it will rise upon you.' Shortly afterwards, the miracle had come to pass. Czarina Elizabeth of Russia, Frederick's most deadly enemy died; her successor became an ally and Frederick went on to victory. Which Czarina was going to die to bring about a change in the fortunes of Benazir? On 17 August 1988 at about 4:35 p.m. Zia, her worst enemy, died in the mysterious crash of his C-130 aircraft. It was like the death of Czarina Elizabeth. With Zia's death, the sun of Benazir's good fortune, which had been hidden behind the clouds, shone upon her. Benazir joined hands with Zia's successor and went on to victory. Such are the weird twists of history.

When I congratulated her on her double victory, she thanked me and graciously offered me a *gulab jaman*, her favourite sweetmeat. People who had come to congratulate her were leaving one by one. I went up to her to take my leave but she asked me to stay back for dinner. She asked her staff to arrange dinner for ten. Soon Farooq Leghari, the President-elect, and Asif Zardari joined us. They had earlier gone to the shrine of a famous saint at Pakpattan for thanksgiving and laying *chaddar*. Others present on the occasion were Ghulam Mustafa Khar, Iqbal Haider, and Aftab Sherpao. At dinner, Farooq said, 'After the swearing-in ceremony tomorrow, I would like to address the nation.' What I heard next stunned me. Benazir Bhutto reacted sharply and told Farooq that it was not necessary for him to address the nation. 'In any case', she said, 'we want to down play the Presidency'. There was a hushed silence. I was most embarrassed, and so was everybody else. This, I said to myself, was not a good beginning. It did not augur well and looked ominous. Was history going to repeat itself in reverse?

Would it now be the Prime Minister breathing down the neck of the President?

At one of the earlier meetings held in my house, Benazir Bhutto had told Farooq that she would like him to take over as the Chief Minister of the Punjab. Farooq did not think it was a good idea and showed no interest. Benazir Bhutto, however, persisted. Farooq dug his heels in and refused. He told Benazir Bhutto that one reason why he was averse to the idea was that he would get no co-operation from his own party in running the affairs of the province. Benazir Bhutto, assuming he wanted the portfolio of the Minister for Finance, told Farooq that she had no intention of making him the finance minister at the Centre because, to quote her, '[she] had [her] own ideas about running the Finance Ministry'. Farooq responded by saying that she did not have to give him any assignment whatsoever at the Centre. Benazir Bhutto, who can be very abrupt, tried to browbeat Farooq but he held his own. Benazir Bhutto can also be very charming, but somehow that did not work either. In retrospect, I think it was very wise on Farooq's part not to go to turbulent Punjab.

I developed great respect for Farooq in 1991, when, as head of the Accountability Cell, I saw the notes submitted by him as the Federal Minister for Water and Power to the then Prime Minister Benazir Bhutto in the case relating to the hiring of a qualified consulting firm to provide consultancy services for the expansion and augmentation of the electricity transmission system in Karachi in accordance with the procedure and guidelines of the donor, in this case the Asian Development Bank. The proposal of M/s Lehmeyer, a consultancy firm, was highest on merit. The evaluation report was duly approved by the Board of Directors of KESC and it was forwarded to the ADB. A copy of the technical evaluation report was also sent to Farooq. The ADB independent evaluation had been carried out by three different members of the bank's consultant selection committee; they unanimously held the proposal of M/s Lehmeyer to be technically sound, and the most attractive bid.

After approval by the ADB, the first-ranked firm, M/s Lehmeyer, was invited for contract negotiations. The second envelope of financial proposals of M/s Lehmeyer was opened in the presence of the representative of the ADB and the bid was found to be the lowest. However, the Chairman of the Prime Minister's Project Evaluation and Monitoring Committee, who worked under the control and guidance of the Prime Minister, directed that the decision regarding the consultancy contract be kept pending until re-evaluation had been carried out by KESC with a different committee. These remarks were conveyed to the Ministry of Water and Power by Major-General (retd.) Naseerullah Babar, Chief of Staff in the Prime Minister's Secretariat.

The Minister for Water and Power, Sardar Farooq Leghari, put up a detailed brief for the Prime Minister in which he took a serious view of the re-evaluation proposal and categorically stated that such a course of action was not desirable as it would cast doubt on the credibility of the institutional framework. He further recommended that KESC be permitted to go ahead with the award of contract on merit in accordance with the prescribed procedure.

Despite this, re-evaluation of the proposal was carried out through a different committee under the supervision of a new Managing Director of KESC. The earlier evaluation in which Lehmeyer was declared number one was reversed. Leghari submitted the re-evaluation report to the Prime Minister's Secretariat and categorically stated that the original evaluation of consultants carried out by KESC and ADB was correct and should not be re-opened or altered. He suggested that KESC be directed to proceed immediately with the agreed award of consultancy contract to M/s Lehmeyer, evaluated as the first-ranking consultant in the original evaluation by KESC and confirmed by ADB.

The Prime Minister's Secretariat responded to the Minister's summary dated 7 January 1990 by conveying the following observation of the Prime Minister: 'If KESC has chosen a consultant, they should be allowed to go through it. In fact KESC should be allowed to run as autonomously as possible so that they are not bogged down w/time log. There should be no further delay.'

Naturally, it was inferred that the summary sent by the Minister, Farooq Leghari, stood approved. Accordingly, specific directions with Leghari's approval were issued to the Managing Director, KESC, to finalize the contract with M/s Lehmeyer.

The Prime Minister's Secretariat took exception to the above-mentioned directions, and taking a very serious view of the matter, directed that, 'remedial action should be taken and a report put up on how directions were changed and what action government should take against those who changed it. The matter be brought before ECC [Economic Committee of the Cabinet] and [the new] head of KESC called to put their case before us'.

Farooq defended his action and the action of his Ministry in the ECC meeting held on 25 June 1990.

The Prime Minister, as Chairperson of the ECC decided that:

KESC as the user organization should finalize the question of award of contract for consultancy service for KESC Fifth Power Sector Project (Transmission system expansion and augmentation) with the ADB. Negotiation should be held by a team comprising Finance Secretary and MD KESC. It would in any case be ensured that ADB loan for this purpose was not lost to Pakistan. In case the Bank was not willing to review its decision, the contract would be awarded to M/s Lehmeyer as originally approved by KESC Board of Directors and ADB.

At a meeting held on 1 January 1990, the Committee consisting of the Finance Secretary and the MD KESC had already been informed by the Resident Representative of ADB head office that a request for a change in KESC's original recommendation would not be entertained. The new MD KESC even proposed presenting the case personally before ADB at Manila. His request was turned down by the ADB.

After the dissolution of the National Assembly on 6 August 1990, the ECC in its meeting held on 9 August 1990 considered the summary submitted by the Finance Division on hiring of consultants for the KESC and decided as follows: 'The ECC took note of the summary dated 8th August 1990 submitted by the Finance Division and directed KESC to conclude and sign the contracts with M/s Lehmeyer Int. within 4 days'.

Farooq had won, although our reference in the case against Benazir, based mainly on Farooq's notes, was thrown out along with others after Benazir became the Prime Minister for the second time. I do not know of any other minister in Benazir's Cabinet who could have put up such a principled fight.

After his election as President, I called on Farooq to discuss matters relating to the Margalla Hills National Park, a special responsibility of the Margalla Hills Society, a non-governmental organization of which I am the President. We also discussed other matters in general and when I was leaving, he said we should meet more often and asked if it would be all right if he came over to my house. I was overwhelmed. Before I could recover from this pleasant shock, he sent for his Military Secretary and told him, 'I have invited myself to dinner at Roedad Khan's house on return from my visit to Iran.' I was deeply touched by the gesture and felt greatly honoured.

With the approval of the President, I only invited the original members of the 'Manhattan Project' set up in early 1993, namely, Aftab Ahmad Khan Sherpao, Habibullah Kundi, and Anwar Saifullah (who joined the Project much later). Unfortunately, Mir Afzal Khan, then Chief Minister NWFP, a key member of the Project was battling with cancer in a London clinic at that time and could not join us.

Chapter 10

Character and credibility

> Fame is a vapour, popularity is accident, riches take wing, and
> only character endures.
> **Horace Greeley**

Peggy Noonan in her assessment of Ronald Reagan writes: 'In a
President character is everything. A President does not have to be
brilliant. Harry Truman was not brilliant and he helped save Western Europe from Stalin. He does not have to be clever, you can
hire clever. White Houses are full of quick-witted people with ready
advice on how to flip a senator or implement a strategy. You can
hire pragmatic and you can buy and bring in policy wonks. But
you cannot buy courage and decency. You can't rent a strong moral
sense. A President must bring these things with him . . ., he must
know why he is there and what he wants to do.'[1] What then were
the dominant qualities of our Presidents?

'Ayub was no Abraham Lincoln or Salahuddin Ayubi, as Bhutto
presented him in the beginning, but he was no charlatan either as
Bhutto portrayed him in the end.'[2] A man of average intellect,
acquisitive but not corrupt, Ayub was basically a decent, kind
person and a gentleman. He stood head and shoulders above all
the Presidents who followed him. With all his faults, he was by far
the best President we have had.

Yahya was a good man but hardly a good President. His dominant quality was his authenticity and transparency. He wore no mask and was totally devoid of hypocrisy. In financial matters, Yahya was scrupulously honest and died almost a pauper. Like Louis XVI, Yahya became President in order to have fun. Yahya always reminded me of Harding who, like Yahya, was a good man but probably the worst President in American history. On being told of his election, he exclaimed: 'God help me, for I need it.' When Columbia University President Nicholas Murray Butler visited him at the White House, Harding told him: 'I knew this job would be too much for me. I am not fit for this office and should never have been here.' Confronted by a tax question on which various advisers gave him conflicting advice, he told a secretary, 'John, I can't make a damn thing out of this tax problem. I listen to one side and they seem right and then — God! — I talk to the other side and they seem just as right, and here I am where I started. I know somewhere there is a book that will give me the truth, but hell, I couldn't read the book. I know somewhere there is an economist who knows the truth, but I don't know where to find him and haven't the sense to know him and trust him when I find him. God! What a job!'

The outstanding quality of Bhutto's character was courage. He was the brightest, most talented, articulate, colourful character ever to inhabit the Presidency. His strengths and weaknesses not only sprang from the same source but could also not exist without one another. In a real sense, his strengths were his weaknesses, his enthusiasms were his undoing, and most of the traits that made him appealing could make him appalling in the flash of an eye. It was impossible not to be charmed by him, just as it was impossible not to hate him.

Ziaul Haq's dominant qualities were his humility and kindness. But he lacked authenticity. Zia always reminded me of Oliver Cromwell with whom he had many traits in common. Both affected simplicity in their manners and appearance. Both were adept in intrigue and assumed a mask of humility. Like Cromwell, Zia seasoned his orations with the words 'God' and 'Virtue'. The power of both Cromwell and Zia rested upon a solid foundation. It was supported by a well-organized military force, without which no dictator can long maintain his authority. There are some important aspects, however, in which these two characters differed widely. Cromwell's power rested on a great military reputation. Zia had no such military achievements to his credit. Unlike Cromwell, Zia was not destitute of humanity but, like Cromwell, Zia was his own master and made full use of the genius of others.

Ghulam Ishaq Khan, the Schultz-look alike bureaucrat as Emma Duncan describes him, was a hardworking man of great personal integrity and incorruptibility. No other President, with the possible exception of Bhutto, worked harder or worked longer hours. Ghulam Ishaq Khan, like Ayub, sometimes seemed excessively technocratic, wooden, humourless, lacking political passion. He was the most fiercely independent of all our Presidents, especially in dealing with the Americans, by whom he was never overawed. If people had known how he used to take on the Americans and how jealously he guarded our nuclear programme, public perception of his record might have been different. He had great gifts, now lost to the nation.

'Richard Nixon said there are two kinds of men who run for the Presidency, those who want to do big things, and those who want to be big — to fulfil some sense of personal destiny to receive self-validation through the hurrahs of the people.'[3] Ayub was the first kind of man in the Nixon formulation. Like Reagan, he did not want to be big, he thought he was already big. He was secure and he did not go into politics to fill an emptiness inside him. There were things bigger than staying in office for Ayub. He had a vision of the future of Pakistan, but a vision is worth little if you do not have the character, the courage, and the heart to see it through.

Yahya does not fit into the Nixon formulation. He did not think he was big and he did not want to do big things. He always wanted to have fun and the Presidency enabled him to have a lot of fun.

Bhutto thought he was already big and wanted to do big things. Like Ayub, Bhutto also had a vision of the future of Pakistan. He failed because he lacked conviction and the strong moral sense which a leader must have if he is to succeed. In the words of Nixon, Bhutto, more than anything else, wanted to fulfil some sense of personal destiny and receive self-validation through the hurrahs of the people. Bhutto introduced socialism in the politics of Pakistan. Zia introduced Islam. Bhutto did as much disservice to socialism as Zia did to Islam.

Zia did not think he was already big. He did not acquire courage and decency in the Presidency: he already had these qualities. Zia knew why he was there and what he wanted to do. He loved power and wanted to stay in office to turn Pakistan into an Islamic society

— not the dynamic, pristine, revolutionary, Islamic society of the early years of Islam, with its emphasis on egalitarianism, social justice, and accountability, but the scholastic, institutionalized, fossilized Islam, co-opted by corrupt rulers. I have no doubt that if Zia had lived, he would have taken us back to the Middle Ages.

Ghulam Ishaq Khan never thought he was big and he never pretended that he wanted to do big things, but he too had a vision of the future of Pakistan. His vision was of a truly dynamic, Islamic society, with its emphasis on social justice and accountability. He failed to turn the tide not because he lacked the courage and the heart to see it through, but because he walked alone and did not have the power. His vision, therefore, remained a poignant dream.

Farooq is personable and intelligent, with a religious bent of mind. He is our most underrated President. Torn between his presidential obligations and his party affiliation, Farooq finds himself in a Hamlet-like situation. Far from being solved, the dilemma appears to be escalating as a result of the increasing political intolerance and blatant, widespread corruption displayed by the party leader. Although not likely to be celebrated as one of our greatest Presidents, he is, mark my words, destined to change the political landscape of Pakistan.

Adieu

> ANTONY: The evil that men do lives after them. The good is oft
> interred with their bones; so let it be with Caesar.
> **Shakespeare**

'Political life is a merciless affair and the man who has been at the top of the tree is most ruthlessly "clawed" to use one of Churchill's favourite words — when he falls or even slips.' In a rare moment of self-pity Churchill told a friend, 'Here I am after almost thirty years in the House of Commons, after holding many of the highest offices of State. Here I am discarded, cast away, marooned, rejected and disliked.' In the dungeon of the Conciergerie, before being taken to the scaffold, Danton (who bore a resemblance to Socrates) too late regretted the blessings of a retired life and said, 'It is better to be a poor fisherman than to govern men.'

'On 26 March 1969, Ayub invited his former Ministers to a farewell meeting. Ayub was in a light grey suit and was wearing dark glasses.' Addressing the ministers, Ayub said: '"The rest of the world was beginning to look up to us but our politicians said 'Don't be in a hurry. We will show you what we really are'. We were really able to bluff the world but our own people called the bluff. I could not sign away the future of the country. I would have much rather committed suicide. We don't know the value of freedom. Our people feel exposed and unhappy in freedom; left to ourselves, we would go back to slavery. I had to step aside. There was no other answer. I never thought our people would go mad like this. Unfortunately, there is no constructive people opinion. My greatest ambition was to transfer power in a democratic manner . . . I doubt if in our political life we will have a good man for a long time. Thank God we have an army. If nothing else, I have held this country together for ten years. It was like keeping a number of frogs in one basket. What sort of Pakistan will emerge, is anybody's guess. There will be either force or mob rule. I hope we can find some answer between the two." The atmosphere was that of a funeral service and as soon as the ritual finished, everyone left quickly without saying a word . . .

'As the car moved out of the porch, Ayub leaned out of the window to wave the final goodbye. The car turned left and went past the gate as the sentries stood to attention'.[4]

Yahya was a beaten man when I went to the President's House on 20 December 1971 to witness the transfer of power. He had played his last card. At the National Defence College in Rawalpindi, his Chief of Staff, Lieutenant General Abdul Hamid Khan, met with angry questions and epithets from the junior officers. They were all shouting 'bastards', 'drunkards', 'disgraceful', and 'shame'. The game was up. After the transfer of power ceremony, I said goodbye to Yahya and left. That was the last time I saw him. That day he was taken into protective custody and detained in the government guest house in Abbottabad. When the Joint Secretary, Ministry of Interior, Zia Hussain, went to serve the order of detention on him, Yahya broke down. All he wanted was to be tried, given a hearing, and, if he was convicted, hanged. If only people had known his side of the story and if only people knew how he defended himself before the Hamoodur Rahman Commission, public perception of his guilt might have been different. I was privileged to have had the Hamoodur Rahman Commission report in my custody for eight long years and I can say without any fear of contradiction that of all the principal witnesses, both civil and military, who appeared before the commission, Yahya's performance was by far the best.

Whatever the merits of the case against Bhutto and whatever the verdict of history on him, his execution continues to haunt me. As the time fixed for execution drew nearer, I recalled two historical parallels, both relating to the turbulent days of the French Revolution. 'When the final determination of the Assembly was read out to Louis, King of France, he requested that he be allowed to see his family; the request was granted. At 8.30 that evening, the family was reunited. No one had yet told them about the King's fate and from behind a glass door Cléry could see the women and children rocking with miseries as he gave them the news. For an hour and three quarters they remained together weeping, kissing and consoling each other as best they could. When it was time to go, none of the family could bear the brutal weight of a final parting. They were on their way out when the Princess Royale, the King's daughter, suddenly threw herself at her father and collapsed in a dead faint.'[5]

'At 10 o'clock, the procession arrived at the scaffold. Beneath the platform Sanson and his assistant prepared to undress the King and tie his hands only to be told by the prisoner that he wanted to keep his coat on and have his hands free. He evidently felt so strongly about the last matter that it appeared for a moment he might even struggle and it took a remark from Edgeworth comparing his ordeal to the Saviour for Louis to resign himself to whatever further humiliations were to be heaped on him. The steps to the scaffold were so steep that Louis had to lean on the priest for support as he mounted. His hair was cut with the professional briskness for which the Sanson family had become famous and Louis attempted finally to address the great sea of twenty thousand faces packed into the square: "I die innocent of all the crimes of which I have been charged. I pardon those who have brought about my death and I pray that the blood you are about to shed may never be required of France". At that moment Santerre ordered a roll of drums drowning out whatever else the King might have had to say. Louis was strapped on to a plank which when pushed forward thrust his head into the enclosing brace. Sanson pulled on the cord and the twelve-inch blade fell, hissing through its grooves to its mark. In accordance with custom, the executioner pulled the head from the basket and showed it, dripping, to the people.'[6]

In my mind's eye, I also recalled Danton standing before the plank, his shirt splattered with the blood of his best friends and his memorable words addressed to Sanson, 'Don't forget to show my head to the people. It is well worth the trouble.'[7]

Bhutto went to the gallows on 4 April 1979 as the clock struck two in the morning. The lever was pulled by Tara Masih, our Sanson. The wooden planks instantly parted and Bhutto fell. A few minutes later, the doctor on duty pronounced Mr Bhutto dead. The evening before, Bhutto had asked for hot water for shaving, saying 'I do not want to die like a bearded *mullah*'. He was asked if he wished to make any will. 'Mr Bhutto said, "I had tried but my thoughts were so disturbed that I could not do it and I have burnt it." . . . He stood alone, unaided, at the scaffold. As the noose was fitted round his neck and hood placed on his head, Mr Bhutto mumbled: "Remove it, remove it."'[8] Thus perished by the hangman's rope, in the fifty-second year of his life, Zulfikar Ali Bhutto, Prime Minister of Pakistan. Whatever might have been his sins, his errors, his excesses, and his indiscretions, they were expiated by his unparalleled suffering. Bhutto's fall reminded me of Antony's words when Caesar fell:

> O what a fall was there, my countrymen!
> Then I, and you, and all of us fell down

Bhutto came to power too early and left too soon.

Zia died in a mysterious air crash on 17 August 1988, two minutes and thirty seconds after take-off. Was it an accident, a criminal act, or sabotage? Nobody would know.

At 2 a.m. on 19 July 1993, Ghulam Ishaq Khan announced that he was resigning his post and leaving his conduct to be judged by history after the dust had settled. He was planning to drive to Peshawar but when Wasim Sajjad, the Acting President, came to know about it, he graciously placed the president's aircraft at Ghulam Ishaq Khan's disposal and he flew to Peshawar. He is leading a peaceful life as a private citizen in Peshawar. A stream of visitors, friends, former colleagues in the civil service, and politicians come to see him daily. He offers his Friday prayers in the mosque attached to the government house, Peshawar, and keeps away from the Press as he has always done.

With the dismissal of the Benazir government on 5 November 1996, President Farooq Leghari set in motion a chain of events which has radically altered the course of Pakistan's history. Three years after he was elevated to the exalted position of President of

Pakistan, Farooq Leghari, like Gorbachev, has transformed the political landscape of Pakistan. Benazir is now out in the wilderness. Her party is in a state of total disarray. The once powerful Presidency which Leghari inherited from former President Ghulam Ishaq Khan is now almost unrecognizable and is a shadow of its former self. Stripped of all powers and with his wings clipped, the President is now like the appendix in the human body, a titular head of state, performing ceremonial functions only. Gone is the aura of omnipotence that surrounded the office of the president, fashioned by Ziaul Haq. He will now have no role to play if the country ever faces a serious crisis as it did before the imposition of martial law, in 1977. The martial law of July 1977, according to General Arif, might have been avoided if the distribution of constitutional powers between the President and the Prime Minister had been balanced and not lopsided as was the case then. With the repeal of the Eighth Amendment, we are back to square one. It seems that, like the Bourbons of France, our rulers have also forgotten nothing and have learned nothing.

The rise and fall of Ayub and his successors has brought to the fore the question of leadership in Pakistan. Bearing in mind their cruel epilogue, their inglorious ending, and exit dance, one could recommend the much misunderstood Machiavelli to our present and future leaders. He has an entire chapter in *The Prince* on why a leader 'must avoid being despised and hated', and about the unpleasant things that happen to a leader who fails to take advice. 'But I will bring this discourse to a conclusion by saying that Princes in our times have this difficulty of giving inordinate satisfaction to soldiers in a far less degree, because, notwithstanding one has to give them some indulgence, that is soon done; none of these Princes have armies that are veterans in the governance and administration of provinces, as were the armies of the Roman Empire, and whereas it was then more necessary to give satisfaction to the soldiers than to the people, it is now more necessary to all Princes, to satisfy the people rather than the soldiers because the people are the more powerful.'

'Governments can err. Presidents do make mistakes,' Franklin D. Roosevelt told the 1936 Convention, 'but the immortal Dante tells us that Divine Justice weighs the sins of the cold-blooded and the sins of the warm-hearted in different scales.'[9] How shall we categorize our Presidents? I tried to, but, on second thoughts, decided to leave it to the reader and to Divine Justice.

Chapter 11

Where does sovereignty lie?
Illusion and reality

'Whereas sovereignty over the entire universe belongs to Almighty Allah alone, and the authority to be exercised by the people of Pakistan within the limits prescribed by Him is a sacred trust'. So says the Preamble to the Constitution of the Islamic Republic of Pakistan.

'Where ought the sovereign power of the state to reside?' asked Aristotle. 'With the people? With propertied classes? With the good? With one man, the best of all, the good? With one man, the tyrant?'

'The sovereignty of [English] Parliament is (from a legal point of view) the dominant characteristic of our political institutions', wrote A. V. Dicey. The principle of parliamentary sovereignty according to Dicey, means neither more nor less than this: that the Parliament has under the English Constitution the right to make or unmake any law, and further, that no person or body is recognized by the Law of England as having a right to override or set aside the legislation of Parliament. It is a fundamental principle with English lawyers that Parliament can do everything but make a woman a man and a man a woman.

Where does sovereignty reside in Pakistan? If the term is used in the legal sense in which it is used by Dicey, sovereign power under our Constitution also resides in our Parliament. But, as Dicey says, the word sovereignty is sometimes employed in a political rather than a strictly legal sense. 'That body is "politically" sovereign or supreme in a state the will of which is ultimately obeyed by the citizens of the state.' In this sense of the word, the people, or in strict accuracy, the electors may be said to be the body in which sovereign power is vested. But, unlike the United Kingdom, the electors in Pakistan are not able to assert themselves or enforce their will. It is also common knowledge that in our country neither parliamentarians nor acts of Parliament reflect the will of the people or the General Will as it is called. In theory, the members of Parliament are trustees for the people but, in practice, once elected they cease to be accountable and have no qualms of conscience in betraying the trust reposed in them by their constituents. No court has so far punished a holder of public office on the ground that he has committed breach of trust. The political sovereignty of the people, in our circumstances, is therefore a myth. To apply the adjective sovereign to the people in today's Pakistan is a tragic farce.

Be that as it may, Pakistan made judicial history — and, in the process, unveiled the *locus in quo* of ultimate power — when a bench of nine judges of the Supreme Court validated the imposition of martial law and the dissolution of Parliament, the legal sovereign, by the Chief of Army Staff, General Muhammad Ziaul Haq on the ground that it was necessitated by considerations of state necessity and public welfare. It held that the CMLA was entitled to perform all such acts and promulgate legislative measures which fell within the scope of the law of security, including the power to amend the Constitution. 'The Court, as an institution did not, with due respect to the Judges, have the power or jurisdiction to circumvent settled constitutional procedures and allow a functionary to tamper with the Constitution. This was an exercise of power without precedent. Not a single dissent was filed.'[1]

'On the strength of this judicial authority, given at the highest level, the CMLA in the years to come was to amend the Constitution wholesale, and cite this judgment of the Supreme Court as an answer to all accusations of abuse of power . . . The regime used the sword supplied to it by the judiciary to strike at judicial power. The Provisional Constitution Order, 1981 (PCO) barred the jurisdiction of the courts to interfere in any matter which fell within the purview of the various Martial Law enforcements or to review or question any act or proceeding before the military courts.'[2]

What is extremely disturbing and surprising is that the Supreme Court, the guardian of the Constitution, without any jurisdiction or power, authorized the CMLA to dismantle the Constitution brick by brick and change it beyond recognition. This was certainly not the finest hour of Pakistan's superior judiciary. We had entered the saddest and darkest period of our not very bright constitutional history.

Shortly before the Dosso case, Justice Munir had declared poetically that 'when politics enter the portals of the palace of Justice, democracy, its cherished inmate, walks out by the back door.'[3] In the *State versus Dosso and another*, the Supreme Court ruled on the legality of the usurpation of power and held that the usurpation of power to create a new regime was valid. Justice Munir, the Chief Justice, held that, 'Where revolution is successful, it satisfies the test of efficacy and becomes a basic law-creating fact'. With this ruling, the Supreme Court legitimized the military regime.

The superior judiciary in Pakistan faced its first real test when the Governor-General, Ghulam Muhammad, with the backing of the army, announced on 24 October 1954 that the constitutional machinery had broken down, and declared a state of emergency. Stating that the constituent assembly had lost the confidence of the people and could no longer function, Ghulam Muhammad effectively dissolved the Assembly and reconstituted the Cabinet. Moulvi Tamizuddin Khan, the Speaker, responded with a petition to the Sindh High Court for writs of mandamus and *quo warranto* to restrain the Governor-General and the new Cabinet from giving effect to the proclamation and dissolution.

The Sindh High Court examined three issues: Whether the Governor-General's assent was needed to validate Assembly actions and whether the Governor-General had the right to dissolve the Assembly; and whether the writ petitions fell within the High Court's jurisdiction. The High Court decided in favour of legislative supremacy and Chief Justice Constantine held that the 'purported dissolution is a nullity in law'. The High Court ruled unanimously against the Governor-General on the issues of assent and dissolution. The Governor-General challenged the High Court's authority to review his actions. The Federal Court headed by Justice Munir, however, held that the Governor-General's assent was required to legalize Assembly actions and dismissed most of the substantive issues raised in the High Court case. The lone dissenter in the appeal was Justice A. R. Cornelius.

In the Asma Jilani case, the Supreme Court considered three related issues: the validity of the revolutionary legality doctrine established in the 1954 Dosso case; the doctrine's applicability to transfer of power to Yayha Khan; and the status of his legal framework. The Court concluded that Yayha Khan had usurped power; that his action was not justified by the revolutionary legality doctrine, and consequently that his martial law regime was illegal. The judgment was, however, given when Yahya Khan was no longer in power.

In March 1981, General Zia promulgated the Provisional Constitution Order 1981 (PCO) 'for consolidating and declaring the law and for effectively meeting the threat to the integrity and sovereignty of Pakistan' and because 'doubts had arisen . . . as regards the powers and jurisdiction of the superior courts'. As a consequence of this Order, judicial powers were extinguished and the 1973 Constitution effectively abrogated. It placed virtually all powers in the hands of the Executive; provided extensive emergency provisions to extend military rule; and gave the President and Chief Martial Law Administrator retrospective powers to amend the Constitution. All orders and actions taken by the regime were considered to have been validly made; and 'notwithstanding any judgement of any court', could not be called into question 'in any court on any ground whatsoever'. Superior Court judges were required to take a new oath to uphold the PCO; not all were invited to do so.

The PCO 1981 was the logical culmination of the process started in 1955 with the judgments in Tamizuddin Khan's case, the 1955 reference, and Dosso's case. Referring to these judgments, Justice Yaqub Ali Khan, in Asma Jilani's case, said, 'The secession of East Pakistan thirteen years later is, in my view, directly attributable to this tragic incident.'[4] This observation was, as before, made after the usurper was dead and gone.

On 29 May 1988, Prime Minister Junejo was dismissed and the National Assembly dissolved by President Zia. The Supreme Court upheld the decision of the Punjab High Court, in declaring that the President's action was invalid in law. The judgments were, however, given after the death of Zia. If the President's action was invalid in law, why was the National Assembly not restored?

On 6 August 1990, President Ghulam Ishaq Khan dismissed Prime Minister Benazir Bhutto and dissolved the National Assembly. That act of dissolution was upheld by the Court.

On 17 April 1993, President Ghulam Ishaq Khan dismissed Prime Minister Mian Nawaz Sharif and dissolved the National Assembly after the Prime Minister had made what amounted to a declaration of war against the President on radio and television and charged him, *inter alia*, with intrigue and conspiring to topple the government. Many people, including Ghulam Ishaq Khan, assumed that after the Prime Minister's declaration of war against the President, in the worst scenario the Court would follow their past pattern by condemning the idea of dissolution but allowing the fact to stand. The Supreme Court, headed by Chief Justice Nasim Hasan Shah, however, appropriated the case in its original jurisdiction (which limited appeals) and then decided against the President. However, many people think that the case against Benazir — which was decided against her — was much weaker than the case against Nawaz Sharif which was dismissed. The Court cited the President for his 'incorrect appreciation of the role assigned to him'. Why was the President's action against Benazir upheld and what were the factors which determined the outcome of the case against her? How was it different from the case against Nawaz Sharif? It is an open secret that the President had the full support of the COAS when he dismissed Benazir and dissolved the National Assembly. When the President took similar action against Nawaz Sharif, he did so only after I had conveyed to him General Waheed's message and after he had satisfied himself that he had the support of the Chief of Army Staff. Knowing Ghulam Ishaq Khan as I do, he would never have taken this action if he had not been sure about the strength of his case or had any doubt about the support of the army. Nobody knew better than Ghulam Ishaq Khan that such momentous decisions are never taken by a civilian head of state in Pakistan without getting the right signal or at least a nod from the Army Chief. But, unknown to us, and almost overnight, 'wiser counsels' had prevailed; General Waheed distanced himself from the President, his benefactor, and joined the rest of the crowd in running him down. Once he lost the support of the coercive power, the party was over for Ghulam Ishaq Khan.

Three centres of power had emerged on the Pakistan political scene. The President, the Prime Minister, and the army represented by the Chief of Army Staff. The Prime Minister as the head of the party in government is directly elected. The President is elected by an electoral college consisting of all MNAs, MPAs, and Senators. The army chief is appointed by the President on the advice of the Prime Minister. The formation of the Council for Defence and National Security (CDNS) may, if it survives, upset the balance of political power between the three members of the troika. For all practical purposes the centre of gravity may shift from the Cabinet to the CDNS. Under the Constitution, it is the Cabinet which aids and advises the President in the exercise of his functions. Now the roles have been reversed and it will be the CDNS, presided over by the President, flanked by the Service Chiefs, which will advise the Prime Minister and, through him, the Cabinet on major national issues!

If any doubt remained as to the locus of ultimate power in Pakistan it was removed when, after the death of Ziaul Haq, the army decided, after internal discussions, not to impose martial law, and asked Ghulam Ishaq Khan, Chairman, Senate, to assume office as the Acting President. The Constitution provided that in the event of the death of the President, the Chairman Senate become the Acting President. He should therefore have automatically stepped into Zia's shoes. But this did not happen. 'The news', according to General K. M. Arif, 'was withheld for over three hours. This was a period of intense behind-the-scenes activity in Islamabad. For three hours the country was without a President and the Pakistan Army without its Chief. Both the appointments had been held by Zia. The Constitution provided that, in the event of the death or absence (of a sitting President), the Chairman of the Senate would become the acting President. Mr Ghulam Ishaq Khan, the then Chairman of the Senate, was thus the automatic choice. The question of succession had been foreseen in the Constitution and its provisions were clear and unambiguous. There was no justification for deviating from the Constitution.'[5]

'In Beg's office', Arif continues, 'two options were considered: one, the Army takes over control of the country and imposes martial law; two, following the constitutional provisions, Mr Ghulam Ishaq Khan becomes the new President. They decided in favour of the latter course. The Army view was firmed. It was time to consult the other two service Chiefs . . . The Service Chiefs agreed with the GHQ view that the Constitution should prevail. Mr Ghulam Ishaq Khan was then requested to visit General Headquarters where he was apprised of the views of the Service Chiefs. The time was now close to 7.30 p.m. (17 August 1988). It was improper for the Military brass to call Mr Ghulam Ishaq Khan to the General Headquarters. Instead, they should have called on him to express their grief and loyalty. Ishaq had the constitutional right to become the President and the military had shown him no favour. He was too nice a person to fuss about the protocol and that too in an hour of national tragedy. It would have been prudent for the top military hierarchy to show him the courtesy.'[6]

Whatever be the constitutional position, one thing is clear that in the final analysis, political sovereignty in Pakistan (*Majestas est summa in civas ac subditoes legibusque soluta potestas*, i.e., 'highest power over citizens and subjects unrestrained by law', in the words of French Jurist Jean Bodin) resides neither in the electorate, nor the Parliament, nor the Executive, nor the Judiciary, nor even the Constitution which has superiority over all the institutions it creates. It resides, if it resides anywhere at all, where the coercive power resides. In practice, it is the *pouvoir occulte* (the hidden power), which is the ultimate authority in the decision-making process in Pakistan. They decide when to abrogate the Constitution; when it should be held in abeyance; when elected governments should be sacked; and when democracy should be given a chance. Behind the scenes, they also decide whether an elected prime minister shall live or die.

But, as Rousseau said, 'However, strong a man is, he is never strong enough to remain master always unless he transforms his might into right and obedience into duty.'

This has been problem of the military dictators of Pakistan, who have ruled for more than half the life of the country. In order to convert their might into right and obedience into duty they devised devious ways and means. This was not a new problem. In the days of the Khilafat, the leader of the Muslims was the Caliph. He was the defender of the Faith, the protector of the territory of Islam, the supreme judge of the state. He was the successor to the Prophet (pbuh), as head of the community, commander of the faithful, leader and ruler of all Muslims. So great was the prestige of the Caliphs that a powerful ruler like Buwayhid Adud-ul-dawlah, made a pretence of complete submission and reverence before the puppet caliph, Tai's, whose name he used to maintain his own authority. Mahmud of Ghazni could threaten the caliph, but he also sought recognition from him. Even the mighty Seljuks, who ruled the largest empire of their day, could not ignore the caliph's legal position. No monarchy could consider itself legally established without recognition by the Commander of the Faithful. Just as the Prophet is the vicegerent of God, the caliph is the vicegerent of the Prophet, the monarch is the vicegerent of the caliph. When the emissaries of the caliph Abu Jafar Mansur Al-Mustansir-billah reached Delhi, it was a day of rejoicing for the newly established empire of Sultan Shamsuddin Iltutmish who was receiving formal recognition from the Commander of the Faithful. When the Caliph Mustasim was executed by Halaku Khan in AD 1258 without leaving any heir, the Sultans of Delhi resolved their problem by the simple device of continuing Mustasim's name on their coins long after his death.

The question of legitimacy has plagued the Muslim world since the death of the Prophet (pbuh) in AD 632. The Holy Quran is silent beyond saying that Muslims should settle their affairs by mutual consultation. The Prophet had abstained from nominating a successor or laying down any rules of political succession. Islam does not recognize hereditary monarchy. In actual practice, the question of succession was decided by the length of the contender's sword and the sharpness of its blade. Therefore, when Munir validated martial law in 1958 or Anwarul Haq sanctified Ziaul Haq's military take-over and usurpation of power, they were both following well-established traditions of Muslim history and were not innovating.

Ayub faced the same dilemma: How was his rule to acquire legitimacy? The Khilafat had fallen long ago. There was no Caliph in Baghdad to grant him recognition. How was he, therefore, to transform his might into right and obedience into duty? He created 80,000 Basic Democrats. Ziaul Haq held a fraudulent referendum on Islamization and, when a small percentage of people voted for Islamization, he concluded that it was a vote of confidence in him and on the strength of this verdict he could rule for five years.

The caliphate disappeared long ago, but the caliph's role in the Muslim world is now played by Washington. No Muslim ruler, the modern sultan, barring some exceptions, considers himself legally established without recognition by the United States of America. The visit of the caliph's emissary used always to be a big event and was celebrated as a day of rejoicing. Feroze Shah, one of the Delhi Sultans, received the caliph's emissaries with great humility and prostrated himself in the direction of the caliph's capital when he received the standards and robes. More or less the same respect is now shown by corrupt and unpopular Muslim rulers to the emissary of the President of the USA. A visit by the American President himself is considered as a dream come true and, in the eyes of the ruler at least, puts the seal of authority on his title to rule. However, sometimes such visits produce unintended results and expedite the ruler's demise as happened in the case of Reza Shah Pehlavi, the King of Kings, after Carter's visit to Tehran and his fulsome praise of the Shah.

Chapter 12

Mandarins

The kind of men we must choose from among the Guardians will be
those who are found to be full of zeal to do whatever they believe is
for the good of the Commonwealth and never willing to act against
its interests.

Plato

The Civil Service of Pakistan is the successor of the Indian Civil Service,
which was the most distinguished Civil Service in the world.

Sir Eric Franklin

'The reason why I wanted to meet you is that I wanted to say a few
words to you, who are occupying very important positions in the
administration of Pakistan in this Province', said Mr Jinnah in an
informal talk to civil officers at Government House, Peshawar, on
14 April 1948.

'The first thing that I want to tell you is this, that you should
not be influenced by any political pressure, by any political party
or individual politicians. If you want to raise the prestige and greatness of Pakistan you must not fall a victim to any pressure, but do
your duty as servants to the people and the state, fearlessly and
honestly. Service is the back-bone of the State. Governments are
formed, governments are defeated, prime ministers come and go,
ministers come and go, but you stay on, and, therefore, there is a
very great responsibility placed on your shoulders. You should

have no hand in supporting this political party or that political party, this political leader or that political leader — that is not your business. Whichever government is formed according to the Constitution and whoever happens to be the prime minister coming into power in the ordinary constitutional course, your duty is not only to serve that government loyally, faithfully, but, at the same time fearlessly, maintaining your high reputation, your prestige, your honour and the integrity of your service. If you will start with that determination you will make a great contribution to the building up of the Pakistan of our conception and our dream — a glorious state and one of the greatest nations in the world.

'While impressing this upon you on your side, I wish also to take the opportunity of impressing upon our leaders and politicians in the same way that if they ever try to interfere with you and bring political pressure to bear upon you, which leads to nothing but corruption, bribery and nepotism — which is a horrible disease and for which not only your province but others too, are suffering — if they try and interfere with you in this way, I say, they are doing nothing but disservice to Pakistan.

'I hope that each one of you will understand his own sphere of duty and responsibility and act with others harmoniously and in complete co-operation, keeping in mind that each one has to do his duty within the sphere to which he belongs. If you on your side start with that determination and enthusiasm — and I hope the other side will also realize what a terrible evil they are raising up and how it demoralizes the services to try and influence this department or that department, this officer or that officer — and if you will stick to your determination you will have done a great service to your nation. Putting pressure and influence on service people, I know, is a very common fault of politicians and those with influence in political parties but I hope that you will now, from today, resolve and determine to act according to my humble advice that I am giving you.

'Maybe some of you may fall victims for not satisfying the whims of ministers. I hope it does not happen, but you may even be put to trouble not because you are doing anything wrong but because you are doing right. Sacrifices have to be made and I appeal to you, if need be, to come forward and make the sacrifice and face the position of being put on the blacklist or being otherwise worried or troubled. If you will give me the opportunity of your sacrifices, some of you at least, believe me, we will find a remedy for that very soon. I tell you that you will not remain on the black-list, if you discharge your duties and responsibilities honestly, sincerely and loyally to the State. It is you who can give us the opportunity to create a powerful machinery which will give you a complete sense of security.'

This was Mr Jinnah's concept of the role of civil servants in independent Pakistan; his vision of their duties; their functions and responsibilities; their obligation to the people and to the state; and their relationship with their political masters. It is a matter of deep regret and shame that this is one of the least known speeches of the Founder of the Nation, and I had to go to the National Archives to dig it out. Neither politicians nor civil servants want to be reminded of Mr Jinnah's concept of the role of the bureaucracy because it does not suit them and is jarring to their ears. Is it there-fore surprising that no reference is made to such an important speech on the government-controlled radio and television? Deliberate attempts have been made by successive governments, and continue to be made, to suppress this speech and keep the people ignorant of its contents.

The Quaid's advice to civil servants was to serve whichever government is formed *according to the Constitution* and whoever happens to be the prime minister, coming into power *in the ordinary constitutional course*. But when a military dictator abrogated the Constitution in 1958, sacked the government, and dissolved the Assemblies, his action was upheld and sanctified by the Supreme Court in accordance with the servile traditions left behind by compliant *qazis* under the Umayyads and Abbassids and nobody in the bureaucracy (and I include myself) withheld his co-operation or refused to serve the martial law government because it was formed in violation of the Constitution. Earlier, in 1953, when the Governor-General had sacked the Constituent Assem-bly of which Mr Jinnah was the first President, his action was up-held by the Supreme Court. The mandarins followed by offering their allegiance to the Governor-General.

The Quaid's advice fell on deaf ears. The service we inherited on independence, known for its integrity, objectivity, and political neutrality was, over the years, thoroughly mutilated, demoralized, emasculated, politicized, corrupted, and changed beyond re-cognition, and is now a ghost of its former self. The most arduous search will not turn up many civil servants anywhere in the country today who do their duty as servants to the people and the state, fearlessly and honestly; who are not influenced by political pressure from any political party or individual politician, and who do not have a stake in supporting one political party or another, or one political leader or another.

A stage has been reached when it is misnomer to call them public servants. Successive governments have reduced government servants to the level of domestic servants. Thousands of party loyalists have been inducted into the civil service, bypassing the Public Service Commission. All holders of public office, including ministers and members of the National and Provincial Assemblies belonging to the ruling party have their quotas in different grades of service against which they can appoint anyone they like, with no questions asked. Is it, therefore, surprising that discipline has collapsed and civil servants look up to their political bosses, instead of to their immediate superiors for postings, transfers, and promotion?

Nearly half a century after Mr Jinnah's informal talk to civil officers at Government House Peshawar, his successor-in-office, President Farooq Ahmed Leghari, in his address on the occasion of the passing-out ceremony of the 23rd Common Training Programme (CTP) at the Civil Academy in Lahore on 2 July 1996, had this to say to young civil servants: 'I hope your training at the Academy has prepared you to work for the welfare of the people, to dispense justice, to work with humility and show respect to the people and their elected representatives. I must warn you that in a democratic set-up public representatives set the agenda for policy goals of an elected government. Each elected government comes to power with certain promises for the electorate. Thus, formulation of policy is the task of elected representatives. The task of the bureaucracy is to assist, advise, and facilitate in judicious and effective implementation of the policies of an elected government. However, in a developing country like ours, the bureaucracy can play a modernizing role and serve as a vanguard for change, and development. It can play a pivotal role in hampering or promoting democratic development in a country. I share the Director General's concern that we are at a critical juncture. If we cling to the past and allow bureaucratic inertia and arrogance to persist, there is a future neither for the bureaucracy nor for democracy nor for the country. As we move towards the twenty-first century, we have to evolve a harmonious relationship between bureaucracy, political institutions, and elected leadership. I believe that democratic consolidation cannot occur without a professionally competent, efficient, and public service-oriented bureaucracy. As you pass out from the Academy, this is your challenge and opportunity. Take up this challenge and seize this opportunity to revitalize the democratic process and democratic institutions to lead Pakistan to progress and prosperity in the twenty-first century. Democratic revolutions and globalization of economy are forcing bureaucracies all over the world to readjust and re-adapt to these changes. Pakistan cannot afford to live in isolation. The Civil Services of Pakistan must adapt to these changes skilfully and with clarity of purpose. I hope training at the Academy has prepared you to meet the challenges that confront Pakistan boldly, imaginatively, and with seriousness of purpose. I am confident that you will not only promote democratic norms but devote yourself to public service and public welfare with humility and honesty of purpose. Unfortunately, the public perception about the civil servants is that they are "arrogant", "inefficient", "inaccessible", and "dishonest". Though I personally know some officers who work with zeal and honesty and who can be compared with the best in any bureaucracy of the world yet this negative image of the civil servant continues to persist and you must all endeavour to change it by your good conduct, personal commitment and devotion to the public service. You have to dedicate yourself for public good and you should always keep in your minds the advice of the Quaid-i-Azam to officers, and I quote:

'"You are not the rulers. Make the people feel that you are their servants and friends, maintain the highest standard of honour, integrity, justice, and fair-play. If you do that, people will have confidence and trust in you and will look upon you as friends and well-wishers." [Address to Gazetted Officers at Chittagong, 25 March 1948]

'You have also to remember that you are a symbol of the federation. Whatever way your careers may take you, you must protect and defend the interests of the Federation and act in accordance with the Constitution of Pakistan. You should be ready and willing to serve in the remotest corner of the country for the welfare of the people as you have chosen a career in the service of the Federation of Pakistan and its citizens — whatever caste, colour, creed, and regional background they may belong to. Serving the Federation of Pakistan and people of Pakistan has to be your primary responsibility, identity, and reference of loyalty.

Once again I would like to recall the words of Father of the Nation, and I quote:

"'Work honestly and sincerely and be faithful and loyal to the Pakistan Government. I can assure you that there is nothing greater in this world than your own conscience and, when you appear before God, you can say that you performed your duty with the highest sense of integrity, honesty and with loyalty and faithfulness.'" [Address to civil officers of Balochistan at Sibi on 14 February 1948]

President Farooq Leghari's speech is full of words of wisdom but it is significant that it contains no reference to Mr Jinnah's informal talk to civil servants at Government House Peshawar on 14 April 1948, and his advice that civil servants must not be influenced by any political pressure, any political party or individual politician. The President's speech also makes no reference to Mr Jinnah's observation that if politicians ever tried to interfere with civil servants and bring political pressure to bear upon them which leads to nothing but corruption, bribery, and nepotism, they would be doing nothing but disservice to Pakistan and his advice to civil servants not to succumb but to resist such pressure even if it involves some sacrifice. Why was this important policy statement of Mr Jinnah omitted from the President's speech? Why was it not brought to his notice? Is it a deliberate omission? Is it because the Quaid's speech, in the opinion of the government, is now out of date and does not reflect the current realities and views of the government on the role of bureaucracy and their relationship with politicians? Why this deviation from the principles laid down by the Father of the Nation? Does it represent a policy change? No wonder the Peshawar speech of Mr Jinnah is one of his least known speeches: neither the politicians nor the civil servants want to be reminded of it.

In the end, the instinct of self-preservation prevails. Most civil servants have therefore, made necessary adjustments. A 'harmonious' relationship now exists between the bureaucracy and the elected representatives. A convergence of interest has taken place. The governing principle is quite clear. If you are not with them, you are against them. If you cannot beat them, join them. Senior civil servants in particular have done precisely that. When some senior civil servants, my former colleagues and friends, grumbled about interference by the prime minister's spouse in the affairs of the government, I asked them why they did not bring their problem to the notice of the prime minister who, I assured them, would take appropriate action. One of them replied: 'The first time you complain about the prime minister's husband, she may nod and say "thank you"; the second time she will ask: "Will nobody rid me of this fool?" Somebody will.' Barring a few exceptions, the bureaucracy has joined hands with the politicians and have become their partners in crime against the people. Together, they loot and plunder in broad daylight with total impunity and no fear of accountability. A culture of amassing unlimited wealth by hook or by crook in the shortest possible time has taken root. Is it surprising that the image of the service is tarnished and public confidence in its integrity, objectivity, and ability to deliver is totally shattered? What contribution can such a service make to the building up of the Pakistan of Jinnah's dream?

Chapter 13

Political succession and the Islamic challenge

> For forms of governments let fools contest,
> That government is best which is administered best.
> **Alexander Pope**

One of the principal causes of the instability of Muslim rule, past and present, all over the world, including Pakistan, is the absence of a law of political succession in Islam, which has inevitably led to uncertainty, civil wars, wars of succession, etc. After the demise of the Holy Prophet Muhammad (peace be upon him), who did not nominate his successor, it was considered necessary to have the institution of the caliphate for the preservation of the religion and the administration of temporal affairs. An *Imam* was required to be appointed by the consensus of the community, but no machinery was evolved or could be evolved at that stage by which the votes of millions of Muslims could be taken as often as the rulers changed or had to be changed.

Abu Bakr Siddiq was elected by a majority but some believed that the Prophet (pbuh) would have wanted Ali Ibn Abu Talib, his cousin and son-in-law, to be his successor. Ali himself accepted Abu Bakr's leadership, but during the next few years he seems to have been the focus of the loyalty of dissidents who disapproved of the policies of the first three caliphs. Ali became the fourth caliph in AD 656, but the Shias would eventually call him the first *Imam* or

Leader of the Ummah. The Shian-i-Ali (those of the party of Ali), led by the Prophet's grandson, refused to accept the Ummayyads who had seized the caliphate after the death of his father Ali Ibn Abu Talib.

'With the advent of the Umayyads to power, the elective aspect of the Caliphate disappeared altogether and the Caliphs began to nominate their successors on dynastic considerations.'[1] The people were required to take oath of allegiance to the successor-designate during the lifetime of the reigning Caliph. The oath of allegiance had to be renewed at the time of succession of the new caliph. More importance was attached to the oath of allegiance by a handful of important personalities like the army generals and the *qazis*. The choice used to be made long before such an assembly was held. Since Islam does not recognize monarchy, or the hereditary right of succession, in practice no Muslim was disqualified unless he suffered from physical infirmities. His title to rule was as good as that of anybody else and was in direct proportion to the length of his sword and the sharpness of its blade.

With the introduction of the Turkish elements in the army, the generals assumed the role of caliph-makers. That the Turkish generals had become the virtual masters of the caliphs can well be illustrated by a story related by Ibn at-Tiqtaqa, the author of *Kitab Al-Fakhri*, who says: 'When Mu'tazz was appointed as Caliph, his courtiers held a meeting and summoning the astrologers asked them how long he [the Caliph] would live and how long he would retain his Caliphate. A wit present in the gathering said, "I know this better than the astrologers". Being asked to specify the time, he replied "So long as the Turks please,"[2] and everyone present laughed.

Soon thereafter, the Turkish Army dragged the Caliph Mu'tazz (AD 853/855–866/869) by the feet and, stripping off his shirt, exposed him to the burning sun. Oppressed by the severe heat, he lifted his feet alternately and the Turks slapped him with their hands. Finally, they put him to death. (cf. Tabari, p.1710). This tradition survives till today and manifests itself in different forms in different Muslim countries.

Pakistan faces the same problem of orderly succession today. Since independence, it has experimented with Constitution, government, and the structure of the state. The military has seized power three times since 1947, ruling directly and indirectly for more than half the life of the country. Pakistan does have a law of political succession enshrined in its Constitution, but it is honoured more in the breach than in observance. It is abrogated or held in abeyance whenever it suits *le pouvoir*. Elected governments are sacked and restored to power at will. We have an elected government today but nobody knows when the axe will fall on it and, when it does fall, no tears will be shed because it is thoroughly corrupt, and the people are sick and tired of fake democracy; commitment to the democratic process in any case is quite weak, if not nonexistent. Pakistan has swung between democracy and dictatorship several times in the past and it does not look as if the pendulum will ever stop swinging from one extreme to the other. Meanwhile, the country remains gripped by fear, uncertainty, and confusion. Development is slowed down and the people suffer. The future of democracy — in fact, the future of Pakistan itself — will depend on the future role of the army in the political history of the country and how the problem of political succession is resolved.

In his 1991 book *Pericles of Athens and the Birth of Democracy*, Donald Kagan, a professor of classics at Yale, propounds a principle that is as valid today as it was 2,500 years ago. Democratic governance, he writes, relies on three conditions: 'The first is to have a set of good institutions; the second is to have a body of citizens who possess a good understanding of the principles of democracy, or who have developed a character consistent with the democratic way of life; and the third is to have a high quality of leadership, at least at critical moments.' Are any of these three conditions present in today's Pakistan?

Today, Pakistan is a democratic country but in the strictly formal sense of the term only. Theoretically, it meets all the criteria for liberal democracy of periodic multi-party elections and guarantees basic rights; but very few Pakistanis will disagree that people have lost faith in the impartiality of the electoral machinery, the independence of the judiciary, and the rule of law, in fact the entire democratic process. In a situation like this and in a largely illiterate society and the sword of martial law hanging over its head, it is hard to imagine liberal democracy, or, for that matter, any democracy working properly or surviving for long.

'To those who bluff themselves, referring to this country as a "democracy", my questions are:

- Can a democracy afford not to have a census for sixteen
  years thus rendering every (repeat every) statistic — fiscal,
  commercial or constituency-wise or otherwise — incorrect?
- In what sort of democracy do known robbers, pillagers, loot-
  ers of public wealth, breachers of trust, misappropriators of
  widows' and orphans' Baitul Maal, Zakat and Iqra funds,
  contest elections to its parliament? — In what sort of a
  democracy does a chief of army staff publicly accept crores
  of rupees from a corrupt banker (later jailed) and preside
  over its dubious expedient disbursement to politicians?
- In what sort of a democracy would a chief of naval staff give
  away the entire seafront of a naval base to the crony of a
  political bigwig, ostensibly to develop a tourist resort?
- In what sort of a democracy would the president, prime
  and other ministers, and senior bureaucrats fly a thousand
  miles (some on special flights) at the people's expense to
  attend the wedding of an offspring of the country's naval
  chief?' (Ardeshir Cowasjee in the daily *Dawn*, 3 January 1997)

To borrow the final questioning death-cry of Ken-Saro-Wiwa, 'What
sort of a nation is this? What sort of a nation is it that permits this?
What sort of a nation is this, within which I take my definition?' Is
it any wonder that democracy, in its twisted, uniquely Pakistani
incarnation, has inspired no passion in the Pakistani body politic?

Today, the number of choices that are available to Pakistan in
determining how it will organize itself politically or economically
are fast diminishing.

As in the rest of the Islamic world, with nearly one-fifth of the
world's population, in Pakistan also, Islam, with its own code of
egalitarianism, morality, concepts of political, economic, and
social justice is emerging as a challenge to liberal democracy,
narrow nationalism, and other forms of government. Both liberal
democracy and military dictatorship have been tried in different
Muslim countries and found wanting.

Islam — not the scholastic, institutionalized, fossilized Islam
co-opted by corrupt rulers — but the true, dynamic, pristine, revolutionary Islam of its early years with its emphasis on egalitarianism, social justice, and accountability, is perceived by the elite as
the greatest threat to the established order. There is a yearning
among the people, especially the poor, for a true Islamic society, a

haven in the words of Shariati, for the disinherited who are plundered, tortured, oppressed, and discriminated against. Therein lies the portent of danger.

Between 1958 and 1997, a period of volatile and oscillating political fortunes, Pakistan has changed its Constitution and its rulers several times with disastrous consequences for its poor and downtrodden people. Within a few decades, we have witnessed the glorious period of Mr Jinnah, the subsequent sickening political rivalries and palace intrigues, the horrors of successive martial law governments, the tragedy of East Pakistan, the false hopes generated by Bhutto's failed promises, the loot and plunder and extravagant court of Benazir and her spouse. And to borrow Balzac's description of France in the nineteenth century, which aptly describes the plight of millions of people in Pakistan today, 'we have liberty to die of hunger, equality in misery, the fraternity of the street-corners.' I have no prescription to offer but, if we are to preserve the honour of our country, is it not time to devise and institute a form, a just, egalitarian, and durable system of rule so that the person, property, honour of it citizens — in short all the fortunes of Pakistan — are not periodically imperilled?

In April 1943 the Quaid had given expression to his views on social justice and economic equality in the Pakistan of his dream. 'Here I should like to give a warning to the landlords and capitalists. The exploitation of the masses has gone into their blood. They have forgotten the lesson of Islam. Do you visualize that millions have been exploited and cannot get one meal a day? If this is the idea of Pakistan, I would not have it.' The hands of the nation's clock stopped the day the heart of the Quaid stopped beating. If the nation is to live, its resuscitation must commence where its heart first stopped beating.

Chapter 14

Supreme Court reborn

> If there is no power of dissolution anywhere, the only means to get rid
> of an unrepresentative Assembly would be a Revolution.
> **Chief Justice Munir**

On the occasion of the deposition of Caliph Qahir, the *qazi* who
was sent to attest the documents declaring the former's abdication
was very upset when the Caliph refused to submit. The *qazi* said,
'What use was it to summon us to a man who had not been forced
to submit?' On hearing this, Ali Ibn'Isa remarked, 'His conduct is
notorious and therefore he must be deposed'. To this the *qazi*
replied, 'It is not for us to establish dynasties — that is accomplished by the men of the swords, we are only suited and required
for attestation.'[1] The next morning the Caliph was found blinded.
It is a matter of deep regret that the performance of our *qazis* ever
since the creation of Pakistan has been no different and no better.

'From the country's first decade, Pakistan's judges have tried
to match their Constitutional ideas and legal language to the exigencies of current politics. Their judgments have often supported
the Government of the day, presumably to retain a degree of
future institutional autonomy. This was their chosen path through
the 1950s when there was no Constitution; during the Martial Law
period of the 1960s, when the Constitution was a moving target;
and under the mixed Constitutional rule of Zulfikar Ali Bhutto in

the 1970s, when hopes for democracy outweighed its reality. To remain open for business, courts accepted limits on their practice that were not always consonant with the conceptual foundations of their rulings — a disjunction that operates today.'[2] 'Judiciary in Pakistan has functioned at the behest of authority and has allowed itself to be used to further the interest of the state against its citizens.'[3]

In Asma Jilani's case, however, 'the Supreme Court concluded that Yahya Khan had usurped power, that his action was not justified by the revolutionary legality doctrine and consequently his martial law was illegal.'[4] Paraphrasing Ayub Khan, Justice Yaqub Ali Khan concluded that the judgment in Tamizuddin Khan's case, the 1955 reference, and Dosso's case had made 'a perfectly good country . . . into a laughing stock, and converted the country into autocracy and eventually . . . into military dictatorship.' He pointedly criticized the abrogation of the 1956 Constitution, observing that 'Iskandar Mirza and Ayub Khan committed treason and destroyed the basis of representation between East and West Pakistan.'[5]

Now that all these usurpers were dead and gone, it was easy for the Justices to vent their decade-long frustration. Yahya Khan could be vilified. The poor man was under detention in the Government Guest House in Abbottabad.

'Like rulings in earlier courts, the court [Lahore High Court] dealing with the challenge to the National Assembly in the 1990 dissolution order took its direction from political winds, refused to examine the soundness of the President's arguments or the sufficiency of his claims and upheld it.'[6] In 1993, however, when President Ghulam Ishaq Khan dissolved the National Assembly and sacked Nawaz Sharif's Government, the objective situation, unknown to the President, had undergone a material change. The Supreme Court took its direction from political winds and reversed his order.

'In America a number of Justices have had in the back of their minds a possibility that they might get the nomination for President and that was not a healthy situation because however strong a man's mentality and character, if he has the ambition in his mind it may tinge or colour what he does and that is exactly what the Founding Fathers wanted to remove from the minds of the Supreme Court, make them perfectly free, knowing that there was no more in life for them than the work of the Court.'[7]

By contrast in Pakistan, for some Justices life begins after retirement. It is also a matter of common knowledge that the ambition to go from the Court to less exalted but more lucrative jobs or assignments in the government has hurt the work of a number of our judges.

Our Founding Father did not realize that one day Supreme Court Judges would be appointed not because of their ability and sterling character but their loyalty to the Executive and their political affiliations. Here, nothing prevented the Executive from court-packing and appointing party loyalists with limited knowledge and experience. If the idea was to degrade the Supreme Court and to find the worst men, some of our governments succeeded brilliantly in doing so. No wonder the people are disgusted at some of the appointments to high judicial offices. These Justices will remain cyphers and will be remembered, if at all, only by their grandchildren.

Hopefully, all this is now behind us. In the history of the Supreme Court in Pakistan no event will have more far-reaching consequences than the judgment delivered by the Supreme Court in the Judges Case on 20 March 1996 which, I am sure, future historians will describe as the Constitutional Revolution of 1996 in Pakistan. When the history of the Supreme Court comes to be written, it may well be divided into two fundamental periods, pre- and post-1996. Henceforth, consultation with the Chief Justice of Pakistan and the Chief Justice of the High Court concerned in the matter of appointment of judges has to be effective, meaningful, purposive, consensus-oriented, leaving no room for complaint of arbitrariness or unfair play. The opinion of the Chief Justice of Pakistan and the Chief Justice of the High Court as to the fitness and suitability of a candidate for judgeship will be accepted in the absence of very sound reasons to be recorded by the President/ Executive; and if the President/Executive appoints a candidate found to be unfit and unsuitable for judgeship by the Chief Justice of Pakistan and the Chief Justice of the High Court concerned, it will not be a proper exercise of power under the relevant article of the Constitution. And finally, appointment of a sitting Chief Justice of a High Court or a Judge thereof in the Federal Shariat Court without his consent will be violative of Article 209 of the Constitution.

This historic judgment, reminiscent of Franklin Roosevelt's proposal to pack the US Supreme Court in 1937, will make the arbitrary appointment of inexperienced, ill-trained, ill-qualified persons of doubtful integrity and party loyalists to the Supreme Court almost impossible. The year 1996 therefore marks a major divide in the Constitutional jurisprudence of Pakistan and in the decisional philosophy of the Supreme Court. The Constitutional Revolution of 1996 will fundamentally alter the character of the Court's business, the nature of its decisions and will help restore public confidence in its independence and objectivity. On 20 March 1996, the relationship amongst the three pillars of the state shifted dramatically. An era of deference by the Supreme Court to the Executive gave way to judicial independence, if not judicial supremacy. A line has been drawn in our judicial history. The Supreme Court on that day underwent a major transformation and will never be the same again. It had altered its views on a major constitutional issue and it had done so because it had been baptized in the waters of public opinion. After years of subservience, it is on its feet and holding its head high. On 20 March 1996, the Supreme Court of Pakistan was reborn.

What a change from the days when a judge had to lobby in order to be elevated to the highest judicial appointment; volunteer assurances of good behaviour; praise the appointing authority to the skies; seek directions from *le pouvoir occulte*; and demean the Court by shifting with political winds!

'During the pendency of the judges' case, the house of the Chief Justice's daughter was raided and his civil servant son-in-law Syed Pervaiz Ali Shah was suspended. After the short order was handed down, the CJ's crested Karachi car was hijacked, its driver thrown down on to the road and told that the toughs knew whose car it was and that the owner would be equally drastically dealt with. The CJ's telephones have been tapped, his offices and houses bugged. The government went to great lengths to try to have him de-notified by the competent authority. Later, death threats were delivered.

'One former Judge has already been killed. That vociferous supporter of the independence of judiciary (together with his son) was shot down in broad daylight in Karachi outside his home . . . Nasir Aslam Zahid, Chief Justice of the High Court Sindh in 1994 was punished and sent to the Federal Shariat Court . . . Justice Fazal Elahi of Supreme Court, who sat on the bench hearing the judges' case, was another victim. His son, a civil servant in NWFP suddenly found himself transferred to Booni, an outpost in Mastuj District of Chitral. The harassment continues.'[8]

In a detailed judgment on petitions challenging the validity of the now repealed Eighth Amendment, a seven member bench of the Supreme Court said, 'It is open to the parliament to make amendments to the constitution of any provision of the Eighth Amendment as contemplated under article 239 as long as basic characteristics of federalism, parliamentary democracy and Islamic provisions as envisaged in the Objectives Resolution/Preamble to the Constitution of 1973, which now stands as a substantive part of the constitution, in the shape of article 2-A are not touched.' The Supreme Court observed that article 58(2)(b) had not tilted the balance of power in favour of the indirectly elected President. The Court observed that much has been said against article 58(2)(b), that it had changed the shape of the constitution from Parliamentary to Presidential, and had concentrated powers in the hands of the President, who was not directly elected as was the Prime Minister. 'Perusal of the constitution, as it is shows that it is not so and the apprehension is unfounded', the Court held. 'The Court further observed "that there was nothing unusual about it [Article 58(2)(b)] — and such provisions enabling the President to exercise such powers could be found in various parliamentary constitutions like in Australia, Italy, India, France and Portugal. In fact article 58(2)(b) has shut the door on Martial Law for ever, which has not visited us after 1977, the Court observed."'

The Court further observed that the Eighth Amendment was brought by a Parliament elected on a non-party basis, but three Parliaments elected on party basis, 'did not touch the Eighth Amendment showing that they had acquiesced to the Eighth Amendment which amount to ratification by implication.'

Now that the Eighth Amendment has been repealed and the President stripped of all powers, the only institution left to safeguard the citizen's civil liberties and check the arbitrariness of the executive is the Supreme Court.

When the history of our benighted times comes to be written, it will be noted that the Supreme Court 'reborn' was the one institution which served the nation most meritoriously in its hour of need. If freedom under law survives in Pakistan, it will be only because of the sturdy independence of the Supreme Court. In the words of Palkhivala, so long as there is a judiciary marked by rugged independence, the citizen's civil liberties are safe even in the absence of cast iron guarantees in Constitution. But once the judiciary becomes subservient to the Executive and to the philosophy of the party for the time being in power, no enumeration of fundamental rights in the Constitution can be of any avail to the citizen, because the courts of justice would then be replaced by government courts. The lesson of history is that when the dykes of law and justice break, revolutions begin.

Chapter 15

Fifty years of independence

> The best lack all conviction while the worst are full of
> passionate intensity.
> **Yeats**

As early as 3 June 1948, Professor Daniel Schuemann, an expert
in International Politics, said in a lecture in New York:

> The State of Pakistan [which] recently came into being in South-East
> Asia, is a State manifest with enormous pitfalls unique to itself. Its
> existence is vulnerable as time will show. In less than half a century,
> the State will collapse because of the people who are born with chains
> of slavery, whose thoughts cannot see love of a free country and whose
> minds cannot function beyond the scope of personal selfish ends —
> I know their insides.

Pakistan today faces its moment of truth. There seems to be a crisis
of public confidence in the country's future and in the institutions
that constitute its political apparatus. Ostensibly, we have representative democracy, with Assemblies, political parties, Cabinets, a
free Press, and the other symbols of democracy. But all these play
no role in determining policy decisions and have (for all practical
purposes) become irrelevant. The shadow military state lurking
behind a corrupt civilian facade is not what Mr Jinnah envisaged
for the country. As Maleeha Lodhi has observed, 'How meaning-

ful is our democratic order, replete with Parliaments, Cabinets, and political parties when real decisions are made elsewhere?' Today, parliamentary membership is the key to material success and a passport and licence to loot and plunder. No wonder the parliament has never served as a check on the arbitrariness of the executive. We are the most corrupt country in the world after Nigeria. The economy is in a mess. According to one report, Rs 123 billion are stuck up in unpaid loans.

Some men in other countries change their party for the sake of their principles; others change their principles for the sake of their party. In Pakistan, no one changes their party for the sake of their principles, nor does anyone change their principles for the sake of their party. Here, they all change their parties and their principles, if they have any, for the sake of base self interest. They call it 'lotacracy' and they have developed it into an ideology the appeal of which is irresistible and which constitutes the greatest challenge to the political party system and the entire democratic structure.

One of the best legacies of the British was the rule of law which formed the basis of Jinnah's Pakistan. But this concept disappeared soon after Jinnah's death. Our past rulers, like their present successors, did not really believe in the rule of law. It is a concept foreign to their ways of thinking. The political will to enforce the rule of law is not there. As Justice Abdul Majid Tiwana of the Lahore High Court has observed, 'Unfortunately our judicial system has come to such a pass that none belonging to a privileged class can be asked by anyone in the country to account for his acts, however unlawful and reckless they may be . . . This is so because the system is meant to punish the less fortunate, the weaker and the helpless, and it cannot even ask, much less punish the wealthy, the powerful and the influential'. Given the present political and socio-economic set-up, the country will never be governed by the rule of law.

Pakistan today presents an image of a country plagued by political, ethnic, and sectarian divisions. Never before has public faith in the country's future sunk so low. There is widespread and growing cynicism among the people. The country as a whole appears to be adrift, lacking confidence about its future. There is no leader able to prepare the country for the twenty-first century. Nobody knows where the country is headed without effective leadership to guide or direct it — and few seem to care.

A friend of mine in Karachi told me: 'I die twice a day, when I leave my flat and when I come back. Otherwise, I go about my business as usual. At any rate, terrorists or no terrorists, this is the only country I have. We do not have a spare country. Fear is in the heart but life goes on'.

It appears as if we are on a phantom train that is gathering momentum and we cannot get off.

God seems to have turned his face away from our country. An historical parallel is to be found in the period of discord in India on the eve of Timur's invasion when men also said that God was angry with the people of Hindustan and the saints were asleep. This is not the country I opted for in the Referendum held in my home province of the NWFP in 1947, and this is not the country I would like to die in. I badly want a Pakistan to defend, a nation I can belong to, fight for, and die for.

These days our country is collapsing into itself. Our people are defenceless against the scourge of rampant corruption at the highest levels. Crime threatens to strangle our country. The extent of criminal activity and corruption, the depth of despair and cynicism among the Pakistani population is immeasurable. People have lost faith in the administrative system, perverted by prolonged politicization. The compulsion to please political parties rather than perform their duty to the State has eroded the authority of the entire administrative system.

Fifty years of independence should be an occasion for celebration but there is little to cheer today. Pakistan today is a land of opportunities for corrupt, unscrupulous, unprincipled politicians, corrupt and dishonest civil servants, smugglers and tax evaders who have bank accounts, luxurious villas, mansions, and apartments in the West. A great divide, a yawning chasm — some call it a new Iron Curtain — separates them from their less fortunate countrymen, whose life is 'nasty, brutish and short'. Because these people can escape from Pakistan's misery, they are different from their countrymen. They have a stake in the *status quo* or system as they call it, and therefore impede the birth of a new order in Pakistan. While life at the top gets cushier, millions of jobless people and those at the bottom of the social ladder are forced to resort to crime, drugs, and vagrancy merely to survive. Many of them are fleeing the country and desperately trying to escape to the false paradises of the Middle East and the West. The rich are getting richer, while the poor are sinking deeper into an abyss of inequality. The middle classes seem defeated. There was a time when they were the key to prosperity and national stability. Now they appear submissive in the face of a drastic drop in the quality of their lives. Passive resignation could lead to bitter resentment and that could end in a new social crisis and dangerous confrontation which could create a menacing storm front and suddenly bring a tempest. If the government does not control inflation and stabilize the balance of payments; if mismanagement of the economy continues and the downward slide is not arrested, a grave economic and financial crisis leading to social chaos and upheaval may soon engulf the country.

In consequence of a bloody civil war, we lost half the country in 1971, which reminds me of the melancholy lines of Jorge Luis Borges, 'Once we had a country. Do you remember? And we have lost it.' Mr Jinnah visualized a great future for Karachi, but today it does not have even an elected corporation to manage its civic affairs. A variety of forces seem to be shaking the country to its very foundations. More and more people are losing faith in the country's future.

Fifty years after its creation, Pakistan's quest for a stable political order remains elusive. Since 1947, Pakistan has been racked by instability and has been subject to recurrent cycles of army rule, turmoil, and divisiveness.

What the country needs is not the dismissal of one corrupt government and its replacement by another, not a mere cosmetic change, but a purifying and cleansing operation to purge the country of all corrupt elements and robber barons, followed by urgent structural changes, institutional reforms, and measures to revive lost faith in democratic institutions and the rule of law. Without this, Pakistan will continue to lurch from crisis to crisis, lacking direction, the will, and the means to meet the enormous challenges ahead.

One of the lessons of our turbulent political history is that when people feel cheated or betrayed by their elected representatives, and resort to agitation, the generals are always there to intervene as final arbiters of the country's political destiny. It is an ironic fact in the history of Pakistan that each time martial law has been imposed, it has — initially at least — been welcomed by the people, mainly because of public outrage against corrupt, inefficient, and unpopular political regimes. Our history can be summed up in one sentence. It is 'the sound of heavy boots coming up the stairs and the rustle of satin slippers coming down'. Will it ever be possible for Pakistan to break out of this vicious cycle of corrupt political governments followed by military regimes, with no radical socio-economic agenda? It is not that there are no other alternatives: the question is whether Pakistan has the capability to grasp one. As we celebrate fifty years of independence, the question that arises is whether this government, like its predecessors, is going to bow to the reality of Pakistan's political life that has remained unchanged since the death of Liaquat Ali Khan: in all important questions the military makes key decisions and the government follows. Is the Nawaz government going to formulate a new tryst with destiny and break new ground by asserting the supremacy of the civilian government?

Chapter 16

Reflections

The soil of common life was at that time
Too hot to tread upon; oft said I then, and not then
only, what a mockery this
Of history; the past and that to come!
Now do I feel how I have been deceived.
Reading of Nations and their works, in faith,
Faith given to vanity and emptiness
Oh! Laughter for the Page that would reflect
To future times the face of what now is!
William Wordsworth

A people that has lost faith in its rulers is lost indeed.
Confucius

Recalling in late middle age what the French Revolution had meant
to his generation, Robert Southey wrote that few persons but those
who had been young at the time could comprehend how the Revolution had opened a visionary world: 'Old things seemed passing
away, and nothing was dreamt of but the regeneration of the human race. Revolutionary France, for the Radical British young held
all their wishes and expectations.'

I was born in slavery. On 14 August 1947, I was a free man, a
proud citizen of a free, independent, and sovereign country which
I could call my own, a country I could live for and die for. I was

young — twenty-four to be precise — full of *joie de vivre*, idealism, hope, and ambition. For me and, like me, for all those who belonged to my generation, Pakistan symbolized all our wishes and expectations. We all shared a seemingly unassailable certainty. We believed in Pakistan. To quote Wordsworth: 'Bliss was it in that dawn to be alive. But to be young was very heaven'.

On that day, we dreamed of a shining city on the hill and the distant bright stars. Today, it is a nightmare of corruption, crime, and despair. Is it any wonder that so few believe in the Pakistan dream today? We thought in those days that we had found freedom, but it has turned out to be just another kind of slavery. As we look back at all the squandered decades, it is sad to think that for Pakistan, it has been a period of unrelieved decline and the dream has turned sour. Once we were the envy of the developing world. That is now the stuff of nostalgia. We seem exhausted, rudderless, disoriented. Our great dreams have given way to a corrosive apprehension, fear, uncertainty, and frustration. The corrupt at the top are doing breathtakingly well and they never had it so good. But the large mass in the middle is struggling hard just to keep its head above water. Those at the bottom are falling out of sight. Ayub, Yahya, Bhutto, and Zia, all powerful heads of state and government, left behind a splintered, ruined country, torn by conflict, hijacked by thugs and robber barons, and in doubt about its future. Each of them started with a blank cheque of goodwill and popular enthusiasm given to him by the people of Pakistan, and each of them ended with a bankruptcy of moral and political support, leaving the country in worse condition than he found it in. A perfectly good country has become the laughing stock of the world.

'All the great leaders have had one characteristic in common. It was the willingness to confront unequivocally the major anxieties of the people in their time. This, and not much else, is the essence of leadership.'[1] The issue Gandhi and Nehru confronted was the independence of India. Jinnah confronted the question of the future of Muslims in an independent subcontinent. Martin Luther King confronted the question of justice and equality for his people. Each one of them committed all his energies to the major anxieties of the people in his time. Few Pakistanis would disagree that, except Mr Jinnah, no political leader in Pakistan confronted the major anxiety of the people. Our leaders have in common a lack of commitment to the country and indifference to the concerns of the people, their poverty, their economic miseries, problems of health, education, law and order, protection of their life and property, etc. Unfortunately, this is not all they have in common: barring a few exceptions, they are all committed to robbing the public. They want to amass unlimited wealth at public expense.

'We turn now to how the rich were singled out for their success', wrote John Kenneth Galbraith. 'In America nothing in the last century and nothing so far in this century, so altered the fortunes of so many people so suddenly as the American or Canadian railroad. The contractors who built it, those whose real estate was in the path, those who owned it, those who shipped by it and those who looted it, could all get rich, some of them in a week. The railroads got built. A great many honest men bent their efforts to their construction and operation. But the business also attracted a legion of rascals. The latter were by far the best known, and they may well have been the most successful in enriching themselves. Spencer's natural selection operated excellently on behalf of scoundrels. Sometimes it tested one set against another.'[2]

In Pakistan, nothing has so altered the fortunes of so many people so suddenly as political power. Here money and power seek each other. The business of politics now attracts the scum of the community and a legion of scoundrels. In the name of democracy, unspeakable sins are committed. These practitioners of the art of grand larceny, loot, and plunder in broad daylight, with no fear of accountability, reminiscent of the situation in the early nineteenth century in India when highway robbers, professional dacoits, and assassins or thugs as they were called, travelled in gangs in the darkness of the night throughout India and when a favourable opportunity occurred, strangled unsuspecting wayfarers by throwing a handkerchief or noose round their neck and then plundered and buried them. The country was rid of this evil only when Captain Sleeman hanged over four hundred members of this Confederacy of robbers. The people of Hindustan heaved a sigh of relief and welcomed the Raj. What is distressing is that the present predation is acquiring an aspect of high respectability and great social distinction.

Every now and then, with a twinkle in her eyes and a mischievous smile, Benazir reminds me what a poor judge of character I have been and how I misjudged some of the key persons in the sordid drama which led to her restoration to power. I concede with painful candour, a feeling of guilt, and a heavy heart that events have proved her right and hindsight proves me wrong, although I believed I was doing the right thing. One lives and learns.

My greatest misjudgement was of Benazir herself. Nature had given her a distinct advantage over all other rulers of Pakistan. 'Sir,' says Samuel Johnson, 'Nature has given woman so much power that the Law cannot afford to give her more.' But with all her glamour, western education, natural and inherited advantages, and awesome powers, Benazir turned out to be a great disappointment as a prime minister. Instead of tackling seriously the country's deep-rooted economic difficulties and addressing other major problems of the people, she tried to escape from these problems and took off, as often as she could, with a plane-load of sycophants for distant lands of little or no interest to Pakistan, at great public expense. There is no evidence that such expensive and lavish peregrinations have given her any new or deeper vision of Pakistan's problems. When the history of her tenure comes to be written — the contours of historical judgement are already emerging — the second Benazir government will be remembered for destroying financial institutions, rampant corruption, loot and plunder, widespread lawlessness, political vindictiveness, and, last but not least, senseless confrontation with the superior judiciary and the President. *Qui deus vult perdere, prius dementat* (Whom the gods would destroy, first they make mad.) We are seeing the proverb justifying itself in the case of Benazir's political doom. When I congratulated her on re-entering the Prime Minister's House, I did not have very high hopes of her but I never realized that her performance would be so poor and she would be such a disaster. Other leaders in Pakistan had only one term in which to govern, but Benazir had the good fortune to receive a second opportunity, and history will not forgive her for frittering away this unique gift. As Talleyrand said of the Bourbon kings, 'They have forgotten nothing and they have learned nothing'. Like the Bourbons, Benazir learned nothing from her first disastrous stint in office, and her second regime has proved to be an even greater catastrophe, perhaps the worst in our history. Despite her ostentatious meanderings all over the world, her only international achievement for Pakistan appears to be its recognition as the most corrupt state in Asia.

'Arrogance of pharaonic proportions is leading her toward political doom', *The Asian Wall Street Journal* editorialized on 23

September 1996 on the death of her brother, Mir Murtaza Bhutto, slain in a police encounter in Karachi. 'Faced with a temporarily united opposition, reluctant IMF lenders and assessments at home and abroad putting Pakistan at the top of the world's most corrupt nations lists, any other leader would be trying to mend her ways. Instead, Ms. Bhutto continues to blame everyone but herself for Pakistan's woes. She recently appointed her husband — dubbed "Mr Ten Percent" by a Pakistani public, that fairly or not sees him as a symbol of corruption — as minister for investments . . . Today, as Ms. Bhutto mourns the death of her estranged brother, many Pakistanis will be asking themselves for the millionth time just how many more blows their battered country can take and what might be the consequences of a total breakdown of social and political order'.

Does a state so shamelessly plundered by a succession of rulers have any legitimate claim on the loyalty of its citizenry? No wonder the social contract between the rulers and the ruled has collapsed and we are back to the state of nature, 'red in tooth and claw'. 'The prudent will,' as the Bible says, 'keep silent in such a time, for it is an evil time'. The better sort of the nation are, therefore, silent, the scum come to the top and rule. Was it not Edmund Burke who said that all that is necessary for the triumph of evil is that the good men do nothing. The state of things has been so insufferable that one longs for it to be decided, as it must be now, one way or another. We have lost the twentieth century. Are we bent on seeing our children also lose the twenty-first? Nothing is so unworthy of a nation as allowing itself to be governed by a gang who loot and plunder. Somewhere in a Raymond Carver story, a character asks: 'We started out such good people. What happened to us?' 'To sin by silence, when we should protest makes cowards of men'. Pastor Martin Niemoeller who was sent to Dachau for resisting the Nazis summed up in his memorable words the plight of people like us who for one reason or another do not speak up. 'They came first for communists, and I didn't speak up because I wasn't a communist. Then they came for the Jews, and I didn't speak up because I wasn't a Jew. Then they came for the trade unionists and I didn't speak up because I wasn't a trade unionist. Then they came for the Catholics and I didn't speak up because I was a Protestant. Then they came for me, and by that time no one was left to speak up.'

Tzu-Chang asked Confucius about government. The Master said: 'The requisites of Government are that there be sufficiency of food, sufficiency of military equipment and the confidence of the people in their rulers'. Tzu-Chang said: 'If it cannot be helped and one of those must be dispensed with, which of the three should be foregone first?'. 'The military equipment', said the Master. Tzu-Chang again asked, 'If it cannot be helped and one of the remaining two must be dispensed with, which then should be foregone?' The Master answered, 'Part with the food. From of old, death has been the lot of all men, but a people that has lost faith in their rulers is lost indeed.'[3] We lost faith in our rulers long ago. Now we have also lost faith in our future and are in danger of losing faith in ourselves. What are we to tell our impressionable youth? Who can assure them that somebody in this country has clean hands? If prime ministers, parliamentarians, holders of public office, senior civil servants, in fact all our rulers, are begrimed with corruption, where do the young turn for inspiration? What is left of the integrity of our political and judicial systems?

One of the lessons of history is that when people lose faith in their rulers, when they lose faith in the sanctity of the ballot box, when elections are rigged and votes are purchased; when judges try to match their constitutional ideas to the exigencies of current politics and shift with political winds; when the judiciary functions at the behest of authority and allows itself to be used against the citizens; when the gap between the rulers and the ruled widens; when there are no ways for people to express political preferences from time to time in an atmosphere free from fear, coercion, or intimidation; when known corrupt people, tax evaders, and smugglers are foisted upon a poor, illiterate electorate unable to make an informed political choice, and then sworn in as Ministers; when elections throw up not the best, not the noblest, not the fittest, not the most deserving but the scum of the community, and a legion of scoundrels only because they are the richest, as is the case in Pakistan today; when hunger and anger come together as happened in March-April 1997, as bread riots erupted in many parts of the country; people, sooner or later, come out on to the streets and demonstrate Lenin's maxim that in such situations, voting with citizens' feet is more effective than voting in elections.

'Technically, the Mughal empire declined because it became increasingly difficult to maintain itself against the Marathas in the South, the Afghans in the North and finally the East India

Company. In reality, the causes of its decay were much more internal than external.'[4] If Pakistan were to decline, it will not be because it could not maintain itself against the resurging power of India. The judgement of history would be that the causes of its decay were, as in the case of the Mughal or the Ottoman empires much more internal than external. The history of the rise and fall of empires shows that no country and no empire disappears overnight. The process of decay starts much earlier. Describing the last years of the Kingdom of Delhi (1782–1803), Percival Spear wrote: 'The symptoms of social collapse are progressive declines in standards of conduct, public and private, and the superiority of centrifugal over centripetal forces. When respect for law and authority declines, the devil of force leaps into its place as the only possible substitute, and in the struggles that ensue every standard of conduct and decency is progressively discarded. Men begin by being realists and end by being satanists. Sometimes synthesis takes place from within, sometimes it is imposed from without. If the original breakdown of authority is caused by a ferment of ideas, a genuine revolution like the French may result. If it is simply due to the decrepitude of authority, the solution is the substitution of fresh authority, but whether the substitute is external or internal depends upon local circumstances.'[5] There are some disturbing similarities here between the last years of the Kingdom of Delhi and present-day Pakistan. Are we heading for a genuine revolution like the French or are we merely witnessing the decrepitude of authority, and its substitution by fresh authority or, what is worse, are we witnessing the twilight of Jinnah's Pakistan? Allah knoweth best.

Today we are on the verge of economic and social collapse. The irony is that it is the armed forces and the armed forces alone which are preventing the country from going into the abyss of disintegration, but the lesson of history is that by itself no army, no matter how strong, has ever rescued a country from internal disorder, social upheaval and chaos or been able to prevent its disintegration. No army was more powerful than the Red Army which in 1941 faced the full might of the German Army, nearly four million troops organized in 180 divisions, with 3350 tanks, 7200 guns, supported by 2000 aircraft, which it destroyed and chased all the way to Berlin; but this mighty army could not prevent the demise of the Soviet Union, a superpower not too long ago, which has now become the laughing stock of the world.

Epilogue

صُبح آزادی

اگست ۱۹۴۷ء

یہ داغ داغ اُجالا یہ شب گزیدہ سحر

وہ انتظار تھا جس کا، یہ وہ سحر تو نہیں

یہ وہ سحر تو نہیں، جس کی آرزو لے کر

چلے تھے یار کہ مل جائے گی کہیں نہ کہیں

فلک کے دشت میں تاروں کی آخری منزل

کہیں تو ہوگا شبِ سست موج کا ساحل

کہیں تو جا کے رُکے گا سفینۂ غمِ دل

This leprous day-break, dawn night's fangs have mangled
This is not that long-looked-for break of day,
Not that clear dawn in quest of which those comrades
Set out, believing that in heaven's wide void
Somewhere the verge of night's slow-washing tide,
Somewhere an anchorage for the ship of heartache.

Faiz Ahmad Faiz

At 11.00 a.m. on 4 November 1996 I left my house and drove to the Presidency for a meeting with President Leghari, not suspecting that the axe was about to fall on Benazir within hours. When I entered the President's office, there was not a scrap of paper on Leghari's table and he looked quite relaxed. The President was calm and affable but, after the usual exchange of pleasantries, I could see that he was gripped with a sense of crisis. He asked me how I viewed the situation. When I told him that never before had public faith in the country's future and its rulers sunk so low and the people felt terribly angry and alienated, the President responded by saying how he had tried on several occasions to impress upon the Prime Minister the urgency of stemming the rot by taking effective action against the rampant corruption in her administration, and had repeatedly warned her that if mismanagement of the economy continued and she did not arrest the downward slide, a grave financial crisis would soon engulf the country. For over an hour, the President then dwelt on Benazir's corruption, maladministration, abdication of authority in favour of her spouse, and the sequence of events leading to the deterioration in their relations. I was stunned by this dramatic change in the situation. I had heard all this before in 1990, when I had met the then President Ghulam Ishaq Khan in the same office on the eve of Benazir's dismissal. Was history going to repeat itself? I realized that the President and the Prime Minister, Benazir Bhutto, were on a collision course and that the fateful decision to sack her and dissolve the Assembly had been taken. As I left the President's office, I knew Benazir's days were numbered and that very shortly she would once again be an ex-Prime Minister.

Around midnight on 5 November, President Farooq Ahmed Khan Leghari, long-time ally, party loyalist, and staunch supporter of Benazir, in exercise of his powers under article 58 (2) (b) of the Constitution, dissolved the National Assembly, sacked the government, sending Benazir out in the cold, and appointed 3 February 1997 as the date for general elections to the National Assembly. A ten-member caretaker cabinet headed by Malik Meraj Khalid was sworn in on 5 November 1996. The caretaker government started with a two point agenda of holding elections within ninety days, as contemplated in the Constitution, and of accountability of the corrupt among the politicians and senior bureaucrats. 'Election and accountability are the two topmost priorities of the caretaker government', declared the caretaker Prime Minister, Meraj Khalid.

On 18 November 1996, the President promulgated the Accountability Ordinance, 1996, which envisages the setting up of an Ehtesab Commission under a serving or retired judge of the Supreme Court. This Commission will investigate corruption cases referred to it by the government or a private person, or on its own motion. The case so investigated within a period not exceeding thirty days will be sent to the High Court, where it will be tried by a bench consisting of three members; the High Court will finalize it within sixty days. Appeal against the verdict will lie before the Supreme Court. The penalties under the ordinance include seven years in prison, dismissal from service in case of government employees, and disqualification for five years for public representatives.

The new ordinance repealed the Holders of Representative Offices (Punishment for Misconduct) Order, 1977 (PPO 16 of 1977) and the Parliament and Provincial Assemblies (Disqualification for Membership) Order, 1977 (PPO 17 of 1977). It is significant that while the offence of misconduct mentioned in the repealed orders has been substituted by the offence of corruption and corrupt practices, the new ordinance does not cover jobbery, favouritism, nepotism, wilful maladministration, and abuse of whatsoever kind of power or position — offences which were covered by the definition of the offence of misconduct in PPO 17 of 1977. It appears that a holder of public office commits no offence under the new law even if he is found guilty of jobbery, favouritism, nepotism, wilful maladministration, or any other abuse of power or position and cannot, therefore, be disqualified. Is it a deliberate omission, intended to protect corrupt politicians and make disqualification of holders of public office almost impossible because under the new law they can be disqualified and sent to prison only if they are found guilty of the offence of corruption or corrupt practices, which, experience has shown, is well nigh impossible under the existing judicial system?

Six weeks after the dismissal of Benazir's government, the caretaker administration appointed to carry out accountability of corrupt politicians has acknowledged that the effort has been largely unrewarding. The new government has publicly stated that it has not been able to gather enough evidence to act against top politicians, including Ms Bhutto, her husband Asif Zardari, and the former Prime Minister Nawaz Sharif. I find this difficult to believe. Either they were not trying hard enough or, what is more likely, a political decision had been taken not to proceed against the mainstream political leaders. Be that as it may, the admission of Prime Minister Malik Meraj Khalid appears to mean that known corrupt people are being foisted upon our poor illiterate electorate and the general elections scheduled for 3 February 1997 will once again be a contest between two sets of corrupt politicians, representing Ms Bhutto's People's Party and the Pakistan Muslim League led by Nawaz Sharif. Many Pakistanis were hoping that both Ms Bhutto and Nawaz Sharif and a large number of their corrupt party men would be disqualified on grounds of corruption from participating in the elections. Instead, the Caretaker Prime Minister is telling the people that it is up to the voters to punish corrupt politicians by denying them re-election. The Prime Minister's admission of failure has provoked a wave of anger and bitter criticism. Many people who had welcomed the Bhutto government's dismissal now feel cheated and are saying that if there was not enough evidence to act against her, why was her government dismissed and the National Assembly dissolved and why had the government squandered an opportunity to set a new course? President Farooq Leghari's credibility has plunged to rock-bottom and he is being held responsible for not initiating action against known corrupt politicians. Is it because it is not in his political interest, now that Benazir has been dislodged from power, to press ahead with his accountability agenda against either of the two mainstream political leaders, and is this the price he had to pay to end his political isolation ? While Leghari has lost the high moral ground he once occupied, the real loser is the country because the same old crooks responsible for bankrupting it are sure to be returned with a fresh 'mandate' to resume their unfinished agenda of loot and plunder.

The formation of the Council for Development and National Security (CDNS) on 6 January 1997 'to give meaning to the role of the President as Supreme Commander of the Armed Forces' and 'to ensure that there would be no element of friction or misunderstanding between the President and the Prime Minister in future' and the surreptitious manner in which it has been constituted has caused a great deal of confusion and resentment in political circles. Whatever its apologists may say, in public perception it represents an attempt to empower the President to take vital decisions having far-reaching consequences, bypassing Parliament and the Cabinet; which it is hoped will become binding on the government because of the presence of the Chiefs of Armed Forces. Subsequent events show, however, that both the President and the Prime Minister, the two civilian pillars of the State will be the losers and it is the *mature* advice of the Service Chiefs that will ultimately prevail in this power game. Whether the CDNS will survive the repeal of the Eighth Amendment remains to be seen.

On 28 January 1997, the Supreme Court upheld the dissolution order passed by President Leghari and rejected Benazir's petition seeking restoration of her government. The court upheld the validity of seven (out of nine) charges brought against her government, including those relating to corruption, extra-judicial killings in Karachi, and violation of several articles of the Constitution. A week later Benazir suffered a humiliating defeat when the Pakistan Muslim League led by Mian Nawaz Sharif scored a resounding victory beyond all expectations in the elections held on 3 February 1997. The landslide victory gave Nawaz Sharif close to a two-thirds majority in the National Assembly. His party is also firmly poised to form a two-thirds majority government in the Punjab Assembly with 211 seats, where the PPP could only get two seats. In the NWFP, the PML (N) is the largest party with 31 seats, while in the Sindh Provincial Assembly, it secured 15 seats. Benazir has been swept out of sight in the Punjab. She has taken a beating in the NWFP and is badly bruised in her home province of Sindh. Benazir, diminished leader of a diminished party, is licking her wounds, not knowing what has hit her. The Mandate of Heaven has passed from her to Nawaz Sharif. The hour of Nawaz Sharif has dawned. It is a solemn moment for him for, as Churchill said, 'With primacy in power is also joined an awe-inspiring accountability for the future'.

Armed with such a massive mandate, Nawaz Sharif should have no problem in forming a strong, stable, and secure government. He can now make or unmake any law. He can even amend the Constitution. Unfortunately, in politics two and two do not always make four, and a massive mandate, as the tragic fate of Bhutto and Mujib, two of our most powerful and charismatic leaders demonstrated, does not necessarily produce positive results. 'Power for the sake of lording it over fellow creatures or adding to personal pomp', according to Churchill, 'is rightly judged base but power in national crisis when a man believes what orders should be given is a blessing'. Nawaz Sharif and his coalition partners had a two-thirds majority in 1990, but, in no time, he developed

serious problems, including unnecessary confrontation first with
the Chief of Army Staff and later with the President, which led to
his dismissal, restoration, and subsequent resignation.

Benazir had been in the wilderness before, but had staged a
come-back, although her pilgrimage from the wilderness to the
centre of the arena had, as subsequent events demonstrated, not
been a very humbling experience for her. Will the sun of her good
fortune rise upon her again or has she lost the Mandate of Heaven
forever and is she through as a political force and has the time
come to write her political obituary? Over the past two years,
corruption, mismanagement, and cronyism had reached unprecedented proportions, and rendered the Benazir government
perhaps the most unpopular in Pakistan history. Public perception
was reinforced in this belief by external events such as the Berlin-
based Transparency International's designation of the government
of Pakistan as the most corrupt in Asia, and by the crisis in Pakistan's relations with the World Bank and the IMF. But perhaps
the most debilitating blow to Benazir's administration was the
murder of her brother and political opponent, Mir Murtaza Bhutto,
by the police force which was under the authority and control of
the Prime Minister. The circumstances and the site of the shoot-
ing, within yards of 70 Clifton — the ancestral family residence,
the home of Zulfikar Ali Bhutto, and a veritable PPP shrine —
added intense poignancy to the act. Public outrage, especially in
Benazir's home province of Sindh, was so great, and suspicion
against her husband Asif Zardari so pronounced, that Benazir was
prevented from being present at the burial of her own brother.
For many observers, this was yet again a stark manifestation of the
dark tragedy that has haunted the Bhutto family. Which Czarina
was going to die this time to bring about a change in her fortunes?
This time the stakes were high and, to add to the multiplicity of
her problems, especially the murder charge against her spouse,
she faced a serious challenge to her political life in her home
province of Sindh from Ghinwa Bhutto, her sister-in-law, widow
of her slain brother, Mir Murtaza Bhutto.

With the repeal of Article 58(2)(b) of the Eighth Amendment,
which is the source of the President's power of dissolving the
National Assembly and appointment of service chiefs, the
President has been defanged, stripped of all powers, and effectively neutralized. He will no longer be a threat to the parliament,
even though he has fortified himself with the help of the Council

for Defence and National Security (CDNS). Nawaz Sharif has undoubtedly scored a major victory, hailed as a political revolution and a defining moment in our history; but the struggle for restoring parliamentary supremacy is not yet over. In fact, it has just begun because ultimate power in Pakistan — that is, highest power over citizens, unrestrained by law — continues to reside where the coercive power resides. Its power to abrogate the Constitution, dissolve the Parliament, and sack elected governments with impunity is not affected by the repeal of 58(2)(b). The sword of martial law will continue to hang over all our democratic institutions as has been the case throughout our troubled political history and *le pouvoir* will continue to play its traditional role of a 'referee' with a strong whistle, in the political power game in Pakistan. Nawaz Sharif's biggest challenge in the days ahead, therefore, will be managing relations with *le pouvoir*, the political sovereign, because it is their will which is ultimately obeyed by the citizens.

Predictably, public euphoria following the dissolution of National Assembly, the dismissal of the Benazir government, and its replacement by another elected government has given way to the sobriety of the morning after. Unrealistically high expectations were awakened during the February 1997 election campaign, and when these expectations were disappointed and remained unfulfilled, frustration set in. No wonder the voters are once again disillusioned with politics and politicians and thus with the entire democratic process. With the IMF breathing down his neck and *le pouvoir occulte* too close for comfort, watching every step he takes, Nawaz Sharif with all his parliamentary strength, consisting mostly of feudal landlords and capitalists has little chance of making Pakistan a world tiger as he had promised during the election campaign. The irony is that the people who gave him the Mandate of Heaven also deprived him of all excuses and expect him to make good on his promises. He is held hostage by his campaign promises, and is now the centre of all expectations. Woe to him if the daunting problems staring him in the face do not fade away and the dark clouds do not roll back.

'The new government', says the *New York Times*, 'will be tightly constrained by the armed forces, which retained decisive behind-the-scenes influence even after surrendering power to civilian governments nearly a decade ago. People have little confidence in Mr Nawaz Sharif's promises and abilities and doubt that the new government, even with its parliamentary strength, will succeed where its predecessors failed in curbing drug trafficking, gun culture that has made a mockery of the police and the courts, and corruption that has virtually bankrupted the government'.

It is an ironical fact that in the history of Pakistan no central government, whatever its mandate, has ever lost power on the floor of the house in consequence of a vote of no-confidence brought against it. It is a unique feature of our stunted, pallid democracy that parliamentary strength does not guarantee the stability or survival of government, and loss of power is invariably brought about by extraneous forces. In a discussion on Pakistan's future at a meeting recently held in Washington, Assistant Secretary of State, Robin Raphel, expressed the opinion that the legislature in Pakistan was not working because it really did not have the power to remove the government. 'The power clearly,' said Raphel, 'rested somewhere else' (*Dawn*, 1 March 1997). It would, therefore, come as no surprise if in spite of the Mandate of Heaven — or perhaps because of it — Nawaz Sharif's 'tryst with destiny ends up in a puff of smoke' as *The Friday Times* editorialized.

The recent of history of China, South Korea, Taiwan, and other Asian Tigers has shown that it is not possible to generate economic growth and cross the poverty line in an impoverished country without enlightened 'authoritarianism' and that only a strong hand can steer a poor country out of economic misery and chaos. Our own experience, on the other hand, has made it abundantly clear that without broad-based economic development, elimination of poverty, eradication of illiteracy, structural socio-economic reforms, and ruthless accountability, ballot-box democracy has no chance of survival, even with well-intentioned leaders, in any developing country. Talking about ballot-box democracy, Stalin used to say, 'It doesn't matter who votes or how many vote. What matters is who does the counting'. Many people in our part of the world have, therefore, great difficulty with the doctrinaire American approach to the promotion of American democratic ideals and what is called 'la pensee unique' — that is, the American-rooted ideology, holding that democracy is good for mankind everywhere at all times and under all circumstances because it is good for America. While this may understandably seem apparent to most Americans, the American experience hardly covers all social and economic scenarios worldwide, and thus extrapolating it to all other situations is both naive and hazardous.

It is not suggested that we in Pakistan are predisposed to live under an authoritarian government or that it is encoded in our genes or embedded in our Islamic culture as Huntington would have us believe; or that we are otherwise unsuited to democracy. All I am saying is that the obstacles to democracy, and they are quite a few, must be removed first and the terrain made more hospitable for the evolution of a civil society. In Taiwan and South Korea, democracy sprouted when per capita income reached about US$ 6000. China is likely to surpass this level by the year 2015 and, as Henry S. Rowen predicts, around that date, we are likely to see the emergence of democracy in China. If, therefore, it is correct that development engenders democracy, we in Pakistan have to attain a certain minimum level of development first and then wait for a critical mass to accumulate, a critical mass of people with democratic principles, a high quality of leadership, and a democratic culture, before we can hope to have a genuine democratic government. There is no other choice if we want to stop Pakistan from swinging between fake democracy and naked dictatorship, going from one extreme to the other as has been the case throughout the troubled history of our country.

Whatever be the ultimate shape of things, today Pakistan is hungry for a person who will light a candle in the gloom of our morale; who has a passion burning within him that will set our nation alight; who will be the standard-bearer of the disenchanted; who can give voice to our humiliation; who helps the nation recover its *elan vital*; who places country above self; who restores the process of national revival; who gives the country a new agenda, one that does not replace one set of corrupt leaders by another; who offers the genuine hope of a new order to take us into a new millennium; who stitches the country back together; whose heart is in the right place; whose hands are clean and will remain clean; who restores the rule of law; who protects the citizen's honour, person, and property; a crusader against high-level corruption, who will purge the country of all corrupt elements, politicians, bureaucrats, both civil and military; who will bring the guilty, those who stole the Pakistan dream, to justice; who will bring back a sense of decency; who will raise the people from the slough of despondency; who will restore the people's faith in themselves, their rulers, and, above all, in their country; who will, as Burke said, 'tell the people not where they want to go but where they ought to go'; who will, as Mercier said, lance the poisoned carbuncle and clean the country of its mess: an essential condition for salvaging the democratic process; and who will 'seize the moment', give the country the 'lift of a driving dream', and drag the nation to its feet again. This is, of course, asking for the impossible. But pursuing the impossible and asking for the impossible is one good definition of a revolution. We live in an age of midgets. The public stage is filled by weak-kneed triflers, mountebanks, and charlatans, begrimed with corruption. But, as Percival Spear said, when the winds blow and the rains descend and the house is about to collapse, such men vanish in a night.

Is the dark long night about to end? And has the time come for us to leave the valley of despair and climb the mountain so that we see the glory of another dawn? The darkest hour is just before the dawn and as generally happens in history, it is at the darkest hour that a bright star arises when you had almost given up hope. When a nation is in crisis, it needs a man to match the time. 'You don't create such a man, you don't discover such a man. You recognize such a man.' The times cry out for leadership. Cometh the hour, cometh the man. The hour will find the man who has the will and the power to restore the Pakistan dream. 'La verite en marche.' The truth is on the march, and nothing shall stop it, and as Margaret Mead said 'Never doubt that a small group of thoughtful, committed citizens can change the world; indeed, it is the only thing that ever has'. Addressing French cadets at St Cyr in 1921, de Gaulle said, 'Remember this lesson. History does not teach fatalism. There are moments when the Will of a handful of free men breaks through determinism and opens up new roads. People get the history that they deserve.' The longer the people allow the waters to rise, the greater the catastrophe that will follow the bursting of the dam.

Our moment of truth has arrived. To borrow the prophetic words of Dostoevsky, I 'have a presentiment of sorts that the lots are drawn and accounts may have to be settled far sooner than one might imagine in one's wildest dreams'.

> Ah Love! could you and I with fate conspire
>   To grasp this sorry Scheme of Things entire,
> Would not we shatter it to bits — and then
>   Remould it nearer to the Heart's Desire!
>
> **Omar Khayyam**

Appendix 1

Summary on the mercy petition filed on behalf of Zulfikar Ali Bhutto

Government of Pakistan
Ministry of Interior

Subject: Mercy Petition in Respect of Condemned Prisoner Zulfikar Ali Bhutto son of Sir Shah Nawaz Bhutto.

    This case relates to the mercy petitions in respect of the condemned prisoner Zulfikar Ali Bhutto son of Sir Shah Nawaz Bhutto, presently confined in District Jail, Rawalpindi.

2. On the day of incident, condemned prisoner Zulfikar Ali Bhutto was holding the office of the Prime Minister of Pakistan. A criminal conspiracy was organised by him to get Mr Ahmad Raza Kasuri, then a Member of National Assembly of Pakistan and his violent critic, assassinated through the members of the defunct Federal Security Force. The other participants in the conspiracy were Masood Mahmood, Director General, FSF, Mian Muhammad Abbas, Director, Operations and Intelligence, Ghulam Mustafa, Arshad Iqbal and Rana Iftikhar Ahmad, Inspector, Sub-Inspector and Assistant Sub-Inspector respectively, and Ghulam Hussain, Inspector of the FSF.

3. The incident took place at about 0.30 a.m. on the night between the 10th and 11th of November 1974, near Shadman-Shah Jamal roundabout in Lahore. Ahmad Raza Kasuri was returning to his house in Model

Town after attending the wedding of one Bashir Hussain Shah in Shadman Colony. He was driving his car bearing No. LEJ-9495. His father Nawab Muhammad Ahmad Khan deceased was sitting next to him, whereas his mother and her sister were occupying the rear seat of the car. As he nego-tiated the roundabout in question, less than a hundred yards from the wedding place, his car was fired upon with automatic weapons by co-ac-cused Ghulam Hussain and the condemned prisoners Arshad Iqbal and Rana Iftikhar. The headlights of the car as well as other parts of its body were hit, and so was his father. The lights of the car went off, but Ahmad Raza Kasuri managed to drive on and to take his injured father to the United Christian Hospital, where the deceased succumbed to his injuries at 2.55 a.m.

4.   The condemned prisoner and the co-accused were tried by the High Court, on its original side, for conspiracy to assassinate Ahmad Raza Kasuri and in pursuance thereof making a murderous assault on him by firing on his car on the night between the 10th and 11th of November 1974, and as a result causing the death of his father Nawab Muhammad Ahmad Khan. The condemned prisoner alongwith the co-accused Mian Muhammad Abbas, Arshad Iqbal, Rana Iftikhar Ahmad and Ghulam Mustafa have been convicted under section 120-B read with section 115 of the P.P.C. and sentence to RI for five years. The condemned prisoner and the co-accused Mian Muhammad Abbas and Ghulam Mustafa have been further convicted under section 307 read with section 109 of the P.P.C. and sentenced to undergo RI for seven years in each case; whereas the remaining two co-accused have been convicted in this behalf under section 307 read with section 34 of the P.P.C. and awarded a similar sen-tence. The condemned prisoner and the co-accused Mian Muhammad Abbas and Ghulam Mustafa have been further convicted under section 302 read with section 301, 109 and 111 of the P.P.C. and each of them has been sentenced to death. A similar penalty has been awarded to the re-maining two co-accused under section 302 read with section 301 and 34 of the P.P.C. The condemned prisoner has also been directed to pay com-pensation to the heirs of the deceased in the sum of Rs 25,000 under section 544-A of the Cr.P.C. or in default to undergo RI for a period of six months. The sentences of imprisonment have been ordered to run con-currently, and shall take effect in case the sentence of death is not carried out. Masood Mahmood and Inspector Ghulam Hussain were also included in the list of accused persons, but were later granted pardon and gave evidence at the trial as approvers.

5.   The sentences were confirmed by the Supreme Court in appeal on 6.2.1979 and were again maintained in review on 24.3.1979.

6.   No mercy petition has been submitted by the condemned prisoner himself. However, on a number of petitions from other persons, the case was considered by the Provincial Government. The Governor, Punjab has

rejected the mercy plea and submitted the case for the orders of the President.

7. Normally, factors of age, sex, mental deficiency, provocation, premeditation, absence of intention to kill, drunkenness, sufficiency of evidence, constructive liability and delay are taken into consideration while examining a mercy petition. In our view, none of the above stated guiding principle is attracted by the facts and circumstances of the instant case.

8. However, during the course of hearing of the review petition, the following submissions were made before the Supreme court by the Counsel of the condemned prisoner:-

> "In any case, even if the conviction of the petitioner is maintained in spite of the error and defects apparent in the majority judgement, it is a fit case where lesser punishment should be awarded for the offence falling u/s 302 PPC read with section 109 and 111 thereof, for the reasons that the petitioner is guilty only of abetment and was not present at the spot at the time of the murder; that the conspiracy was to kill Ahmad Raza Kasuri and not his father who was hit by accident; that the conviction of the petitioner is based on the evidence of approvers; that there has arisen a difference of opinion between the learned Judges of this Court (Supreme Court) as to the petitioner's guilt; that with the introduction of the Islamic Laws in the country with effect from the 12th of Rabi-ul-Awwal, 1399 H (i.e. the 10th of February, 1979), it would be anomalous to impose death penalty for an unintentional murder, especially when the Shariat laws do not recognise as approver, and the witnesses have to fulfil strict qualifications as to integrity and character before their testimony can be acted upon; and that the fact that the petitioner was compelled to boycott the proceedings in the trial has also bearing on the question of sentence."

9. While dismissing the review petition, the Supreme Court has made the following observations:-

> "Although we have not found it possible in law to review the sentence of death on the grounds urged by Mr Yahya Bakhtiar, yet these are relevant for consideration by the executive authorities in the exercise of their prerogative of mercy."

10. It has been contended in the mercy pleas that the observations of the Supreme Court on the quantum of sentence constitutes a recommendation for commutation of death sentence and that such recommendations have always been honoured by the executive. The contention is misconceived and erroneous. According to the guiding principles, the recommendation of the court to the executive to consider the question of commutation of death sentence is not binding and is not meant to be honoured in every case but is to be considered keeping in view the facts and circumstances of each case and even in such cases the scope of interference by the executive is of a very limited character. On the question of quantum of sentence the Supreme Court observed as under:-

"Taking now the question of sentence, I will at this stage deal with the case of appellant Zulfikar Ali Bhutto in the first instance. The facts summarised in the preceding paragraphs establish beyond any doubt that the appellant used the apparatus of Government, namely, the agency of the Federal Security Force, for a political vendetta. This was a diabolic misuse of the instruments of State power as the head of the administration. Instead of safeguarding the life and liberty of the citizens of Pakistan, he set about to destroy a political opponent by using the power of the Federal Security Force, whose Director General occupied a special position under him. Ahmad Raza Kasuri was pursued relentlessly in Islamabad and Lahore until finally his father became the victim of the conspiracy, and Ahmad Raza Kasuri miraculously escaped. The power of the Prime Minister was then used to stifle proper investigation, and later to pressurise Ahmad Raza Kasuri in rejoining the Pakistan People's Party. All these facts go to show that there are no extenuating circumstances in favour of the appellant, and the High Court was accordingly right in imposing the normal penalty sanctioned by law for the offence of murder as well as its abetment."

11. Another ground taken for clemency is that commutation of death sentence of the condemned prisoner would be in accordance with the Islamic canons of law. The question has been examined in detail by the Law Division. Their views are at annexure 'A'.

12. In view of the finding of the Supreme Court on the quantum of sentence the advice of the Law Division and our views in para 7, no case for commutation of death sentence appears to have been made out.

13. However, while examining a mercy petition, all the circumstances of the case including those which may not have been before the court, having no direct bearing on the issue of guilt of the condemned prisoner are to be taken into account. The responsibility of carrying out a death sentence is awesome and in its decisive phase full and anxious consideration to all factors of the case is to be given before taking final responsibility for so irreparable and irreversible a decision. The exercise of prerogative of mercy does not depend upon principles of strict law or justice or any well-defined rules and regulations. It is a question of policy and judgement in each case and decisions in such cases have to be arrived at after a careful balancing of conflicting considerations.

14. This is an unprecedented case which has caused deep concern at home and has generated a lot of interest abroad. The general reaction, particularly in USA and Western Europe, to the execution of the sentence would be strong and adverse and would cause aversion and do immense damage to the image of Pakistan abroad. According to the Guiding Principles "cases in which there are special or political considerations are to be dealt with on merit of each case. It may sometime be necessary to take account of public opinion and to commute the sentence in deference to a widely spread or strong local expression of public opinion lest the execution

should arouse sympathy for the murderer rather than otherwise."

15. Be that as it may, the President has unfettered powers under Article 45 of the Constitution to pass any orders he deems fit in his judgement.

16. The Minister for Interior has seen and approved the summary.

17. Submitted for orders.

Sd/-

ROEDAD KHAN

Secretary

COS to the President, CMLA's Secretariat, Rawalpindi
Ministry of Interior u.o. No. 3/19/79-Ptns, dt: 1.4.1979

18. As indicated in Para 6, the mercy petitions received by the Provincial Government have been considered by the Government of Punjab. The Governor has rejected them. In addition some petitions received by CMLA Secretariat were sent to the Ministry of Interior for consideration. These are placed with the case. The points raised in them are in most cases identical in rules and are reflected in this Summary.

19. The advice given by the Ministry of Law (Flag/A) may also be seen.

Sd/-

The President

Petition is rejected.

Sd/-

Zia-ul-Haq

Appendix 2

References filed against the former Prime Minister, Ms Benazir Bhutto

Reference 1: In the Special Court of Mr. Justice Mohammad Amir Malik

Reference by the President of the Islamic Republic of Pakistan under Article 4 of the Parliament and Provincial Assemblies (Disqualification for Membership) Order 1977 (PPO No. 17 of 1977)

Ms. Benazir Bhutto,
wife of Mr. Asif Ali Zardari,
Ex-Prime Minister of Pakistan,
Bilawal House,
Karachi.

..... RESPONDENT

The following Reference is made under Article 4 of PPO No. 17 of 1977 to the Honourable Special Court for appropriate action:

That the Respondent, Ms. Benazir Bhutto, was elected as a member of the National Assembly from Constituency No. NA-166 Larkana-III during the general election held on 16th November, 1988, under the Constitution of the Islamic Republic of Pakistan, and held the office of Prime Minister of Pakistan from 2 December, 1988 until 6 August, 1990.

2. That during her tenure as aforesaid, the Respondent committed or caused to be committed acts of misconduct within the meaning of the said PPO 17 of 1977 in that, *inter alia*.—

Concise Statement of Facts

(1) That the Intelligence Bureau of the Government of Pakistan works directly under the authority of the Prime Minister and the Director of the Intelligence Bureau reported and was responsible to the Prime Minister.

(2) That on 26 October, 1989, a resolution for a vote of no-confidence was moved in the National Assembly against the Respondent, the ex-Prime Minister of Pakistan, under the provisions of the Constitution of the Islamic Republic of Pakistan. It is also on record that the elections in Azad Kashmir were held on 21 May, 1990, and the election of the Prime Minister of Azad Kashmir was on 29 June, 1990. Earlier from April to June, 1989, there were, and continued to be, problems concerning Provincial Assembly members for the NWFP Government.

(3) The Respondent, and, under her authority, her Party members and the bureaucracy at her disposal, made every effort to win over as many members as possible of the National Assembly of Pakistan, the Legislative Assembly of Azad Kashmir for the election of the Prime Minister of Azad Kashmir, and, earlier, the NWFP Provincial Assembly, by wilful misapplication and/or diversion of public moneys, namely, in the present case Secret Service Funds, for a purpose other than that for which the same were meant and otherwise abused her power and position as Prime Minister. In any event, the said public moneys were misapplied and/or diverted and/or misconduct otherwise committed by the Respondent, in that, "The Secret Service Fund is intended only for the purpose of buying information, and for no other purpose," and the procedures laid down for the proper utilization of the SS Fund were totally disregarded. A copy of the detailed instructions regarding the administration, proper utilization and maintenance of accounts of the Secret Service Fund which provides, *inter alia*, as follows:-
"The Secret Service Fund is intended solely for the purpose of buying information, and for no other purpose. No expenditure which is legitimately debitable to 'contingencies' or any other 'head' of account must be incurred from the Fund.......
"All receipts shall be entered ....
giving details of the nature of transaction ....
"On the 'Payment' side ....
Every entry shall be clear enough to indicate the entry of payment."

(4) That the Secret Service (SS) Fund for 1988-89 was Rs 3.2 million under the budget grant for the year. However, from April 1989 to June, 1989, Supplementary Grants amounting to Rs 15.284 million were sanctioned. Of this, the sum of Rs 4.084 million was

required for intelligence operations. The remaining Rs 11.2 million was disbursed as follows:

Date	Name of Payee	Amount	Remarks
15.6.89	Chief Minister, NWFP through Mr. M. Akram	Rs 5,000,000 (Five million)	Receipt of the C.M. NWFP attached.
14.4.89	Mr. Mohibullah Shah, Addl. Secretary PM Sectt. through Maj (Retd) Masood Sharif Khan, *Ex*-Joint Director.	Rs 4,000,000 (Four million)	Copy of IB letter No. 7/Budget/81(20)81 dated 11.9.90 to Mr Masood Sharif and his reply dated 12.9.90 are attached as Annex 'E'.

(5) In the Budget for 1989-90, a sum of Rs 5.8 million was provided on account of regular Secret Service Fund for the Intelligence Bureau. In view of the political situation as aforementioned between October 1989 and June 1990. Supplementary Grants of Rs 124.3 million were made to the SS Fund as follows:

S. No.	Date	Special Grant	Amount
(i)	16.10.89	Special Grant-I	Rs 20,000,000 (Twenty million)
(ii)	26.10.89	Special Grant-II	Rs 50,000,000 (Fifty million)
(iii)	10.02.90	Special Grant-III	Rs 2,500,000 (Two point five million)
(iv)	19.03.90	Special Grant-IV	Rs 13,000,000 (Thirteen million)
(v)	10.04.90	Special Grant-V	Rs 20,000,000 (Twenty million)
(vi)	06.05.90	Special Grant-VI	Rs 10,000,000 (Ten million)
(vii)	14.06.90	Special Grant-VII	Rs 8,800,000 (Eight point eight million)
		Total	Rs 124,300,000

(6) Of the said sum of Rs 124.3 million, the Supplementary Grants at V and VII above, amounting to Rs 28.8 million were made on the demand of the Intelligence Bureau for its normal operations with the approval of the competent authority. The remaining Grants, namely, the aforementioned amounts totalling Rs 95.5 million were drawn on orders of the Prime Minister's Secretariat without any formal request from or requirement of the Intelligence Bureau.

(7) Out of the SS Funds of Rs 95.5 million so received by the Intelligence Bureau, the following major payments were made:-

Date	Name of Payee	Amount	Remarks/Receipts
25.10.89	Malik Waris Khan	Rs 10,000,000 (Ten million)	IB's letter No. 7/Budget/81/(20)-1 dated 11.9.90 to Mr. Sharif Khan and his reply dated 12.9.90 are attached as Annex 'R' and 'S'.
25.10.89	Mr Aftab Khan Sherpao, CM, NWFP through Maj (Retd) Masood Sharif Khan Ex-Joint Director	Rs 10,000,000 (Ten million)	IB's letter No. 7/Budget/81/(20)-1 dated 11.9.90 to Mr. Sharif Khan and his reply dated 12.9.90 are attached as Annex 'R' and 'S'.
26.10.89	Maj Gen (Retd) Nasirullah Khan Babar, Special Assistant to the PM through Maj (Retd) Masood Sharif Khan, Ex-Joint Director.	Rs 30,000,000 (Thirty million)	IB's letter No.7/Budget/81/(20)-1 dated 11.9.90 to Mr. Sharif Khan and his reply dated 12.9.90 are attached as Annex 'R' and 'S'.
28.10.89	The then Prime Minister of Pakistan through Maj (Retd) Masood Sharif Khan, Ex-Joint Director.	Rs 20,000,000 (Twenty million)	IB's letter No. 7/Budget/81/(20)-1 dated 11.9.90 to Mr. Sharif Khan and his reply dated 12.9.90 are attached as Annex 'R' and 'S'.
12.6.90	Mr Hanif Khan, Minister for Kashmir Affairs.	Rs 10,000,000 (Ten million) Rs 8 million + Rs 2 million	Receipt Receipt
16.6.90	Mr Hanif Khan, Minister for Kashmir Affairs.	Rs 1,200,000 (One point two million)	Receipt
18.6.90	Mr Hanif Khan, Minister for Kashmir Affairs.	Rs 100,000 (One lac)	Receipt
19.6.90	Miss Naheed Khan	Rs 500,000 (Five lac)	DIB Minute
25.6.90	Miss Naheed Khan	Rs 500,000 (Five lac)	Receipt
25.6.90	Miss Naheed Khan	Rs 500,000 (Five lac)	Receipt
16.6.90	Miss Naheed Khan	Rs 100,000 (One lac)	DIB Minute
30.6.90	Miss Naheed Khan	Rs 1,000,000 (One million)	Receipt

(8) The following affidavits are filed in support of payments referred to above and made in 1988-89 and 1989-90:-
    (i)   Affidavit of Mr Masood Sharif Khan, Joint Director IB.
    (ii)   Affidavit of Mr Ghulam Mujtaba Cashier, IB.
    (iii)   Affidavit of Col (Retd) Mohammad Ikram-ul-Haq, Deputy Director, Administration, IB.

It may also be noted that Major General (Retd) Nasirullah Khan Babar, former Special Assistant to the *ex*-Prime Minister was duly authorised to communicate the *ex*-Prime Minister's verbal orders of an executive or administrative nature *vide* letter of 22.2.1989 from the Secretary to the Prime Minister and the Cabinet Secretary's letter of 26.2.1989.

3. The facts narrated above and circumstances under which large amounts of SS Funds were first provided to the Intelligence Bureau during 1988-89 and 1989-90 and then paid on instructions from and/or under the authority of the Respondent to Mr. Mohib Ullah Shah, Additional Secretary (E&F), Prime Minister's Secretariat, Maj Gen (Retd) Nasirullah Khan Babar, Special Assistant to the Prime Minister, Malik Waris Khan Afridi, the then Minister of State for Frontier Regions, Mr Aftab Ahmed Khan Sherpao, the then Chief Minister of NWFP, Mr Hanif Khan, the then Minister for Kashmir Affairs and Northern Areas, Miss Naheed Khan, the then Political Secretary to the Prime Minister and last but not the least the Respondent Ms Benazir Bhutto, *ex*-Prime Minister herself, not for "buying of information" of intelligence value clearly shows that public moneys were wilfully misapplied and/or diverted under the direction of the then Prime Minister for a purpose other than that for which they were meant and thus the Respondent committed an act of misconduct. Office Note of Sardar Noor Illahi Leghari, the Director, Intelligence Bureau, from 5.9.1989 to 9.8.1990 states, *inter alia*, as follows:-

"Special SS Fund

All amounts received by the Intelligence Bureau as Special Supplementary Grants are disbursed under the instructions of the Chief Executive and the authorised officer to handle this account in the DIB."

(*Note*.—In this statement the dates 20.10.89 and 19.4.90 are typographical errors and should read 26.10.89 and 10.4.90 respectively).

The misconduct of the Respondent is further aggravated when the payments of Rs 70,000,000 out of DIB's SS Fund were made between 25 and 28.10.1989, including a payment of Rs 20 million to the *ex*-Prime Minister, (without receipts from the actual recipients) are seen in the perspective of the "No Confidence" motion which was moved in the National Assembly on 26.10.1989 against the Respondent and other facts as stated above. The misconduct of the Respondent as stated above resulted in a considerable loss of Rs 95.1 million to the national exchequer in the financial years 1988-89 and 1989-90.

4. The President is satisfied that on the material submitted herewith, there are reasonable grounds for believing that the Respondent has committed an act of misconduct within the meaning of Article 4 of PPO No. 17 of 1977 and accordingly the above Reference is made to the Honourable Special Court with the request to enquire and decide the case relating to the misconduct of the Respondent and record its findings and pass a ppropriate orders in accordance with law.

5. As the Reference relates to the SS Fund and is therefore of a confidential nature, the material submitted herewith may, it is respectfully requested, be treated as such, and any further material subsequently available/submitted in support of the above Reference to the Honourable Special Court may also receive the same confidentiality.

By Order of the President.

Sd/-

FAZLUR RAHMAN KHAN,
Secretary to the President.

Reference 2: In the Special Court of Mr Justice Rashid Aziz Khan

Reference by the President of the Islamic Republic of Pakistan under Article 4 of the Parliament and Provincial Assemblies (Disqualification of Membership) Order 1977 (PPO No. 17 of 1977)

Ms Benazir Bhutto, wife of
Mr Asif Ali Zardari,
Ex-Prime Minister of Pakistan,
Bilawal House, Clifton,
Karachi.

..... *RESPONDENT*

The Reference herein is made under Article 4 of PPO No. 17 of 1977 to the Special Court.

That Ms Benazir Bhutto w/o Mr Asif Ali Zardari, resident of Bilawal House, Karachi, was elected as a member of the National Assembly from Constituency No. 166 Larkana-III during the general election held on 16 November, 1988, under the Constitution of the Islamic Republic of Pakistan, and held the office of Prime Minister of Pakistan.

2. On perusal of the documents placed on record herewith, the President is satisfied that there are reasonable grounds for believing that an act of misconduct has been committed by the Respondent in abuse of her position by manipulating and managing the issue of a letter of intent by the Capital Development Authority (CDA) contrary to all Rules and

Regulations to favour International Guarantee Trust Company (IGTC) for allotment of 287 acres of prime land for a hotel and related facilities, which area was reserved for the National Athletic Centre in the CDA Master Plan.

3.   The concise statement of facts is hereunder:

a.   The CDA Land Disposal in Islamabad Regulations 1988 provided at para 16 as follows:

"*Commercial and Business Plots.*—100 per cent by Public Auction with exception of plots reserved/to be earmarked for University or any other agency by the Government. The bidder can bid for any plot put to auction. The Authority, however, reserves the right to reject a bid without assigning any reason and may also resort to open negotiations if the auction bid falls below the reserve price and is rejected." The standard plot size for a five star hotel is 5 acres in Islamabad.

b.   IGTC a London based Firm with no hotel management background or construction experience applied directly to the then Prime Minister, Ms Benazir Bhutto on 17.10.1989 for allotment of 287 acres of land north of Rawal Lake in Islamabad for construction of a 350 room hotel plus other facilities. This land, in fact, "forms part of an area reserved for the National Athletic Centre in the Master Plan. The area is meant for such athletic installations like rowing, canoeing and yachting and a standard size Golf Course."

c.   The London address given by IGTC, namely, 11 White Horse Street, Mayfair, London SW1, is that of a night club/disco by the name of Club Royale at that address. One Muzaffar Mustafa Khan, a first cousin of the Respondent, is a Director of this club. His visiting card bears the name and insignia of Club Royale and the same London address, telephone No. and fax No. as that appearing on the IGTC application addressed to the Respondent for allotment of land. There is no separate office of IGTC at the said address.

d.   On 8.11.89 the Additional Secretary to the Prime Minister, in respect of the said IGTC proposal, "requested that Secretary Cabinet, Chairman CDA and Mr Javed Pasha, Chairman, Prime Minister's Project Evaluation Committee, may please go through this proposal and formulate views for a subsequent meeting and presentation to the Prime Minister. The exact date and time for the meeting and presentation to the Prime Minister will be conveyed by the Military Secretary to whom a separate reference is made."

e.   Mr Shafi Mohammad Sehwani, Member Planning, CDA, opposed the proposal *vide* his note dated 23.11.89 pointing out that the proposed site was not for hotels but a reserved area under the CDA Master Plan; and that a list of parties desirous of setting up 5-star hotels had already been submitted to the Prime Minister for "planned sites" for such hotels to which IGTC's name may be added.

f. The Committee constituted by said letter of 8.11.89 met on 30.11.89 and the Cabinet Secretary, Acting CDA Chairman and Mr Javed Pasha, together with Miss Seema Aleem, decided that the questions, *inter alia*, of land use and planning be discussed within 3-4 days. In the absence of permanent incumbent on leave Mr Inamul Haq, Additional Secretary, Cabinet Division (administrative Ministry of CDA) was informally holding additional charge of CDA.

g. Before this second meeting could be held the Respondent, Ms Benazir Bhutto, gave additional charge of Chairman, CDA to Mr Iqbal Jaffar on 3.12.1989 who at that time was the Additional Secretary in the Prime Minister's Secretariat.

h. Within a few days, on 9.12.1989 Mr Iqbal Jaffar Acting Chairman CDA directed a note be prepared for the Prime Minister regarding the said hotel project.

i. A draft note was prepared and submitted by the CDA on 11.12.1989 on the same lines as the note dated 23.11.1989 by the Member Planning. This note was not acted upon and instead on 2.1.1990 the new CDA Chairman (Mr Iqbal Jaffar was appointed Chairman CDA on 27.12.89) sent a note to the Prime Minister's Secretariat "fully" supporting IGTC's proposal with slight changes. The procedure prescribed was not followed for changes of land use and the Master Plan, where as previously such changes were placed before the Cabinet for approval.

j. Meanwhile, Mr Sehwani the Member Planning was removed from CDA on 14.1.1990. Thereafter, the new CDA Chairman discussed the matter on 13.2.90 with one Rafiuddin, representing IGTC, and the same day the Chairman CDA sent a note to Mr Javed Pasha, Chairman Prime Minister's Project Evaluation and Monitoring Committee wherein, *inter alia*, the allotment of the said land on leasehold basis was suggested. To hasten the finalization of the deal, and without even waiting for the response of Javed Pasha, Mr Jaffar the CDA Chairman discussed the matter with the Prime Minister and within 24 hours, on 14.2.1990, recorded his minute as under:-

> "The proposal made in the letter dated 13.2.1990, addressed to Mr Javed Pasha was discussed by me with the Prime Minister on the same day. The Prime Minister was pleased to approve the general idea of the proposal made in the letter. The letter of intent may now be issued to the sponsors containing the proposal made in the said letter."

k. Accordingly, the letter of intent was prepared and handed over to Mr Rafiuddin in the office of the Chairman, again within 24 hours, on 15.2.90.

l. On the next working day, at the instance of said Mr Rafiuddin, Mr Wahid, Director, PE&C, CDA, immediately worked out the cost of land with the approval of the Chairman. The following rates were communicated to IGTC through Mr Rafiuddin *vide* letter dated 17.2.90 signed by Mr Qanait Ali, Director CDA:-

"a. Land under hotel/towers/buildings   Rs 1,008.00
                                                per square yards.

b. Recreational land and other areas   Rs 400.00
                                                per square yards.

c. Green Area/Golf Course   Rs 17.00
                                                per square yards.

d. Annual Ground Rent   Rs 0.25
                                                per square yards."

Departing from earlier precedents the land "under" buildings was to be charged at different rate as compared to open areas comprising the hotel limits. Moreover the prices, particularly for the hotel land, were far below even the reserve price for commercial property sold by the CDA; and in sales through auction the prevailing rates were, in fact, Rs 15,000 approximately per square yard of commercial land in 1987, thus involving a potential loss to the CDA and the Exchequer of hundreds of crores of Rupees.

m. During the entire processing of the case, the Law Officer of the CDA was never consulted although this was a requirement of CDA Rules, the advice tendered by Planning was totally disregarded, and other Branches of CDA were never given a chance to play their legitimate role.

n. Next, a draft allotment letter was submitted to the Chairman CDA on 1.3.1990. By this time however, the deal was reported in the Press on 26.2.1990. An Adjournment Motion was also subsequently moved in the National Assembly by Lt General (Retd) Abdul Majid Malik on 21.3.1990.

o. Meanwhile a draft Allotment Letter was submitted by the Cabinet Secretary to the Prime Minister with a summary dated 10.3.90. It points out that the letter of intent was issued by the CDA to IGTC "after obtaining the approval of the Prime Minister"; and moreover that, "the contents of draft Allotment Letter are almost the same as that of the Letter of Intent" in respect of 287.5 acres for the proposed project.

p. The draft Allotment Letter was then further processed by Mr Mohammad Nawaz Malik, Additional Secretary Prime Minister's Secretariat, who, *inter alia*, made the following observations, on the relevant file on 4.4.90, against the said allotment of land:-

"A big chunk of land located in the National Park Area is proposed to be allotted for Hotel. It is not indicated anywhere on the file documents whether the approved Master Plan of Islamabad allows such use. If not, whether permission of the competent authority has been obtained for such a deviation. "The site of the proposed hotel is located in the most prized/ exclusive area with the Constitution Avenue and the Diplomatic Enclave on the North and Rawal Lake on the South. The land in this area is known to be very costly. The rates quoted in para 2 of the Draft Allotment Letter and in other available papers do not suggest whether they are competitive. It can be safely presumed that, by auction the proposed land would fetch much higher return."

q. On receipt of the aforesaid note of Mr Mohammad Nawaz Malik, the Respondent noted:

"Views of CDA be sought on points raised above and then re-submitted.

"Once views of CDA are obtained it may be put by the CDA Chairman alongwith these reservations to a Committee comprising Ministry of Water and Power, Ministry of Railways and Chairman PMPEC by the CDA Chairman."

The Committee met on 6.5.1990 and at this late stage, for the first time, asked the sponsors to produce, *inter alia*, documents showing their financial position and other details. After this no other meeting of the Committee took place.

r. However to overcome precondition in CDA Land Disposal Regulations 1988, which stipulates that all commercial lands shall be sold by public auction, the CDA was manipulated to cover the special concessional terms already offered to the IGTC through a special provision added to the Regulations on 10 May, 1990, with the approval of the Respondent, to read, *inter alia*, as follows:-

"Notwithstanding anything contained in the Regulations, the Authority may, in suitable cases, make allotments of land vesting in it on the recommendations of a Committee to be constituted by the Government."

s. The Respondent's actions throughout were not in the Public interest.

t. Writ Petition No. 432/1990 was filed in the Lahore High Court, Rawalpindi Bench, Rawalpindi, by two MNAs at the time, namely, Syeda Abida Hussain and Lt General (Retd) Abdul Majid Malik and the said High Court on 5.6.90 admitted the Petition and ordered *"status quo"* to be maintained. Thus the efforts of the Respondent to allot the land to IGTC through the CDA were frustrated.

u. To achieve the above purpose of showing undue favour to M/s IGTC at the cost of CDA the Respondent removed the Chairman CDA and Mr Sehwani, Member Planning, from their appointments; and, also, thereafter to facilitate this transaction, changed the CDA Regulations to accommodate the proposal of M/s IGTC. Respondent created a committee for allotment and dispensed with the well-established system of auction. Had the deal gone through it would have caused a loss of hundreds of crores of Rupees to the CDA and the Exchequer and equivalent undue gain to M/s IGTC.

v. The above facts disclose that in disregard of CDA Ordinance/Regulations/Rules thereunder, in violation of CDA Master Plan and by ignoring the available expert advice of CDA officials, the Respondent had the letter of intent issued to M/s IGTC for their proposal at extremely low rates and then made an attempt to issue letter of allotment which action was eventually frustrated by order of *status quo* by the Lahore Court dated 5.6.90. The Respondent thereby committed act of misconduct within the meaning of PPO 17/77.

5. The above Reference is made to the Special Court with the request to enquire and decide the case relating to the misconduct of the Respondent and record its findings and pass appropriate orders in accordance with law.

6. It further material subsequently becomes available in support of the above Reference it will be submitted respectfully to the Honourable Special Court.

By Order of the President.

Sd/-

FAZLUR RAHMAN KHAN,
Secretary to the President.

Reference 3: In the Special Court of Mr Justice Mohammad Amir Malik

Reference by the President of the Islamic Republic of Pakistan
under Article 4 of the Parliament and Provincial Assemblies
(Disqualification of Membership) Order 1977 (PPO No. 17 of 1977)

Ms Benazir Bhutto, wife of
Mr Asif Ali Zardari,
Ex-Prime Minister of Pakistan,
Bilawal House, Clifton,
Karachi.

..... *RESPONDENT*

Reference is herein made under Article 4 of PPO No. 17 of 1977 to the Special Court.

That Ms Benazir Bhutto w/o Mr Asif Ali Zardari, was elected as a member of the National Assembly from Constituency No. 166 Larkana-III during the general elections held on 16th November, 1988 under the

Constitution of the Islamic Republic of Pakistan, and held the office of Prime Minister of Pakistan.

2. On perusal of the facts and documents placed on record herewith, the President is satisfied that there are reasonable grounds for believing that an act of 'misconduct' within the meaning of PPO No. 17 of 1977, has been committed by the Respondent in abuse of power and position during her tenure of office as Prime Minister.

Concise statement of facts:

3. Combined Opposition Parties served a notice of no confidence against the Prime Minister under Article 95 on 23.10.89. The notice was communicated by Secretary National Assembly to the House on 24.10.89 and the House granted leave for moving the resolution on 26.10.89 which was to be voted upon by the House on 1.11.89.

4. In consequence of the above notice hectic activities started and the Members of Federal Cabinet together with members of National Assembly of PPP led by the former Prime Minister made various statements and laid various accusations and held the move as unconstitutional and against democracy.

5. As the lobbying for and against no confidence picked up speed and meetings and visits between the MNAs and the other lobbyists became more frequent the Respondent conceived an innovative plan of transporting the members of the National Assembly to Peshawar initially and then to Saidu Sharif subsequently with the ostensible object of taking them to a place not easily accessible to the opposition and thus denying the political leaders and members of the National Assembly an opportunity to freely meet, discuss and form an independent and objective opinion for voting on the day of no confidence motion.

6. The plan envisaged the use of Service Aircrafts of Pakistan Air Force by operating Special Flights — non-operational for non-military use from 26 October to 1 November 1989 to pick up MNAs as and when they became available irrespective of the capacity of each flight. Initially, the MNAs were transported from PAF Base Chaklala to PAF Base Peshawar. They were carried in 2 PAF Boeing 707 flights on 26.10.89 and 27.10.89, and in one PAF Fokker flight on 27.10.89. After delivering the members of National Assembly at Peshawar, Ministers Hanif Khan, Farooq Leghari, Iftikhar Gillani, Ahmad Saeed Awan and Mir Baz Khan Khethran returned to Chaklala Air Base by PAF Fokker flight. At this time plans had been changed to take the MNAs to Saidu Sharif and therefore those MNAs who were located at Peshawar were shifted to Saidu Sharif using two flights of C-130 each, carrying 88 and 34 passengers respectively. Remaining members of National Assembly who were still at Chaklala including the Respondent herself were moved by two flights of PAF Fokker Friendship on 28.10.89 and 30.10.89 including one flight kept stand-by throughout

the period at Chaklala/Saidu Sharif. Passenger manifest in r/o C-130, 44 carrying "delegation of 68 MNA" from Saidu Sharif to Chaklala is not immediately available. Thus a total of 12 flights using PAF's C-130 aircrafts, Boeing and Fokker Friendship were used for carrying approximately 113 MNAs, MPAs and other staff/families in violation of PAF Regulations.

7.   The above action of transporting the MNAs from Chaklala to Peshawar and from Chaklala to Saidu Sharif and from Peshawar to Saidu Sharif was widely condemned in the press by prominent personalities.

8.   PAF's position had to be defended by Air Chief himself who said that PAF was to obey orders, the purpose of flights was to be explained by the Government. After having concentrated the MNAs in Saidu Sharif the Respondent arranged three flights of C-130 Aircraft of PAF out of which one was kept stand-by and two were used to carry the 113 passengers including all the MNAs who had been transported there, from Saidu Sharif to PAF Base Chaklala. From Chaklala they moved straight into the Parliament House to participate in voting during no confidence resolution on 1.11.89 — the day of voting.

9.   The PAF Aircrafts were used in violation of the Air Force Instruction 8 of 1975. AFI 8/75 Regulation Governing Provisions of Passages, in Service Aircrafts provides:

a.   Special Flight has been defined as, "flights arranged for conveyance of particular individual/individuals on a specific load for purpose other than military". Persons entitled to the use of special flights are listed in para 3 of the Regulations. These persons are the President, the Prime Minister, Ministers of Pakistan, Governors of provinces, Chief Ministers of provinces, Speaker of the National Assembly, Deputy Speaker of the National Assembly, Chairman of Senate, Deputy Chairman of the Senate, Secretaries of the Federal Government, Chief Secretaries of the Provincial Governments, the Chief of the Staff, Pakistan Army, the Chief of the Naval Staff, Pakistan Navy, The Chief of the Air Staff, Pakistan Air Force, important visitors to Pakistan and Civil Departments. Para 4 of the Regulations lays down the procedure for requisitioning of special flights which reads, "Requisition for special flights other than those for the President of Pakistan, the Prime Minister of Pakistan, the Defence Minister; the Governors/Chief Ministers of Provinces and the three Chiefs of Pakistan Armed Forces will be routed through the Ministry of Defence by the Department concerned". Para 5 of the Regulations lays down the Financial Adjustments which reads, "With the exception of the President of Pakistan, the Prime Minister of Pakistan, the Defence Minister and three Chiefs of the Pakistan Armed Forces a debit will be raised against the Government department concerned on the basis of the charges assessed from time to time by the Air Force authorities in consultation with the Financial Adviser (Air Force)".

b. In this particular case the MNAs (and MPAs) were unentitled persons and so were a number of other persons who used the air passage facility on the clandestine journey. The aircrafts were used in a callous manner so that their seating capacity was grossly underutilized and passengers loaded on as "available" basis without regard to operational importance of the aircraft. The requisition for the flights was not moved through the Ministry of Defence and the PAF Headquarters were verbally ordered by the Respondent's staff on behalf of the Respondent to make the arrangements. The operation was overseen and conducted by the Federal Ministers. The expenditure was debited to PAF Budget thus causing it a loss of over Rs 10 lacs. In addition for Respondent's political motives an unnecessary stress and strain was caused to the PAF Service Aircrafts and PAF personnel who worked round the clock from 26.10.89 to 1.11.89 by operating at least one to two flights per day. The clandestine operation also reduced the number of hours of life of precious military equipment primarily meant for the operational use of the PAF to enable the Respondent to save her Government from falling in a constitutional move.

10. From the above facts and statements it is clear that the Respondent in gross violation of national interest used the PAF operational equipment for saving her own government in violation of the PAF Regulations for ensuring the loyalties of members of the National Assembly in abuse of the power and position, launched a clandestine operation to keep the members away and in her personal and direct custody, bringing them to the Parliament House for voting a few minutes before the debate was a commence and thus managed to defeat the no-confidence motion by a narrow margin of 12 votes.

11. The aforesaid act on the part of the Respondent constitutes misconduct, through wilful mal-administration, wilful misapplication and diversion of public money and resources and therefore attracts the provisions of PPO 17 of 1977.

12. The President is satisfied that there are reasonable grounds for believing that the Respondent has committed an act of misconduct within the meaning of Article 4 of PPO No. 17 of 1977 and accordingly the above Reference is made to the Honourable Court with the request to enquire and decide the case relating to the misconduct of the Respondent and record its findings and pass appropriate orders in accordance with law.

13. If further material subsequently becomes available in support of the above Reference it will be submitted to the Honourable Special Court.

By Order of the President.

Sd/-

FAZLUR RAHMAN KHAN,
Secretary to the President.

Reference 4: In the Special Court of Mr Justice Rashid Aziz Khan

Reference by the President of the Islamic Republic of Pakistan under Article 4 of the Parliament and Provincial Assemblies (Disqualification of Membership) Order 1977 (PPO No. 17 of 1977)

Ms Benazir Bhutto,
Ex-Prime Minister of Pakistan,
Resident of Bilawal House,
Karachi.

..... *RESPONDENT*

Reference is herein made under Article 4 of PPO No. 17 of 1977 to the Special Court.

That Ms Benazir Bhutto w/o Mr Asif Ali Zardari, resident of Bilawal House, Clifton Road, Karachi was elected as a member of the National Assembly from Constituency No. NA-166, Larkana-III, during the general election held on 16th November, 1988 under the Constitution of Islamic Republic of Pakistan, and held the office of the Prime Minister of Pakistan from 2nd December, 1988 to 6th August, 1990.

2. On perusal of the facts and documents placed on record herewith, the President is satisfied that there are reasonable grounds for believing that an act of 'misconduct' within the meaning of PPO No. 17 of 1977, has been committed by the Respondent in abuse of power and position during her tenure of office as Prime Minister.

3. Concise statement of facts is hereunder:-

a. Till middle of 1989 production of liquified petroleum gas (LPG) was 324 tons per day.

b. This production was marketed by six marketing companies, *viz.* (i) Burshane, (ii) Lifeline — Private Sector Companies, (iii) Foundation Gas, (iv) Sui Northern Gas Pipeline Ltd., (v) Southern Gas Company Ltd., and (vi) Pakistan State Oil Company Ltd., (PSO) — Public Sector Companies.

c. An additional production of 60 tons/day of LPG from Adhi and 25 tons per day from Dakhni fields was envisaged to be available by July/August 1989.

d. The Ministry of Petroleum and Natural Resources considered the requests of twenty six applicants for the distribution and marketing rights and allocation of product from these two new sources, and decided in October 1988 that no new company or an individual should be inducted in the LPG marketing.

e. In November 1988, it was decided that allocation of additional product be given to the existing marketing companies in equal proportion on the consideration that they would market 15% in

Azad Kashmir, 20% in hilly areas and 15% in NWFP including FATA area. However, Al Shifa Trust (a charitable Trust Hospital located at Rawalpindi) in joint venture with Pakistan State Oil and Oil and Gas Development Corporation (OGDC) was allowed in October 1988 on humanitarian grounds entire allocation of LPG *ex*-Dakhni (25 tons). The entire production of LPG *ex*-Adhi was to be equally distributed among the other five marketing companies *viz.* Fon Gas, Burshane, Lifeline, Southern Gas Co. Ltd., and Sui Northern Gas Pipelines Ltd.

f.   Accordingly, a letter was issued to Al Shifa Trust on 30.10.88, and to the other aforesaid companies on 28.11.88.

g.   Subsequently, after the PPP Government took over and the Respondent became the Prime Minister a review meeting of LPG allocations was held on 7.2.89 in the Ministry presided by Secretary Petroleum, and it was decided to suspend the allocations made to the aforesaid companies and the letters of allocation issued to them were cancelled on 15.2.89.

h.   Thereafter the allocation of LPG from Adhi and Dakhni fields made earlier was again reviewed by the Minister for Petroleum, and it was decided that the allocation of two private sector companies *viz.*, Lifeline and Burshane be cancelled and in order to overcome infrastructure problems the four Public Sector Companies were allowed to continue with their construction/development plans on provisional basis for approximate period of 8–10 months.

i.   A summary was submitted by the Ministry to the Prime Minister on 3.4.89, giving background on LPG allocations made by the Ministry with two suggestions (in paras 7 and 8 of the summary):

   1.   12.5 tons of LPG *ex*-Dhakni be reallocated to a new party namely Lub Gas (Pvt) Ltd.,

   2.   The allocation made to the four public sector companies *ex*-Dhakni/Adhi can be altered, if so desired.

j.   Ms Benazir Bhutto in her capacity as Prime Minister, ordered on the summary dated 3.4.1989 submitted by the Secretary, Ministry of Petroleum and Natural Resources, in connection with distribution of Liquid Petroleum Gas (LPG) that, "Air Marshal Zulfiqar Ali Khan, Gulzar Khan, Tariq Akbar Khan, Mian Assad Ehsan have also applied for liquid petroleum gas permission. They may be given in PREFERENCE to others because they suffered unduly in the past dictatorial regime." Sd/- BB (Benazir Bhutto) dated 10.4.1989.

k.   The aforementioned four beneficiaries of permission were neither mentioned in the said summary, nor were they shown as applicants in the summary; nevertheless the Respondent on her own initiative without proper inquiry gave them benefit of permission purely to favour them so that they may obtain pecuniary gain.

l. Later on, according to the records of the Ministry, the name of Tariq Akbar Khan was dropped, and instead Lub Gas Ltd., a Private Limited Company belonging to Mr Tariq Islam, (a first cousin of the Respondent) was added in a meeting held on 15.4.1989, under the chairmanship of the Minister of Petroleum, and the allocation for Lub Gas was 15 tons *ex*-Dakhni, as against the proposed 12.5 tons in the summary dated 3.4.1989. All the four individuals/companies namely ACM (Retd) Zulfiqar Ali Khan, Gulzar Khan, Mian Assad Ehsan and Lub Gas Ltd., were advised by the Minister that 50% dealers would be appointed by him.

m. Subsequently a letter was received from M/s Lub Gas dated 10.5.1989 requesting that their address should be changed as 7 Egerton Road, Lahore, instead of Spencers & Co. (Pak) Ltd., I. I. Chundrigar Road, Karachi, and that future correspondence could be signed by Mr Iqbal Z Ahmed or his nominee.

n. The *ex*-Prime Minister despite full knowledge that Lub Gas Ltd., belonged to her cousin Mr Tariq Islam, did not only cause the approval in favour of Lub Gas Limited *i.e.*, her cousin Mr Tariq Islam but also, unjustifiably and without reason in abuse of her position and power got cancelled the earlier allocation letters validly issued by the ministry to Public Sector Companies launching joint venture of Al-Shifa Trust and the Respondent without inquiry or application on record permitted four other newcomers who were her close associates, friends or relatives namely Air Chief Marshal (Retd) Zulfiqar Ali Khan (a close friend later appointed Ambassador of Pakistan in USA on 12.7.89), Gulzar Khan (a friend and Special Assistant to Prime Minister), Tariq Islam (a first cousin), Mian Assad Ehsan (a friend) to obtain benefit of LPG marketing rights/permission.

o. While the approval was granted in favour of these four persons on 10.4.89 by Respondent's orders on Summary dated 3.4.89 and 15.4.89, they applied for grant of LPG marketing licences many days thereafter as indicated below:-
    (1) Mr Gulzar Khan   19.4.1989
    (2) Mr M A Ehsan   2.5.1989
    (3) M/s Lub Gas (Pvt) Ltd. (Proposed)   10.5.1989
    (4) ACM (Retd) Zulfiqar Ali Khan   27.5.1989
    This was done by depriving four Public Sector Companies and a Charitable Trust in joint venture with two Public Sector Companies.

p. The order of allocation of LPG to the above named four persons inclusive of Tariq Islam, owner of Lub Gas Ltd., was in breach of Rules known as Liquified Petroleum Gas (Production and Distribution) Rules, 1971 promulgated under Section 2 of the Regulation of Mines, Oilfields and Mineral Development (Government

Control) Act 1948 (XXIV) of 1948, by the Central Government as shown below:-

1. Rules 3, 4 and 5 of Part II have been violated and the four allottees mentioned above did not fulfil the requirements set out in the said Rules.
2. There were no applications before the Respondent from the above named four persons, when she made the order of allocation in their favour on 10.4.89. (The Respondent wrongly noted on the said Summary that they "have also applied").
3. That the requirements of the Rules and the application as prescribed thereunder were not fulfilled before the Respondent gave the allocation to the four concerned persons.
4. The names of these four allottees do not appear in the list of 26 applicants annexed to the summary and these allottees did not exist according to Rules.
5. No inquiry was held or allowed to be held as per rules particularly Rules 3 to 5 before the Respondent bestowed the allocations on the four allottees.
6. In any case, the Summary of the Secretary dated 3.4.89 did not relate to any application of the four allottees and no order could be passed on this Summary in their favour.

4. In the light of the foregoing facts and circumstances there is reason to believe that the aforementioned acts of the Respondent besides being in breach of statutory rules, arbitrary, discriminatory and without reasonable basis, constitute 'misconduct' within the meaning of PPO No. 17 of 1977 and further disclose acts of favouritism, nepotism wilful maladministration and abuse of power and position.

5. The above Reference is made to the Special Court with the request to enquire into and decide the case relating to the misconduct of the Respondent and record findings and pass appropriate orders in accordance with the law.

6. If further material subsequently becomes available in support of the above Reference, it will be submitted respectively to the Honourable Special Court.

By Order of the President.

Sd/-

FAZLUR RAHMAN KHAN,
Secretary to the President.

Reference 5: In the Special Court of Mr Justice Mukhtar Ahmad Junejo

Reference by the President of the Islamic Republic of Pakistan under Article 4 of the Parliament and Provincial Assemblies (Disqualification of Membership) Order 1977 (PPO No. 17 of 1977)

Ms Benazir Bhutto, wife of
Mr Asif Ali Zardari,
Ex-Prime Minister of Pakistan,
Bilawal House, Clifton, Karachi.

..... *RESPONDENT*

Reference is herein made under Article 4 of PPO No. 17 of 1977 to the Special Court.

That Ms Benazir Bhutto w/o Mr Asif Ali Zardari, was elected as a member of the National Assembly from Constituency No. 166 Larkana-III during the general elections held on 16th November, 1988 under the Constitution of the Islamic Republic of Pakistan, and held the office of Prime Minister of Pakistan.

2.   On perusal of the documents placed on record herewith, the President is satisfied that there are reasonable grounds for believing that an act of misconduct has been committed by the Respondent as Prime Minister holding the portfolio of Finance Minister, and by virtue of office functioning as Chairman of the Economic Committee of the Cabinet (ECC), whereby the Respondent allowed/arranged/caused to be awarded a contract/deal in favour of a firm known as Ralli Brothers by which a Government Statutory Corporation, namely the Cotton Export Corporation (CEC) working under the Ministry of Commerce, was made to suffer a loss of about US$ 4.6 million *i.e.* over Rs 10 crores.

3.   The concise statement of facts is hereunder:

a. Mr Paul Southworth, Managing Director M/s Ralli Brothers and Coney of Liverpool, submitted by hand in the first week of May, 1990, an undated, unaddressed proposal to Secretary Finance, Mr R A Akhund, for purchasing 6–8 lac bales of raw cotton from the Cotton Export Corporation of Pakistan.

b. Secretary Finance forwarded this proposed on 10.5.90 to Secretary Commerce and Chairman, CEC, as the subject was to be dealt with by that Division.

c. Immediately thereafter, on 12.5.90, the Commerce Ministry, as directed, submitted a summary for the ECC concerning the offer from M/s Ralli Brothers and Coney, for consideration at the ECC meeting on 14.5.90. On 13.5.90, the Respondent directed that a summary on the progress of export of cotton be also brought before the ECC meeting the very next day *i.e.* 14.5.90.

d. At the ECC meeting on 14.5.90, the Respondent, as Chairman ECC discussed two summaries (i) relating to export of cotton and (ii) sale of cotton to Ralli Brothers. The CEC's views were that the offer of Ralli Brothers was "not acceptable" because, *inter alia*, (i) unsold stock of cotton was less than 6 lac bales while uncommitted stocks were only 2 lac bales and that also "provided the private sector can cover its outstanding commitments"; (ii) the quantity of 2 lac bales is the minimum for carry over; (iii) any supplies to Ralli Brothers had to be made at the cost of the private sector (Pakistani parties) which "would generate a new controversy"; (iv) private sector uncovered commitments are at an average price of US cents 69 per lb against the average of US cents 51.5 offered by Ralli Brothers and that the present international prices are "firm in the range of US cents 69-70 per lb."; (v) discount visualised in the of-fer of Ralli Brothers would "result in estimated loss of US$ 30 mil-lion or Rs 665 million at US cents 13 per lb, on average"; and (vi) "if at all a bulk deal has to be struck with international buyers with the condition of encashing L/C before 30th of June 1990, offers from other bidders are also required to be invited to conform the deal to the requirements of competition and openness." The Min-istry of Commerce endorsed the above views of the CEC, adding that "a similar contract of 1988 between CEC and Ralli Brothers is under investigation by FIA on charges of malafide.

e. The ECC decided on 14.5.90 to set up a Secretaries Committee for negotiating cotton prices with different international Firms specifically including only Ralli Brothers by name.

f. The Secretaries Committee examined bids from 7 parties on 27.5.90 but finding none of them satisfactory extended the date to 29.5.90. A comparative chart of the bids received on 29.5.90 is set out at page 3 of the Secretaries Committee Report. It shows that out of the 7 types of cotton available, Ralli Brothers had bid for only three and for only one type covering 6300 bales were Ralli Brothers the highest bidders. The Secretaries Committee recommended, *inter alia*,

    i. Bids for fast moving types should not be accepted because of wide differential between the Minimum Export Price and prices quoted by the bidders, and bright prospects for export at a higher price.

    ii. Bids for the slow moving Aadnas, 1210, Nemis etc. types may be accepted at the highest price offered by the bidders on CEC terms. These are as follows:-

        a. Nemis 1 "6300 bales at 66.00 US cents per lb to M/s Ralli Bros.

        b. Aadnas 1 "15000 bales at 61.00 US cents per lb to M/s A M Jones.

    c. 1210 1 "15000 bales at 57.25 US cents per lb to M/s A M Jones.

    d. Baram 11/32 "3200 bales at 68.50 US cents per lb to M/s Conti Cotton."

g. The Commerce Minister at the time noted that the bids were markedly below the Minimum Export Price and suggested that all bids be cancelled and the whole issue be reconsidered.

h. On 3.6.90, a summary was submitted to the ECC where in it was proposed by the Ministry of Commerce that, as New York prices had gone up by 2 cents per lb. CEC be directed to expedite the sale of 1.5 lac bales subjects to its standard terms. No specific party or parties were recommended. The summary of 3.6.90 was considered at the next meeting of the ECC on 6.6.90 under the Chairmanship of the Respondent. The proposal submitted in the summary was totally disregarded by the Respondent in the said Meeting and the Ministry of Commerce was instead directed to hold negotiations specifically with Ralli Brothers (thereby excluding all other parties) for the sale of the entire quantity of 1.5 lac bales against their highest offer for 6300 bales of only one type. The Respondent as Prime Minister and Chairman of ECC influenced the above decisions to be taken and thereby caused the contract to be awarded to Ralli Brothers at a price much lower than the prevailing Minimum Export Price.

j. The contract was concluded with Ralli Brothers on 13.6.90 at an average price of US cents 61.37/lb which was substantially lower than the prevalent Minimum Export Price of around US cents 69.78 Lb and against the Government's own Directive that CEC would not be allowed or permitted any sale below Minimum Export Price. This resulted in a loss of about US$ 4.6 million or over Rs 10 crore to the Exchequer on the sale of 147,309 bales.

k. Both the Karachi Cotton Association (KCA) and All-Pakistan Textile Mill Owners Association (APTMA) throughout protested vehemently to stop the deal (an appeal published in Press and, after the deal was finalized in favour of Ralli Brothers, called upon the Government to institute a full-scale inquiry into the sale of cotton to one single buyer. In a press release in June 1990 the KCA raised a number of objections to the deal *inter alia* (i) that the sale was confined to one buyer when at least 15 registered regular buyers were willing to pay higher prices than Ralli Brothers and all were willing to accept CEC terms; (ii) that the advice of KCA and APTMA was ignored about rising international prices and that bulk sales would be against national interest; and (iii) that the MEP mechanism established by Government was totally ignored.

l.   Incidentally, only 7224 bales were shipped upto 30.6.90 and a considerable quantity has yet to be shipped.

4.   The above facts disclose and there is reason to believe, that in disregard of advice from CEC, the Secretaries Committee and the Ministry of Commerce, and despite the clamour by KCA and APTMA regarding the impropriety of the deal, and in violation of the established rules and procedures for the sale of cotton, the Respondent as stated above in abuse of her power and position as Prime Minister and Chairman CEC manipulated and managed the decision of the ECC for securing the contract/deal in favour of Ralli Brothers a pre-designated Firm, causing a loss of approximately US$ 4.65 million *i.e.* over Rs 10 crores.

5.   The above Reference is made to the Special Court with the request to enquire and decide the case relating to the misconduct of the Respondent and record its findings and pass appropriate orders in accordance with law.

6.   If further material subsequently becomes available in support of the above Reference it will be submitted respectfully to the Honourable Special Court.

By Order of the President.

Sd/-

FAZLUR RAHMAN KHAN,
Secretary to the President.

Reference 6: In the Special Court of
Mr Justice Wajihuddin Ahmad

Reference by the President of the Islamic Republic of Pakistan
under Article 4 of the Parliament and Provincial Assemblies
(Disqualification of Membership) Order 1977 (PPO No. 17 of 1977)

Ms Benazir Bhutto, wife of
Mr Asif Ali Zardari,
Ex-Prime Minister of Pakistan,
Bilawal House, Clifton, Karachi.

..... *RESPONDENT*

The Reference herein is made under Article 4 of PPO No. 17 of 1977 to the Special Court.

That Ms Benazir Bhutto w/o Mr Asif Ali Zardari, resident of Bilawal House, Karachi, was elected as a member of the National Assembly from Constituency No. 166 Larkana-III during the general elections held on 16th November, 88 under the Constitution of the Islamic Republic of

Pakistan, and held the office of Prime Minister of Pakistan from 2nd December, 1988 to 6th August, 1990.

2.   On perusal of the documents placed on record herewith, the President is satisfied that there are reasonable grounds for believing that an act of "misconduct" within the meaning of PPO No. 17 of 1977 has been committed by the Respondent during her tenure of office as Prime Minister of Pakistan, in abuse of her power and position as such.

3.   Concise statement of facts is hereunder:-

a.   The Karachi Electric Supply Corporation (KESC) is managed and controlled by Water & Power Development Authority (WAPDA) working under the Ministry of Water and Power.

b.   The Asian Development Bank (ADB) had provided a loan of US$ 100 million to Government of Pakistan alongwith a concurrent loan of another US$ 100 million provided by Exim Bank, Japan for expansion and augmentation of KESC transmission system at Karachi.

c.   According to the ADB procedure and guidelines, the KESC were required to engage a qualified consulting firm to provide consultancy services.

The following firms were short-listed by the KESC:

1.   M/s Electricite-De-France, France;
2.   M/s Fichtner Consulting Engineer, West Germany;
3.   M/s Gilbert Commonwealth, USA;
4.   M/s Lahmeyer International, West Germany; and
5.   M/s Electro Consult, Italy.

d.   Invitation letters, terms of reference and evaluation, criteria were prepared and after scrutiny by the Asian Development Bank, were issued to the above Consulting Firms. As per ADB's guidelines, two-envelope system was adopted, requiring bidders to submit technical and financial proposals separately.

e.   All the above-mentioned five firms submitted their technical proposals on 12.6.1989 to the KESC. Technical evaluation of the proposal was carried out by a Board of senior officers of KESC. The proposal of M/s Lahmeyer was declared number one on merit, followed by that of Fichtner as the second in order of ranking. The evaluation report was duly approved by the Board of Directors of KESC, and it was forwarded to the ADB. A copy of the technical evaluation report was also sent to the Minister for Water and Power. The ADB also carried out its independent evaluation by three different members of the Bank's consultant selection committee, who unanimously held the proposal of M/s Lehmeyer as a technically sound, proper and most attractive bid.

f.   After approval by the ADB, the first ranked firm, M/s Lehmeyer was invited for contract negotiations to be held on 12.9.1989. The second envelope on financial proposals of M/s Lehmeyer was opened in the presence of the representative of the ADB, and it was also found to be the lowest; the second ranked firm being twice as expensive as is shown in the following table:-

	Foreign man months	Local man months	Total
First Ranked Firm : Lehmeyer International	137.0	349.3	486.3
Second Ranked Firm : Fichtner	311.0	815.0	1126.0

As per average man months rate, Lehmeyer was found cheaper than Fichtner by Rs 101.3 million. Accordingly, a contract with M/s Lehmeyer was initiated on 21.9.1989.

g. Messrs Atcon the local partners and representative of M/s Fichtner, made a representation on 1.8.1989 to Chairman WAPDA, the Secretary, Ministry of Water & Power and to the Prime Minister, requesting re-evaluation of the technical proposals.

h. The Chairman of the Prime Minister's Project Evaluation and Monitoring Committee (PMPEMC), Mr Javed Pasha, who operated under the control and guidance of the Respondent, on 29.8.1989 called for the evaluation report and also directed that the decision of the consultancy contract award should pend until the evaluation report had been examined.

i. The Pakistan Associate of Messrs Atcon Ltd., Mr Rao Nasim Hashim is the son of Rao Hashim Khan, who contesting on PPP ticket was defeated in the general elections of 1988 but was appointed as Chairman of the Federal Law Commission.

j. The Managing Director, KESC, on 19.9.1989 submitted the evaluation report to PMPEMC. The Chairman, PMPEMC, sent a u.o. note 75/PMPEMC/89 dated 28.10.89 to Gen (Retd) Nasirullah Khan Babar in the Prime Minister's Secretary, observing therein that the proposal of Lehmeyer was deficient and advising that revaluation be carried out by the Ministry of Water & Power or by KESC with a different committee. These remarks of Chairman PMPEMC received by Gen Babar were conveyed to Ministry of Water and Power by the Prime Minister's Secretariat *vide* u.o. No. 4(61)/89-EAF-III, dated 10.12.1989.

k. In the meanwhile, Mr S T H Naqvi, Managing Director KESC who had handled this case so far was changed and Mr Bashir Ahmed Chaudhry, a retired officer of KESC was appointed Managing Director KESC on 6.11.89.

l. The Ministry of Water and Power accordingly directed the new Managing Director, KESC to carry out re-evaluation with a different team, *vide* their D.O. No. P-III-1(24)/89, dated 18.12.1989.

m. The Minister for Water and Power, Sardar Farooq Leghari, however, put up a detailed brief for the Prime Minister in which he took a serious view of the re-evaluation *vide* his u.o. No. P-III-

1(24)/89, dated 7.1.1990. He categorically stated that such a course of action was not desirable as it would cast doubt on the credibility of the institutional framework. He further recommended in it that the KESC be permitted to go ahead with the award of contract on merits in accordance with the prescribed procedure.

n. The re-evaluation of the proposals was now carried out through a different committee under the supervision of the new Managing Director, KESC. The earlier evaluation in which Lehmeyer with 975 marks was leading Fichtner by 11 marks, was reversed. As a result of this re-evaluation, Fichtner got a total score of 973 marks, giving it a lead of 5 marks over Lehmeyer who was given a total of 968 marks.

o. The Chairman, WAPDA, who is also the Chairman KESC Board of Directors scrutinized this re-evaluation report and made detailed comments rejecting the report with the remarks that the re-evaluation carried out by new Managing Director, KESC, was "arbitrary, without any reasons and against the ADB guidelines", and was totally biased. He communicated his views in a letter addressed to the Secretary, Ministry of Water & Power, on 12.2.1990, adding that he had taken a serious note of the fact that re-evaluation committee report was sent to the Ministry without getting it approved by the Board of Directors of the KESC.

p. The Ministry of Water and Power submitted the re-evaluation report to the Prime Minister's Secretariat on 14.2.1990, categorically stating that the original evaluation of consultants carried out by the KESC, which had been approved by the Board of Directors of the KESC and the ADB, was correct and should not be reopened or altered. It was further suggested that the KESC be directed to proceed immediately with the already agreed award of consultancy contract to M/s Lehmeyer, evaluated as the first ranking consultant in the original evaluation by the KESC and affirmed by the ADB.

q. The Prime Minister's Secretariat responded to the Minister's summary dated 7.1.1990 referred to at para 3, (m) above by conveying the following observations of the then Prime Minister:

"If KESC has chosen a consultant, they should be allowed to go through it. In fact KESC should be allowed to run as autonomously as possible so that they are not bogged down w/time lag. There should be no further delay."

Naturally, it was inferred that the summary sent by the Minister on 7.1.1990 stood approved and it was understood that KESC was free to proceed in employing the consultants whereby the evaluation exercise carried out by KESC would remain intact. Accordingly, specific directions with the approval of the Secretary and Minister of Water & Power, were issued to Managing Director KESC, to finalize the contract with M/s Lehmeyer *vide* telex No. P-III-1(24), 89, dated 29.4.1990.

r. The Prime Minister's Secretariat, however, *vide* their u.o. No. 1929/DS-E&F-1/90, dated 17.5.1990, taking exception to the above-mentioned telex and "a very serious view" of the matter, directed that:-

> "Remedial action should be taken and a report put up on how directions were changed and what action Government should take against those who changed it.
>
> "The matter be brought before ECC and head of KESC called to put their case before us."

s. In the meeting of the ECC held on 25.6.1990, the Minister for Water & Power submitted a detailed brief.

t. In the same meeting, the Managing Director, KESC, misrepresented the facts as reported in the minutes by stating that:-

> "re-evaluation report was seen by the original evaluation committee who agree with second evaluation which did not deviate from the Asian Development Bank guidelines. The Asian Development Bank had threatened cancellation of loan not because of re-evaluation but due to delay in the decision regarding award of contract. As a matter of fact, second evaluation report was not given to Asian Development Bank. He maintained that there was substance in the representation of M/s Fichtner as first evaluation was not done properly."

u. The other opinion expressed in the ECC meeting was that "the real evaluation was done by the ADB and the quality of consultants approved was very high and that it was an international practice that a proposal once evaluated should not be re-evaluated. It was emphasised that a decision to award contract needed to be taken soon as a loan of US$ 200 million was at stake."

v. The Prime Minister also being Chairperson of the Economic Coordination Committee, decided that:-

> "KESC as the user organization should finalize the question of award of contract for consultancy services for KESC Fifth Power Sector Project (Transmission System Expansion and Augmentation) with the Asian Development Bank. The negotiations should be held by a team comprising Finance Secretary and Managing Director, KESC. It would in any case be ensured that Asian Development Bank loan for this project was not lost to Pakistan. In case the Bank was not willing to review its decision, the contract would be awarded to M/s Lehmeyer as originally approved by KESC Board of Directors and Asian Development Bank."

The decision of the ECC was conveyed to Secretary, Ministry of Water & Power *vide* u.o. dated 26.6.1990.

w. A meeting was held on 1.7.1990 by the team referred to earlier consisting of Secretary Finance and Managing Director, KESC, with the Resident Officer of ADB at Islamabad who informed them that ADB would not reverse its decision. It was further confirmed by telex dated 23.7.1990 from ADB Head Office intimating that request for a change in KESC's original recommendations would not be entertained. Mr Bashir Ahmad Chaudhry, Managing Director, KESC, even proposed to present the case personally before ADB at Manila, but his request was turned down by the ADB.

x.   After the dissolution of National Assembly on 6.8.90 the ECC in its meeting held on 9.8.1990 considered the summary on hiring of consultants for KESC submitted by the Finance Division and decided as follows:-

> "The ECC took note of the summary dated 8th August 1990 submitted by the Finance Division and directed KESC to conclude and sign the contract with M/s Lehmeyer International within 4 days."

4.   In the light of the foregoing facts and circumstances there is reason to believe that the Respondent in disregard of opinion of Minister of Water and Power, decision of competent Board of Directors of KESC and concurrence of ADB made every effort to attempt to exclude the lowest and most qualified bidder of the tender, namely M/s Lehmeyer, and to award the contract to M/s Fichtner at a higher rate, and thereby attempted to cause loss to the Government of Pakistan to the extent of Rs 101.3 million as stated in sub-paragraph (f) above and also delayed utilization of loan for approximately one year.

5.   All the above facts further disclose that there is reason to believe that the Respondent attempted to commit favouritism, wilful mal-administration and misapplication of public moneys. All these acts constitute "misconduct" under PPO No. 17 of 1977.

6.   The documents listed below may be read in support of this Reference and facts stated therein may be considered:-

(1)   Enlistment of firms to provide consultancy services.

(2)   Evaluation report declaring M/s Lehmeyer as number one on merit, duly approved by the Board of Directors of KESC.

(3)   Evaluation of the Asian Development Bank agreeing to the report.

(4)   Invitation to M/s Lehmeyer for negotiation.

(5)   Request of M/s Atcons for re-evaluation.

(6)   Ministry of Water & Power's direction to the KESC to supply the evaluation report.

(7)   Direction of the Prime Minister's Project Evaluation & Monitoring Committee (PMPEMC) to the KESC to pend decision for award of consultancy.

(8)   Letter of Chairman, PMPEMC, to Lt Gen (Retd) Nasirullah Khan Babar, advising for re-evaluation.

(9)   Ministry of Water and Power's direction to the KESC to carry out re-evaluation by a different team.

(10) Brief of former Minister for Water and Power addressed to the former Prime Minister taking a serious view of the re-evaluation.

(11) Re-evaluation report declaring M/s Fichtner as number one on merit.

(12) Scrutiny by Chairman, WAPDA, of the re-evaluation report stating that it was "arbitrary" and that it had not been approved by the Board of Directors.

(13) Note of Secretary, Ministry of Water & Power, addressed to the Prime Minister's Secretariat recommending that the KESC be directed to award consultancy to M/s Lehmeyer evaluated as the first-rating consultant in the original evaluation report.

(14) Directions of the Ministry of Water and Power to the KESC to finalize the contract with M/s Lehmeyer on the assumption that the summary of the Minister had stood approved.

(15) Note of Prime Minister's Secretariat taking "a very serious view" of the matter and directing remedial action, a report on officials responsible for it, and orders to place the matter before the ECC.

(16) Submission of a detailed report by the Minister for Water & Power before the ECC.

(17) Extract from the minutes of the meeting of the ECC in which the new Managing Director of the KESC misrepresented the facts.

(18) Note of the Cabinet Division communicating decision of the ECC to the KESC.

(19) Telex from the ADB Head Office stating that a request for a change in the KESC's original recommendation would not be entertained.

(20) Proposal of the new Managing Director, KESC, to plead the case personally in Manila to justify the recommendation contained in the re-evaluation report.

(21) Telex turning down the request for a personal appearance in Manila.

7.   The above Reference is made to the Special Court with the request to enquire into and decide the case relating to the 'misconduct' of the Respondent and record its findings and pass appropriate orders in accordance with law.

8.   If further material subsequently becomes available in support of the above Reference, it will be submitted respectively to the Honourable Special Court.

By Order of the President.

Sd/-
FAZLUR RAHMAN KHAN,
Secretary to the President.

Note: Documents at Para 6 not reproduced.

Notes

Prologue

1. *Gazetteer of the Peshawar District 1897-98* (Lahore: Sang-e-Meel Publications, 1989), 11.
2. Ravi Dayal, *We Fought Together for Freedom* (New Delhi: Indian Council of Historical Research, Oxford University Press, 1995), 187.
3. Ibid., 187.
4. Lal Baha, *NWFP Administration Under British Rule* (Islamabad: National Commission for Historical and Cultural Research, 1978), 216.
5. William Shawcross, *The Shah's Last Ride* (Oxford: Oxford University Press, 1989), 46-7.
6. Gul Hassan Khan, *Memoirs of Lt. Gen. Gul Hassan* (Karachi: Oxford University Press, 1993), 342.
7. David Eisenhower, *Eisenhower at War 1943-45* (New York: Random House, 1986), 801-2.
8. Martin Gilbert, *First World War* (New York: Henry Holt and Company, 1994), 500.

Chapter 1: Ayub

1. Mohammad Ayub Khan, *Friends Not Masters* (Karachi: Oxford University Press, 1967), 70.
2. Ibid., 71.
3. Ibid., 71.

4.   Altaf Gauhar, *Ayub Khan: Pakistan's First Military Ruler* (Lahore: Sang-e-Meel Publications, 1994), 488-9.
5.   Ibid., 479.
6.   Ibid., 277-8.
7.   Ibid., 278.
8.   Ibid., 485.

Chapter 3: Yahya

1.   Gauhar, *Ayub Khan*, 480.
2.   G. W. Choudhry, *The Last Days of United Pakistan* (Karachi: Oxford University Press, 1993), 124.
3.   Don Cook, *Charles de Gaulle* (New York: G. P. Putnam and Sons, 1983), 324.
4.   Ibid., 325.
5.   Ibid., 327-8.

Chapter 4: Bhutto — triumph and tragedy

1.   General K. M. Arif, *Working with Zia* (Karachi: Oxford University Press, 1995), 111.
2.   Ibid., 110.
3.   Stanley Wolpert, *Zulfi Bhutto of Pakistan: His Life and Times* (New York: Oxford University Press, 1993), 288.
4.   Robert A. Wilson (ed.), *Character Above All* (New York: Simon & Schuster, 1995), 106.
5.   Ibid., 106.
6.   Ibid., 106.
7.   Ibid., 106-7.
8.   Ibid., 108.
9.   Stephen E. Ambrose, *Nixon* (New York: Simon & Schuster, 1989), 10.
10. Ibid.

Chapter 5: Ziaul Haq

1.   Wilson, *Character*, 38.
2.   Altaf Gauhar, *Dawn*, Karachi.
3.   Cook, *de Gaulle*, 302.
4.   Craig Baxter, *Zia's Pakistan* (Boulder and London: Westview Press, 1985), 2.
5.   Sir Morris James, *Pakistan Chronicle* (Karachi: Oxford University Press, 1993), 209.
6.   Diego Cordovez and Selig Harrison, *Out of Afghanistan* (New York: Oxford University Press, 1995), 56.

7. Ibid., 250.
8. Ibid., 20.

Chapter 6: Ghulam Ishaq Khan

1. Ronald Reagan, *Ronald Reagan Autobiography* (New York: Simon & Schuster, 1990), 19.

Chapter 7: Towards confrontation

1. *Pakistan Political Perspective* (Islamabad: Institute of Policy Studies, Islamabad, March 1993), 6.
2. Ibid., 12.
3. Ibid., July 1993.
4. Ibid., August 1993.
5. James Cannon in *Character*, 146.
6. Peggy Noonan in *Character*, 217.
7. David McCullough in *Character*, 42·

Chapter 10: Character and credibility

1. Noonan in *Character*, 202.
2. Gauhar, *Ayub Khan*, 493.
3. Noonan in *Character*, 203.
4. Gauhar, *Ayub Khan*, 479-81.
5. Simon Schama, *Citizen* (New York: Alfred A. Knop, 1989), 668.
6. Ibid., 669.
7. Ibid., 820.
8. Arif, *Working with Zia*, 208-9.
9. Doris Kearns Goodwin in *Character*, 20.

Chapter 11: Where does sovereign lie? Illusion and reality

1. Makhdoom Ali Khan, *Introduction to the Constitution of the Islamic Republic of Pakistan* (*Pakistan Law Manual*, 1986), xxxvii.
2. Ibid.
3. Paula R. Newberg, *Judging the State* (Cambridge: Cambridge University Press, 1995), 75.
4. Ibid., 121.
5. Arif, *Working with Zia*, 401.
6. Ibid., 402.

Chapter 13: Political succession and the Islamic challenge

1.   Amir Hasan Siddiqi, *Caliphate and Sultanate* (Karachi: Jamiyet-ul-Falah Publications, 1963), 13.
2.   Ibid., 42.

Chapter 14: Supreme Court reborn

1.   Siddiqi, *Caliphate*, 51.
2.   Newberg *Judging the State*, 5.
3.   Ibid., 12.
4.   Ibid., 120.
5.   Ibid., 121.
6.   Ibid., 216.
7.   William E. Leuchtenburg, *Supreme Court Reborn* (New York: Oxford University Press, 1995), 44.
8.   Ardeshir Cowasjee, '*Ehtesab* or *Intikhab*' (Karachi: *Dawn*, 3 January 1997).

Chapter 16: Reflections

1.   John Kenneth Galbraith, *Age of Uncertainty* (London: British Broadcasting Corporation, 1973), 330.
2.   Ibid., 49.
3.   Confucius, *Analects*, C (49 BC).
4.   Paul Kennedy, *The Rise and Fall of the Great Powers* (New York: Random House, 1987), 13.
5.   Percival Spear, *Twilight of the Mughals* (New York: Oxford University Press, 1980), 10-11.

Index